TRANSITION FROM SCHOOL TO POST-SCHOOL LIFE FOR INDIVIDUALS WITH DISABILITIES

Dr. Edward M. Levinson is a professor of educational and school psychology at Indiana University of Pennsylvania (IUP), and previously worked for eight years as a school psychologist and vocational assessment coordinator in the public schools of Virginia. He is a nationally certified school psychologist (NCSP), and holds certification as a school psychologist in Pennsylvania, Virginia, and New York. In a 1997 School Psychology International article which listed the top 50 authors in the school psychology literature from 1987–1995, Dr. Levinson was ranked 16th. He has published three books and over 80 book chapters and journal articles, and in May of 1996 received IUP's distinguished faculty award for research. Dr. Levinson has served on the editorial boards of *Psychology in the Schools, Career Development Quarterly, Journal of Counseling and Development* and the *Journal of Employment Counseling,* and has been an ad hoc reviewer for *School Psychology Review* and *School Psychology Quarterly.* He has made close to 100 presentations at local, state, and national meetings on the topics of vocational assessment, transition, and stress and burnout.

TRANSITION FROM SCHOOL TO POST-SCHOOL LIFE FOR INDIVIDUALS WITH DISABILITIES

Assessment from an Educational and School Psychological Perspective

Edited by

EDWARD M. LEVINSON, ED.D.

CHARLES C THOMAS • PUBLISHER, LTD.
Springfield • Illinois • U.S.A.

Published and Distributed Throughout the World by

CHARLES C THOMAS • PUBLISHER, LTD.
2600 South First Street
Springfield, Illinois 62704

ISBN 0-398-07480-1 (hard)
ISBN 0-398-07481-X (paper)

Library of Congress Catalog Card Number: 2003056436

With THOMAS BOOKS *careful attention is given to all details of manufacturing and design. It is the Publisher's desire to present books that are satisfactory as to their physical qualities and artistic possibilities and appropriate for their particular use.* THOMAS BOOKS *will be true to those laws of quality that assure a good name and good will.*

Printed in the United States of America
SR-R-3

Library of Congress Cataloging-in-Publication Data

Transition from school to post-school life for individuals with disabilities : assessment from an educational and school psychological perspective / edited by Edward M. Levinson.
p. cm.
Includes bibliographical refernces and index
ISBN 0-398-07480-1 -- ISBN 0-398-07481-X (pbk.)
1. Youth with disabilities--Vocational education--United States. 2. Youth with disabilities--United States--Psychology. 3. School-to-work transition-- United States--Evaluation. I. Levinson, Edward M., 1952-

LC4019.7.T73 2004
371.9'0473--dc22

2003068732

CONTRIBUTORS

HEATHER BEAUCHAMP, ED.S., NCSP
School Psychologist
Lake Forest School District
Felton, Delaware

DANIEL CANE, M.S.
School Psychologist
Lincoln Intermediate Unit #12
New Oxford, Pennsylvania

MEGAN COSTANZA, ED.S.
School Psychologist
Fox Chapel Area School District
Pittsburgh, Pennsylvania

LESLIE A. EGET, ED.S., NCSP
School Psychologist
Charles County Public Schools
LaPlata, Maryland

Larry Fultz, Ph.D.
School Psychologist
Baltimore County Board of Education
Towson, Maryland

KELLEY E. GOSS, ED.S., NCSP
School Psychologist
Appalachia Intermediate Unit #8
Altoona, Pennsylvania

DEBORAH A. HOUCK, M.A., C.A.S.
School Psychologist
Charlotte-Mecklenburg Schools
Charlotte, North Carolina

M. ALICIA JENKINS, ED.S., NCSP
School Psychologist
Baltimore County Public Schools
Towson, Maryland

KATHLEEN R. KIEWRA, ED.S.
School Psychologist
Fox Chapel Area School District
Pittsburgh, Pennsylvania

CHAD KINSEY, MS, NCSP
School Psychologist
Fleetwood Area School District
Fleetwood, Pennsylvania

JENNIFER SMITH KUZEMCHAK, ED.S.
School Psychologist
ARIN Intermediate Unit #28
Indiana, Pennsylvania

NICHOLE LEHMAN, ED.S., NCSP
School Psychologist
Lincoln Intermediate Unit #12
New Oxford, Pennsylvania

EDWARD M. LEVINSON, ED.D.
Professor of Educational and School Psychology
Indiana University of Pennsylvania
Indiana, Pennsylvania

MARK NEVILL, MSED
School Psychologist
Blast Intermediate Unit #17
Williamsport, Pennsylvania

KIRSTEN STIFFLER, ED.S.
School Psychologist
Blacklick Valley School District
Nanty Glo, Pennsylvania

KRISTEN YOUNG, ED.S.
School Psychologist
Butler Area School District
Butler, Pennsylvania

PREFACE

According to the U.S. General Accounting Office, one-third of young workers ages 16-24 do not have the skills they need to perform entry-level, semiskilled jobs. Additionally, nationwide studies conducted by the National Career Development Association and the Gallup Organization suggest that adults who consciously plan and prepare themselves for a job make up only one-third of those currently working. Consequently, the remaining two-thirds of employed adults enter their jobs as a result of chance, the influence of others, or took the only job available. Most importantly, only half of these workers are content with their jobs.

In particular, individuals with disabilities are at especially high risk for failure or dissatisfaction with their jobs. When compared with their non-disabled peers, individuals with mild disabilities experience a higher rate of unemployment and underemployment, lower pay, and greater dissatisfaction with their job. Moreover, there is a high dropout rate among students with disabilities, and as a result, this population has not received the vocational training necessary to make a smooth transition from school to work. Studies that have compared special education dropout rates with control group dropout rates (normative data) have consistently demonstrated that students with disabilities leave school more often than students without disabilities. Students with learning disabilities and emotional disabilities are at an especially high risk of dropping out of school. Some studies have reported dropout rates exceeding 40 and 50 percent, respectively, for these populations. Hence, this population of students is especially in need of effective school-to-work transition services.

This high dropout rate may be attributed to several factors. Many schools focus their curriculum on college-bound students rather than those who plan to enter the work force following high school. Statistics indicate that only 15 percent of freshmen entering high school graduate and obtain a degree from a four-year college within six years of their high school graduation. As a result, focusing resources on college-bound students leaves the majority of non-college-bound students lacking in the skills necessary for success in the work force. The 21st Annual Report to Congress reported that students with disabilities were more likely to stay in school and even more likely to be employed after high school if they were provided with some form of vocational training and school-to-work transition service.

This book is designed to assist professionals in developing and implementing transition services for students with disabilities. Specifically, this book focuses on the importance of assessment in transition planning and targets the various domains which should be included in any school-to-work transition assessment. The book advocates a transdisciplinary school-based approach to transition assessment which involves not only school-based professionals in the assessment process but community agency representatives as well. As such, the book may be useful to a variety of professionals including regular education teachers, special education teachers, vocational education teachers, school counselors, school psychologists, and school administrators, as well as professionals employed by community agencies like Vocational Rehabilitation, Mental Health/Mental Retardation, and Social Services.

Most books on transition are written from a special education or vocational rehabilitation perspective by authors with extensive backgrounds in those fields. This book, however, is written from an educational and school psychological perspective and is designed to complement the existing literature on transition by offering a slightly different perspective on the process. All authors are practicing school psychologists who have had extensive experience in the schools working with students with disabilities. Authors were assigned chapters based upon their interests and experiences and were asked to write their chapters in a way that blended a review of the literature with their personal and professional experiences in working with students with disabilities. It is my sincere hope that their efforts and the resulting chapters prove to be in some way helpful to those professionals involved in transition planning, and in particular, to those involved in the very important assessment component of the process.

In particular, I would like to thank Karen Wolff, our administrative assistant extraordinaire for her help with this project. I would also like to thank the students, faculty and staff of the Department of Educational and School Psychology at Indiana University of Pennsylvania for their effort toward and support of this project. This book is dedicated to them.

EDWARD M. LEVINSON

CONTENTS

TRANSITION FROM SCHOOL TO POST-SCHOOL LIFE FOR INDIVIDUALS WITH DISABILITIES

Chapter 1

INTRODUCTION TO TRANSITION ASSESSMENT

EDWARD M. LEVINSON

INTRODUCTION: TRANSITION ASSESSMENT

In the last several years, schools have increasingly focused upon providing students with the services and skills they need in order to obtain and maintain employment and to function effectively and independently in the community. More often than not, this effort has been focused upon students with disabilities, in that these students are those who historically have had greater difficulty achieving such goals once they leave school. Through this effort has been termed "transition," the term transition has been used to refer to different processes within the school environment. Several years ago, I was teaching a doctoral seminar in school psychology and one of the students asked if she could make her required presentation on the topic of transition. I was thrilled; however, my attempts to provide the student with needed information were met with quizzical looks and blank stares. "What does all this have to do with preschool assessment and kindergarten transition programs?" she asked. Slightly embarrassed, I explained that I misunderstood her topic, took back the reference materials I had provided to her, explained that the term "transition" meant different things to different people, and told her that the topic was nonetheless acceptable!

Though the term transition has been used to refer to different processes within the educational environment (for example, it has been used to describe movement from preschool to kindergarten, or from elementary school to junior high school, etc.), for the purposes of this book, the term transition will be used solely to described the process of facilitating the post-school adjustment of students, particularly students with disabilities. Post-school adjustment will be broadly defined to include adjustment to work, leisure, and independent functioning in the community.

DEFINITIONS OF TRANSITION

Wehman, Kregel, and Barcus (1985) offered the following definition of vocational transition:

> Vocational transition is a carefully planned process, which may be initiated either by school personnel or by adult service providers, to establish and implement a plan for either employment or additional vocational training of a handicapped student who will graduate or leave school in three or five years; such a process must involve special educators, parents and/or the student, an adult service system representative, and possibly an employer.

This definition clearly suggests that transition efforts must involve a variety of school and community personnel and must include the parents of the student or the student themselves. Moreover, the definition suggests that transition is a planned and systematic process that occurs well before the student is eligible to leave school.

Although the definition provided by Wehman et al. (1985) emphasizes school-to-work transition, many transition specialists argue that transition programs must focus upon community adjustment and other aspects of adult life as well. In the landmark document "OSERS Programming for the Transition of Youth with Disabilities: Bridges from School to Working Life," Madeline Will of the Office of Special Education and Rehabilitative Services defined transition as follows:

> The transition from school to working life is an outcome-oriented process encompassing a broad array of services and experiences that lead to employment. Transition is a period that includes high school, the point of graduation, additional postsecondary education or adult services, and the initial years of employment. Transition is a bridge between the security and structure offered by the school and the opportunities and risks of adult life. Any bridge required

> both a solid span and a secure foundation at either end. The transition from school to work and adult life requires sound preparation in the secondary school, adequate support at the point of school leaving, and secure opportunities and services, if needed, in adult situations. (Will, 1986; p. 10)

In October, 1990, Congress enacted the *Education of the Handicapped Act Amendments of 1990* (P.L. 101-476), an amendment of P.L. 94-142, the Education of the Handicapped Act (EHA). Under this new law, the name EHA was changed to the Individuals with Disabilities Education Act (IDEA). Though this legislation will be discussed again later in this chapter, IDEA includes a definition of transition that is currently the basis for many school-based transition programs. Section 602(a) of IDEA defines transition services as:

> A coordinated set of activities for a student, designed within an outcome-oriented process, which promotes movement from school to post-school activities, including post-secondary education, vocational training, integrated employment (including supported employment), continuing and adult education, adult services, independent living, or community participation. The coordinated set of activities shall be based upon the individual student's needs, taking into account the student's preferences and interests, and shall include instruction, community experiences, the development of employment and other post-school adult living objectives, and, if appropriate, acquisition of daily living skills and functional vocational evaluation (Education of the Handicapped Act Amendments of 1990, P.L. 101-476, Section 602(a) [20 U.S.C. 1041(a)].

P.L. 101-476 requires that a student's Individual Education Plan (IEP) address the issue of transition, and that transition planning be initiated by at least age 14. Specifically, IDEA lists the following additional requirements for the IEP:

> (D) a statement of needed transition services for students beginning no later than age 16 and annually thereafter (and, when determined appropriate for the individual, beginning at age 14 or younger), including when appropriate, a statement of the interagency responsibilities or linkages (or both) before the student leaves the school setting, and (F) in the case where a participating agency, other than the educational agency, fails to provide the agreed upon services, the educational agency shall reconvene the IEP team to identify alternative strategies to meet the transition objectives.

Additionally, the law specifies that if the IEP team determines that services are not needed in one or more of the areas specified in the legislation, the IEP must include a statement to that effect and the basis upon which the determination was made.

TRANSDISCIPLINARY TRANSITION MODEL

The Transdisciplinary Transition Model (TTM) that I advocate is depicted in Figure 1.1. The term "transdisciplinary" is used instead of "multidisciplinary" in order to depict the need to involve professionals "across disciplines" in the transition process. Traditionally, the term "multidisciplinary" has been used in education to depict the need to involve educators from different fields *within* education in a particular process. For example, "multidisciplinary teams" responsible for identifying students with disabilities are often comprised of school psychologist, teachers, guidance counselors, school nurses, and school administrators, all of whom are educational personnel based in schools. These multidisciplinary teams do not typically include professionals from outside of the schools (they include professionals from multiple disciplines *within* schools). As the figure indicates, the model encompasses services from a variety of community agencies in addition to the schools, and consists of the following phases: Assessment, Planning, Training, Placement, and Follow-up. The reader should note that these phases are not conceptualized as separate processes that occur at only one distinct point in time. Rather they are considered to be ongoing interacting processes that affect each other. Moreover, each phase represents a process that may occur repeatedly over a period of time. For example, a student may be assessed as having interest and aptitude in automotive mechanics, and a plan may be developed and training initiated to prepare the student for placement in an automotive mechanics training program. During the course of training, however, the student's interests may change or the student may demonstrate limitations that render placement in an automotive mechanics program inappropriate. This may require a reassessment of the student and development of a new plan. This entire process may be repeated at different points during the school years. For example, it may occur when considering placement in a vocational program, or later, when considering placement in a job or residence. While the assessment phase is the focus of this book and will be discussed in more detail in subsequent chapters, a brief review of each phase of the model follows.

Components of Transition Planning

Assessment			Planning		Training			Placement			Follow-up
Needs in	Utilizing	By	Objectives in	By	Skills in	In	By	Vocationally in	Residentially in	by	
Intellectual/ Cognitive Area	Tests	School Psychologist	Employment Area	School Personnel	Intellectual/ Cognitive Area	School Setting	Teachers	Competitive Employment	Independent Living in • Single Family Home • Group Home	School Personnel	Provide Needed Supported Services
Educational/ Academic Area	Interviews	Teachers	Residential Living Area	Vocational Rehabilitation Personnel	Educational/ Academic Area	Residential Setting	School Psychologist	Supported Employment	Supported Living in • Family's Home • Group Home	Vocational Rehabilitation Personnel	Evaluate Adequacy of Services Provided
Social Interpersonal Area	Observation	Counselors	Community Functioning Area	Mental Health/Mental Retardation Personnel	Social/ Interpersonal Area	Community Setting	Vocational Rehabilitation Counselors	Sheltered Employment	Institutional Living in • Nursing Home • Hospital	Mental Health Mental Retardation Personnel	
Occupational Vocational Area	Rating Scales	Vocational Evaluators		Social Services Agency Personnel	Occupational/ Vocational Area		Social Workers			Social Service Agency Personnel	
Independent Living Area	Work Samples	Social Workers		Employers	Independent Living Area		Job Coaches			Parents	
Physical/ Sensory Area	Situational Assessment	Speech Therapists		Parents	Physical/ Sensory Area		Employers				
		School Nurses		Students			Parents				
		Occupational/ Physical Therapists					Speech Therapists				
							Occupational/ Physical Therapists				

Figure 1.1.

Assessment

An initial first step in transition planning is an assessment of a student's skills and individual needs. As the figure suggests, a variety of domains need to be assessed and these include the following: intellectual/cognitive, educational/academic, personality/social skills, vocational interests/aptitudes, and career maturity/self advocacy, and life skills. Different assessment approaches and techniques can be utilized to gather information about a student, different domains may be targeted for assessment at different points in the student's educational career, and the purposes of assessment may vary from one assessment to another. Assessment should not be the responsibility of one professional, but instead should be conducted by a team of professionals, each of whom is responsible for gathering specific information about the student. Professionals involved in this process may be employed by the schools or by community agencies. As mentioned previously, this phase of the transition process will be highlighted in the remaining chapters of this book.

Planning

Following a thorough assessment of the student's individual needs and skills, the information gathered is used by the transdisciplinary transition team to develop a transition plan for the student to be included in the student's IEP. This plan should specify goals and objectives regarding employment, residential living, and community functioning, and should identify which professionals and agencies are responsible for providing needed services. Additionally, a time frame for service provision should be included.

Training

Following the development of a transition plan as part of the student's IEP, instruction and training are initiated. In addition to school personnel, professionals from a variety of agencies may be involved in training the student. Additionally, this training may take place in a variety of settings including the school, the workplace, the community, and the residence.

Placement

Once instruction and training have been completed, the student is ready to be placed in a job, in a residence, and/or in a postsecondary educational setting for additional training. A variety of employment, residential living, and postsecondary placement options exist for a student, and the appropriateness of any one option for a student depends upon their level of functioning. Employment options may include competitive employment, supported employment, or sheltered employment. Residential living options may include independent living, supported living, or institutional living. Postsecondary educational options may include community colleges, four-year colleges, universities, private, technical and trade schools, and so forth.

Follow-up

The final phase of the transdisciplinary transition model specifies that an evaluation must be made of the degree to which a student is functioning successfully in various post-school settings. Termination of some support services, initiation of other services, and/or a change of placement may result from this follow-up evaluation.

The model also assumes that transition is part of the broader phenomenon of career development. That is, rather than conceptualizing transition planning as a separate process that is initiated at age 14 or 16, the model conceptualizes transition planning as a natural part of the lifelong process of career development and career planning. That is, the knowledge and skills individuals need in order to make a successful transition from school to work and community living actually begin to develop at birth, and continue throughout the life span. Hence, issues like understanding oneself and getting along with others, which should be addressed as early as the elementary school years will ultimately affect transition. Hence, assessment and planning for a student's successful transition actually beings in elementary school and continues throughout their educational career. Hence, the model conceptualizes transition assessment and planning as an ongoing process that is inextricably linked to career development. Consequently, it is important for professionals involved in transition assessment to understand career development theory and to use it as a guide when establishing transition assessment programs. The following section briefly discusses career development theory. This section will be followed by an application of career development theory to the transdisciplinary-transition planning model advocated by the author.

Career Development Theory

Career development has been defined as "the total constellation of psychological, sociological, educational, physical, economic, and chance factors that combine to shape the career of any individual over the life span" (Sears, 1982). Developmental theories assume that the choice of a career is an orderly and rather predictable process that consists of a series of well-defined and hierarchical stages. These stages identify the issues, roles and conflicts that most individuals confront at given points in their lives, and provide a birth-to-death perspective of vocational maturation. As with other aspects of development, the age and rate at which individuals progress through each of these vocational stages will vary. Although vocational development theorists provide age ranges that are associated with each of these stages, one must interpret these age ranges cautiously and not rigidly. Just as some children begin to walk at ten months and others at 13 months, there is normal variability inherent in the age ranges associated with these stages. The ages associated with the stages, however, do provide some guidelines which can be used to assess whether a student is progressing at an average rate in their vocational development and what career-related goals and objectives might be appropriate to set for individuals at varying points in their educational careers. As such, career development theory can be used as a guide when establishing transition objectives for individuals throughout the school years.

As Isaacson (1986) has suggested, probably no one has written as much about, or had as much influence on the field of vocational development as has Donald Super. Super has devoted almost 50 years to the study of vocational development (Super, 1942), and is one of the most widely known and respected career development theorists in the world. His theory was first proposed in a relatively complete form in 1953, and has been continually modified ever since.

Super proposed the existence of five major stages: Growth, Exploration, Establishment, Maintenance, and Decline. Each of these major stages is comprised of several substages, and each is associated with several developmental tasks. Figure 1.2 summarizes these stages, substages, and developmental tasks. Although only two major stages generally occur during the traditional school years (Growth and Exploration), all stages are listed and summarized in keeping with the birth-to-death perspective inherent in developmental theory. Relatedly, in that a major goal of transition is to provide individuals with the knowledge and skills they need in order to function successfully in society, recognition of the developmental issues which will confront individuals years after they leave school is important. That is, transition services should not only afford individuals the ability to successfully negotiate the developmental tasks that confront them just prior to and just after exiting school, but should empower and prepare them more generally to confront the major developmental issues that will confront them throughout life as adults.

The following ten propositions underlie Super's theory:

1. People differ in abilities, interest, and personality.
2. Individuals are qualified, by virtue of these characteristics, each for a number of occupations.
3. Each of these occupations require a characteristic pattern of abilities, interests, and personality traits–with tolerance wide enough, however, to allow for both some variety of occupations for each individual and some variety of individuals in each occupation.
4. Vocational preferences and competencies–the situations in which people live and work, and hence their self concepts–change with time and experience, making choice and adjustment a continuous process.
5. This process (item 4 of this list) may be summed up in a series of life stages characterized as those of growth, exploration, establishment, maintenance, and decline. These stages can be subdivided into (a) the fantasy, tentative, and realistic phases of the exploratory stage, and (b) the trial and stable phases of the establishment stage.
6. The nature of the career pattern is determined by the individual's parental socioeconomic level, mental ability, and personality characteristics, and by the opportunities to which he or she is exposed.
7. Development through the life stages can be guided, partly by facilitating the process of maturation of abilities and interests and

Super's Stages of Career Development

Stage	Growth			Exploration			Establishment		Maintenance	Decline	
Substage	Fantasy	Interest	Capacity	Tentative	Transition	Trial	Commitment and Stabilization	Advancement		Deceleration	
Age Range	0–10	11–12	13–14	15–17	18–21	22–24	25–30	31–41	45–64	65–70	71 and on
Primary Tasks	Increase self-awareness and awareness of the world of work			Explore various vocational options and implement a vocational choice			Settle and advance within chosen occupation		Preserve vocational status and gains	Cope with declining vocational abilities and begin to adjust to retirement	

Figure 1.2. Note: From Children's Needs II (p. 537) by G. Bear, K. Menke, and A. Thomas (Eds.), Washington, DC: National Association of School Psychologists. Copyright 1997 by the National Association of School Psychologists. Reprinted by permission of the publisher.

partly by aiding in reality testing and in development of the self-concept.

8. The process of vocational development is essentially that of developing and implementing a self-concept; it is a compromise process in which the self-concept is a product of the interaction of inherited aptitudes, neural and endocrine make-up, opportunity to play various roles, and evaluations of the extent to which the results of the role playing meet with the approval of superiors and fellows.
9. The process of compromise between individual and social factors, between self-concept and reality, is one of role playing, whether the role is played in fantasy; in the counseling interview; or in real-life activities such as school classes, clubs, part-time work, and entry level jobs.
10. Work satisfactions and life satisfactions depend on the extent to which the individual finds adequate outlets for his or her abilities, interests, personality traits, and values; they depend on his or her establishment in a type of work, a work situation, and a way of life in which he or she can play the kind of role that growth and exploratory experiences have led him or her to consider congenial and appropriate.

Simply put, Super believes that each of us has a relatively unique set of personality characteristics (interests, abilities, values, attitudes, etc.), which qualify us for a vast array of occupations. Although all occupations require a given set of abilities interests, and personality traits, there is enough variability (tolerance) inherent in each characteristic set of traits so as to accommodate a variety of different kinds of people (providing the variability inherent in the traits possessed by these individuals are within the occupation's tolerance range). Super believes, as do most vocational theorists, *that there is no one right occupation for anyone.* There are *many* right occupations for everyone. The traits that characterize one's personality and thereby qualify them for jobs develop as a result of one's progression through the five stages detailed in Figure 1.2, and are influenced by environmental factors like socioeconomic status, parents, family, friends, and schooling.

Super believes that the early years of life are a time of growth during which people develop the interests, skills, values, and attitudes (including attitudes about work), which become part of their personality. This is also the time during which one begins to learn about themselves, and to develop a self-concept. In adolescence, teens explore and "test out" their self concepts via school, leisure, and part-time work experiences. Self-concept is further refined as a result of these experiences, and eventually a career and leisure activities are chosen in which one believes they can fully implement their self-concepts and experience satisfaction.

Once having selected and entered a career, there is an initial "settling in" period during which the individual assesses the job's suitability (i.e., the degree to which the job allows one to fully implement their self-concept). There may be several job changes before the individual stabilizes and feels comfortable and secure in their career choice. Following this stabilization and commitment, the individual puts effort into "climbing the corporate ladder" so to speak. Advancement in one's career becomes of paramount importance when people reach their 30s and 40s. This is generally considered to be the time of peak performance. When people reach their late 40s and 50s, individuals, having accomplished much in their careers, attempt to preserve their accomplishments in the face of competition from younger, achievement-oriented colleagues (those, most likely in the advancement stage). When people reach their 60s, physical and mental skills begin to deteriorate, work activities change, and individuals begin to look toward non-work activities for self-concept implementation and satisfaction. Disengaging from work, and adjusting to retirement are major developmental tasks during these years.

Applying Career Development Theory to Transdisciplinary Transition Planning

When one reviews the career developmental objectives that confront individuals during the school years, several major themes emerge. Career development is an ongoing process that involves a series of decisions. In order to empower individuals and render them capable of making realistic and informed decisions independently (and as such, to negotiate the developmental tasks that will confront them throughout life), they must be provided with opportunities to learn about themselves, learn about the world of work, and learn how to make decisions in a logical rational manner. Hence, improving self-awareness, improving occupational awareness, and improving decision-making abilities should be major objectives throughout the school years. Figure 1.3 elaborates on these three major themes, and lists specific vocational/ career objectives by grade level. One goal of transition assessment is to determine the extent to which students have successfully achieved these objectives, and to what extent they may need assistance and support in doing so. Transition planning which emanates from this assessment should have the purpose of assisting students in accomplishing these objectives. Hence, the transdisciplinary transition-planning model advocates periodic assessment of the degree to which students have accomplished these vocational/career objectives. Based upon this assessment, plans may be developed which specify activities designed to facilitate accomplishment of these objectives.

As an example, consider a student who is initially evaluated and identified as having a disability in third grade. As part of this initial evaluation, self-awareness and social/interpersonal skills may be assessed, deficient skills identified, a plan designed to remediate these deficiencies developed and incorporated in the student's IEP, and training initiated. Each year as the student's IEP is reviewed and revised, an informal assessment of the student's progress can be made, plans can be revised, and training redirected if indicated. When the student reaches the sixth grade and is reevaluated, an assessment can be made of the student's interests and understanding of the world of work. Based upon this assessment, career exploration activities appropriate for this student can be planned and initiated. Again, an assessment of the extent to which the student is gaining an understanding of careers of interest to him/her can be made in conjunction with the annual IEP review and revision. Based on this, plans may be altered and instructional activities changed as indicated. When the student is in the ninth grade and subjected to another reevaluation, an assessment can be made of the student's aptitudes, decision-making skills, and independent living skills. Based upon this, continuing career exploration activities may be planned, instruction and training in decision-making or aspects of independent living may be initiated, and placement in a vocational training program consistent with the student's interests and aptitudes may be considered. Again, progress can be reassessed and monitored annually via the IEP, and plans and training altered as indicated. Finally, when the student is again subjected to a reevaluation in the twelfth grade, the assessment can focus upon the immediate task of

Phases of Career Education

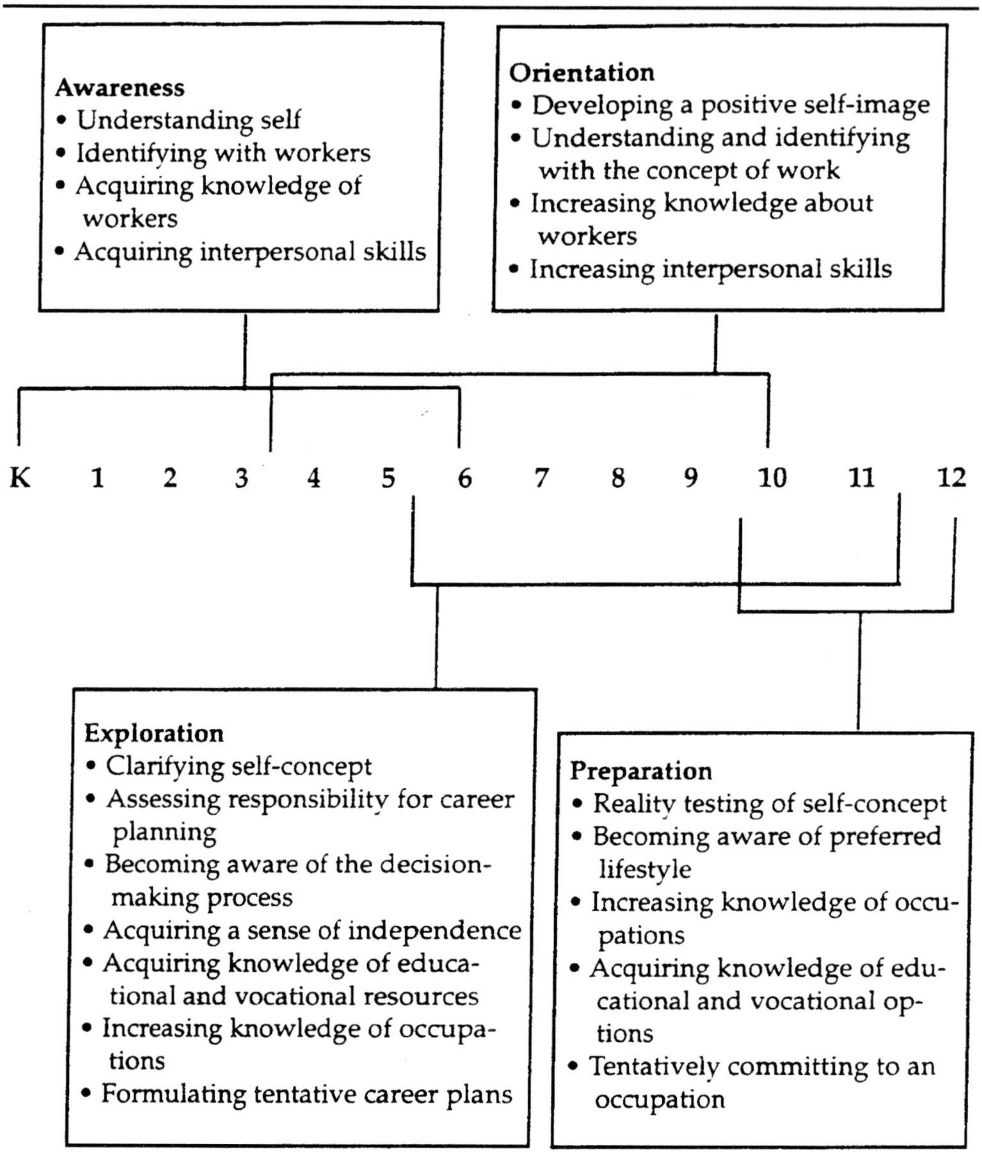

Figure 1.3. From *Children's Needs II* (p. 540) by G. Bear, K. Menke, and A. Thomas (Eds.), Washington, DC: National Association of School Psychologists. Copyright 1997 by the National Association of School Psychologists. Reprinted by permission of the publisher.

placement in a job consistent with previous training, and in a residence consistent with the independent living skills acquired by the student.

The previous example is simply provided to illustrate how the transdisciplinary transition model may be linked to career development theory and objectives, and the reevaluation and Individual Education Plan processes, which are mandated by law for students with disabilities. Additionally, the example illustrates how the model conceptualizes transition as an ongoing, longitudinal process rather than a single time event. Lastly, the example illustrates how the various phases of the model (assessment-planning-training-placement-follow-up) are ongoing and interactive rather than separate and distinct.

The assessment of individual student needs is a necessary first step in transition planning. Assessment is designed to identify an individual's strengths and weaknesses, and is used to identify what skills a student may need to acquire in order to make a successful transition. It can also identify those skills, which have already been acquired by the student and thus, do not have to be targeted for development. Given that, all planning and instruction is based upon assessment, a thorough and valid assessment of a student's needs is perhaps the most important part of the transition process. That is, if an inadequate or inaccurate assessment of a student is conducted, skills which have not yet been acquired by the student may not be identified, may never be included in the student's transition plan, and may never be acquired by the student prior to leaving school. Additionally, a faulty or inaccurate assessment could also lead professionals to target skills for instruction which the student has already developed, thus, wasting valuable instructional time. In either case, effective transition planning will be seriously compromised by an inaccurate assessment.

The accuracy of the assessment process is largely influenced by the accuracy of the assessment instruments used, and the skills of the assessor. To illustrate the importance of these two factors, consider the following scenario taken from Levinson (1993). Suppose you are having your blood pressure taken as part of a comprehensive physical examination. If the gauge used to take your blood pressure is faulty (it yields inaccurate readings), you may be incorrectly diagnosed as having high (or low) blood pressure and may be placed on unnecessary medication, which over a period of time may have a negative impact on your health. Additionally, faulty equipment could also lead to dangerously high (or low) blood pressure going undetected, and needed medication never being prescribed. Similarly, if the blood pressure gauge is not faulty, but the measures yielded are misread or misinterpreted by inadequately trained medical personnel, your health may also be adversely affected.

Assessments, which are conducted for the purpose of assisting in the development of transition plans, can be viewed in a similar fashion. If faulty or inaccurate instruments are used to assess individuals, and measures from these instruments are used in transition planning, inappropriate transition programming may result. However, accurate instruments do not, in and of themselves, guarantee that professionals involved in the transition process will use results accurately. Only in the hands of competent and skilled assessment professionals may accurate assessment instruments yield data which may significantly and positively contribute to a student's transition planning.

A Multitrait-Multimethod Approach to Multifactored Assessment

Assessment for transdisciplinary transition planning should involve a variety of school and community-based professionals, utilize a variety of assessment techniques and strategies (multimethod), and require that assessment information be gathered in a variety of domains (multitrait). Scores from measuring instruments are often affected by factors other than the trait being assessed by the instrument. Sometimes scores are more influenced by the person that administered the instrument or the type of assessment device being used than by the trait being assessed. For example, when being interviewed about their vocational aspirations, students may respond one way to their parents and a different way to their teacher. In such an instance, the results of the interview may be a function of the "interviewer" rather than of the trait being assessed by the interview (vocational aspirations). Similarly, the vocational aspirations the student may communicate in an interview may differ from the aspirations the student might communicate on a paper and pencil test. That is, the type of assessment technique used, as well as who conducts the assessment may influence assessment results. In either case, the student's response is not a true reflection of "vocational aspirations," and hence, the assessment information gathered is inaccurate.

In order to take these factors into account and to increase the accuracy of assessment data gathered for transition planning, different transition team members should be asked to gather similar information about a student using different assessment techniques. For example, a teacher could be asked to assess a student's vocational interests by interviewing the student and by observing the student during leisure time. A school psychologist or guidance counselor could also be asked to assess the student's interests by interviewing the student's parents, and by administering a vocational interest inventory. Should the results of this interest assessment conducted by different team members using difference sources of information and different assessment techniques agree, considerable confidence can be placed in the results. In such a case, it is likely that the results of the assessment were overly influenced by either the method used to measure interests or the individual conducting the assessment. Should there be inconsistencies, however, less confidence can be placed in the results of this "interest assessment."

Assumptions Underlying Assessment

Several assumptions underlie the accurate assessment of any skill or trait (Salvia & Ysseldyke, 1991). Those professionals involved in assessment for transition planning must recognize these assumptions in order to properly interpret assessment data. If any of the following assumptions are not met, assessment results may be invalid. The reader should note that while the term "test" is used frequently in the following sections, the term as it is used here is meant to mean any assessment technique which may be used to collect assessment information, including rating scales, observational procedures, interviews, etc.

The Person Conducting the Assessment is Skilled

When assessment results are interpreted and used by transdisciplinary teams in transition planning, there is an inherent assumption that the test was administered, scored, and interpreted accurately. Whether this assumption is met will depend upon whether the person conducting the assessment has the appropriate training, experience, and skills needed. The test administrator must be knowledgeable about general assessment practices and must also be familiar with the administration guidelines of the test being used. The less experienced and skilled an individual is, both in regard to general testing and assessment practice, and in regard to administering, scoring, and interpreting the particular test being used, the less likely it is that accurate results will be obtained from the test.

Error Will Be Present

All tests contain some degree of error. No test score is a perfectly accurate measure of the trait being assessed. The amount of error inherent in a test can be estimated, and is reported as a measure of the test's "reliability." Reliability will be discussed shortly.

Test scores should not be interpreted rigidly, and instead, should be interpreted as estimates. As an example, consider the scale I use to weigh myself each morning. When I get on and off the scale twice in rapid succession, I generally get two different readings. Obviously, I have not gained or lost weight in that time period. I recognize that my scale yields different measures on multiple weighings, and I know I can never be sure which of these different measures (if any) is my current weight. Therefore I take multiple weighings, average them, and consider the average an estimate of my current weight.

Tests are not unlike weight scales in this regard. Due to the error inherent in them, tests will generally yield different scores when administered several times to the same student. Thus, we can never be sure that the score obtained on a test is the one score that perfectly accurately estimates the degree to which the student currently possesses the trait being measured by the test. Hence, we must treat scores as estimates, and interpret these scores with some degree of flexibility.

The Test is Appropriate to Use with a Particular Student

When selecting a standardized norm reference test for use with a particular student, it is important to insure that the background and experiences of the students comprising the norm group do not differ markedly from the background and experiences of the students to whom the test is being administered. If this is not the case, the score yielded by the test will be the result of an unfair or an inappropriate comparison and will be inaccurate. As an example, consider that an adult male who is 5'11" tall and weighs 180 pounds is generally considered to be of average height and weight when compared to the entire population of men in the U.S. However, if this person were to be compared with only male professional football and basketball players (an unfair and inappropriate comparison), they would inaccurately be labeled as short and underweight.

Additionally, if tests require skills of the test-taker that are not the focus of the assessment and not possessed by the student, the results of the test will be inaccurate and misleading. For example, a test that requires vision will yield inaccurate results for blind individuals and a test that requires hearing will yield inaccurate results for deaf and hearing-impaired individuals. A test that requires a seventh grade reading level will yield inaccurate results for an individual who only reads at the fourth grade level, etc.

The Test Measures What it Purports to Measure

As Salvia & Ysseldyke (1991) suggest, we cannot rely on a test's name in defining what the test measures. We must analyze the content of the test and ensure that the items adequately reflect the trait or traits supposedly being measured. Unfortunately, many tests have titles that do not accurately describe the nature of the test's content, and do not correspond to what research on the test has suggested the test measures. Whether a test measures what it purports to measure is generally considered to be an issue of "validity," a concept which will be discussed shortly.

Situational Factors Which Influence Assessment Results

Test users must be aware of various situational factors that may influence a student's performance on a particular test. In that these factors may influence or distort test results, test scores must be interpreted in light of such factors. This section discusses the following situational factors: the physical environment in which the test is administered, the emotional climate associated with the testing, the test type and administration procedures, the examiner's test administration skills, and the test-taker's background and life circumstances.

Physical Environment

The physical environment in which testing is done may affect test performance. Inadequate lighting, heating, and ventilation may detract from an individual's test performance. Similarly, testing a student in a crowded room or in a room with many distractions may prevent the student from performing at an optimum level, and may result in test scores that are inaccurate.

Emotional Climate

Emotional climate refers to the degree of comfort a student feels in a testing situation. This is a function of many factors including the physical environment in which the testing is done, the nature of the interaction between the test-taker and examiner, and the time or day during which testing is completed. For example, students may be unnerved when being tested in front of others or in a small crowded room, may feel uncomfortable with the examiner's reaction to them, or may be annoyed that they are being tested instead of participating in their normally scheduled class or activity. All of these factors may result in inaccurate test scores.

Test Type and Administration Practices

The type of test used, the number of students administered the test at a given time, and the amount of testing done in any one sitting (without break) will also influence test performance. Some students perform optimally on essay tests, while others perform optimally on more structured types of tests like multiple choice. Similarly, some students are intimidated and distracted by large group settings while others are not. Some students are capable of maintaining sustained attention on a task for longer periods of time than are other students and can better manage lengthy tests.

Examiner Skill

As previously mentioned, the expertise possessed by the examiner will influence the test score derived. Skill in organizing and arranging the test materials and test environment, skill in administering and scoring the test, skill in motivating the student and managing the student's behavior, will all influence student test performance and ultimately, the score derived from the test.

Current and Past Life Circumstances of the Student

Assessment results must be considered in light of the student's current health and nutrition, family life, background, and attitude at the time of testing. Significant events in the student's past, like deaths, divorces, serious illnesses, etc. are likely to influence student test performance and must be considered when interpreting test scores. For these reasons, comprehensive medical, social, and developmental histories should be a part of all comprehensive assessments designed to aid in transition planning.

Reliability and Validity

In order to properly select, use, and interpret assessment results, one must have a general understanding of the issues of reliability and validity. The following section is meant to briefly introduce the reader to these topics.

Reliability

Reliability refers to the degree of consistency and stability inherent in scores yielded by a measuring instrument. When measures are reliable they are relatively free from error. The less reliable a test is, the more error will be present in the test's scores, and the less accurate these scores will be. By estimating reliability, we can determine how accurate our test scores are. Tests that possess less than adequate reliability are relatively useless and should not be used.

Three methods exist for estimating a test's reliability: Test-retest, Alternative forms, and internal consistency. Each of these methods yields a "reliability coefficient" symbolized by "r." Reliability coefficients range from .00 (indicating the absence of reliability) to 1.00 (indicating perfect reliability). The closer the reliability coefficient is to 1.00, the more consistent are the scores yielded by the test.

Test-Retest Reliability

When assessing reliability using this procedure, the same test is administered to the same group of people at two different points in time. The two sets of scores are then correlated. As such, test-retest reliability is an estimate of the stability of scores over time.

Alternate Form Reliability

Using two equivalent forms of the same test assesses this form of reliability. One group of individuals are given Form A of the test and then Form B of the test. The other group of individuals is given Form B of the test following by Form A of the test (alternating the order of administration of the two forms of the test controls for any systematic inflation of scores on any one form of the test due to practice). Scores from the two forms of the test are then correlated to yield a reliability coefficient for the test.

Internal Consistency Reliability

This form of reliability is based upon one administration of the test to one group of individuals. The test is divided into two equivalent forms and scores from both forms are then correlated. The most common method for splitting a test into two equivalent forms is to divide the test into even-numbered items and odd-numbered items. It is important to note that internal consistency reliability estimates are inappropriate to use for timed tests, and do not estimate changes which may occur over time. Hence, estimations of both internal consistency reliability and test-retest reliability should be considered when evaluating tests. Other methods for measuring internal consistency reliability exist as well and use formulas such as the Kuder-Richardson Formula 20, and Cronbach's Alpha.

When evaluating a test's reliability, one should consider the type of reliability provided as well as the reliability coefficients. Ideally, evidence of several forms of reliability should be provided. While reliability coefficients of .90 or higher are considered to be good, coefficients of .80 or higher are generally considered to be adequate (Sattler, 1990).

Validity

Whereas reliability refers to the extent to which a measuring instrument is consistent, stable, and free of error, validity refers to the extent to which the instrument actually measures what it purports to measure. It a test is reliable, it may or may not be valid. That is, it may be consistently measuring something other than what it purports to measure. However, if a test is valid (measuring what it purports), then it is also reliable (it is not "measuring" error). Three types of validity exist: content validity, criterion-related validity (consisting of both concurrent validity and predictive validity), and construct validity.

Content Validity

Content validity refers to the extent to which items on a test are representative of the domain the test purports to measure. Clearly, a test which contains only subtraction problems cannot be considered a valid test of mathematics. Such a test also needs to include addition, multiplication, division, algebra, geometry, etc. as well as subtraction. Thus, the items on this hypothetical test do not adequately represent the domain of mathematics, and the test cannot be considered to possess adequate content validity. Content validity is not assessed via statistical methods, but instead is often judged by a panel of experts familiar with the domain measured by the test.

Criterion-Related Validity

There are two types of criterion-related validity: concurrent validity and predictive validity. Concurrent validity is generally assessed by correlating scores on the test of interest with a well-established test that is known to be a valid measure of the trait(s) supposedly measured by the test of interest. If the two tests are highly correlated, it is assumed they are measuring the same trait(s), and that the test of interest is a valid measure of the trait(s) it purports to measure.

Predictive validity refers to the correlation between a test and a criterion in which there is a time-lapse between administration of the test and performance on the criterion measure. The assumption being made is that if a test is measuring what it purports to measure, it should be able to predict the kinds of occurrences that valid tests of this type are capable of predicting. For example, aptitude tests are generally capable of making predictions about an individual's performance on certain types of tasks. Hence, to assess the predictive validity of a test believed to be measuring "mechanical aptitude," one might correlate scores on the test with performance in an automotive mechanics-training program, for example. High correlations between scores on the test and performance in the program would suggest that scores could be used to predict performance and that the test probably does measure some type of mechanical aptitude.

Just as reliability is reported in the form of a coefficient that ranges between 0 and 1.00, so, too, is validity. As Gay (1987) has suggested, there is no "magic number" a validity coefficient should reach. Generally, the higher the validity coefficient, the more valid the instrument is. Hence, professionals who are considering selecting instruments for possible use in transition planning should compare the validity evidence of several instruments which could be utilized to assess a particular trait, and base their evaluation on this comparison.

Evaluating Tests

Many factors must be considered when evaluating the adequacy of tests, and when interpreting scores obtained from them. Both practical and technical issues need to be considered when evaluating tests for possible use in transition planning. From a practical standpoint, issues such as the ease with which the test can be administered, the clarity of the directions provided, the ease of scoring, and the attractiveness and durability of the test materials must all be considered. From a technical standpoint, the reliability and validity of the test must also be evaluated along with other factors that are beyond the scope of this brief review. Readers can obtain information about all published tests from two major sources: the *Mental Measurements Yearbook* (MMY) (Mitchell, 1985) and *Test Critiques* (Keyser & Sweetland, 1984–1985). In that the effectiveness of transition planning partially depends upon whether or not information collected on a student is accurate, professionals involved in transition planning should evaluate each and every assessment instrument used to collect information. The selection of assessment instruments for use in transition planning should not be taken lightly, and only instruments that are reliable and valid (and hence, are likely to result in accurate information being generated) should be utilized.

Assessment Techniques

As discussed earlier in this chapter, this author advocates a multitrait, multimethod approach to assessment for transdisciplinary transition planning. As such, each domain to be assessed should be assessed using multiple assessment techniques. Several different assessment techniques can be utilized by transdisciplinary transition team members for planning purposes and include paper and pencil test, interviews, observations, situational assessment, and work samples. Each of these techniques has distinct advantages and disadvantages which should be recognized by those who use them. The following section briefly summarizes these advantages and disadvantages.

Paper and Pencil Tests

Paper and pencil tests are of two types: criterion-referenced and norm-referenced. Criterion-referenced tests identify an individual's status with respect to an established standard of performance, and as such, determine the student's mastery of certain skills (Sattler, 1988). For example, a criterion-referenced test may be used to determine how many competencies a student has acquired in a vocational training program. Statements such as "Sue has mastered 95 percent of the skills taught in Diesel Mechanics I" can be made with criterion-referenced tests. Norm-referenced tests compare an individual's performance to other individuals. Statements like "Sue's interest in automotive mechanics exceeds 80 percent of all other students her age across the country" can be made on the basis of norm-referenced tests. Paper and pencil tests have the advantage of being relatively inexpensive, and quick and easy to use. Additionally, they often possess adequate reliability and validity. Because they allow for comparisons to be made, tests are useful in selecting students for certain programs. For example, vocational aptitude tests are often used to assist in determining in which vocational training program a particular student should be placed. However, norm-referenced tests have been criticized for a variety of reasons. They frequently create tension and anxiety in students that interferes with their performance and are often used to label and categorize students in ways that do them harm (Sax, 1980). Tests have also been said to discriminate against minorities (Sax, 1980), although this has been debated (Reschly, 1990; Sattler, 1988). Tests have also been said to penalize very bright and creative students in that unique or innovative responses are often penalized and scored as incorrect. Perhaps most importantly, tests have been criticized for providing information that has little value from an instructional planning process.

Interviews

As Sattler (1988) has indicated, interviews provide an opportunity for professionals to encourage a student to provide information the student would not have ordinarily and otherwise volunteered, and to gather information about students that may not be obtainable in any other way. The interview is an extremely flexible data-gathering strategy that can be modified or changed at a moment's notice to accommodate and integrate any new information. It also can be used to gather information about a wide range of topics, and as such, is extremely versatile.

The interview also possesses some disadvantages as an assessment tool. Reliability and validity are difficult to establish, and interviewer and interviewee biases may distort the information obtained. Interviews are often time-consuming to conduct and require skills that some professionals do not possess. Hence, many professionals may need to be trained in order for them to effectively conduct interviews.

Observation

Much information can be gained about a student by simply watching and listening to the student. However, unsystematic and poorly planned observations are likely to yield inaccurate information. Ideally, observation of a student's behavior should take place in a variety of settings, be conducted at different times, and be completed by several different transdisciplinary transition team members. The use of multiple observers and different observational settings can assist in determining the reliability and validity of the observational data gathered and also increases the representativeness of the behavior observed. Correct use of behavioral observation provides objective data that strengthen inferences that are made about students from the use of other assessment techniques, such as paper and pencil tests. For example, observing a student competently mixing mortar and laying brick supports the inference of "high aptitude in masonry" which may have been made based upon scores from an aptitude test. Similarly, observing the student while involved in the task of mixing mortar may offer support for or against the inference of "high interest in masonry" which may have been derived from a paper and pencil interest inventory. While tests are generally limited to measuring one specific trait, observations can be used to measure many traits. Based upon an observation, for example, inferences can be made about a student's interests, aptitudes, work habits, and so forth. Few other assessment techniques have such versatility. Observations can also be conducted in a way so as to allow social comparisons to be made. For example, by observing the amount of "on-task" time Sue (an "average" student) spends working on a project in a vocational class, we now have a basis for comparing any other student in the class. So if Bob's work habits are of concern, his "on-task" time can be observed and compared to Sue's, to determine if his work habits are "below average."

Additionally, an observation provides a picture of a student's spontaneous behavior in natural settings, and allows for a comparison to behavior in more contrived settings like a test situation. Observations of behavior also provide information on students that may not be gained in other ways from uncooperative students.

Several common problems exist in behavioral observation. Despite the attempt to observe *naturally* occurring behavior, the presence of an observer creates an *artificial* situation, and may influence the student being observed. Students may act differently in the presence of an observer than they do when the observer is not present. Additionally, the values and expectations that observers possess may also bias their observations. That is, observers are more likely to notice and record behaviors they expect to notice. Relatedly, the first impressions observers form about a student often bias their later judgments and ratings of the student. Unless multiple observations are made at various times in different settings, the observer may fail to obtain a representative and generalizable sample of behavior. If an unrepresentative sample of behavior is obtained, it is likely that inaccurate inferences will be made, and inappropriate programming (based upon these inferences) will be enacted. Hence, obtaining valid observational data can be time-consuming. Lastly, errors in recording behavior often occur because observers are unfamiliar with the recording system being used, have insufficient time to record what they have observed, or experience a lapse in attention and concentration frequently referred to as observer drift (Salvia & Ysseldyke, 1991).

Work Samples

A work sample is "a well-defined work activity involving tasks, materials, and tools which are identical or similar to those in an actual job or cluster of jobs . . . and are used to assess an individual's vocational aptitude, worker characteristics and vocational interest" (VEWAA-CARF, Vocational Evaluation and Work Adjustment Standards with Interpretation Guidelines and VEWAA Glossary, 1978). For example, a clerical work sample might require a student to respond to phone calls, perform typing and filing activities, and so forth. The administration of a work sample often takes several hours, and usually consists of a demonstration/training phase and assessment phase. During the demonstration/training phase, the student is trained to perform certain work tasks following a live or audio-video demonstration. Following this, the student is often given an opportunity to practice the task and receive feedback on their performance. Following this demonstration/training phase, the student performs the task and is evaluated. The student's performance is usually compared to age-based norms or industrial standards.

As summarized by Levinson (1993), advantages of work samples include the following: (1) they provide students with an opportunity to explore and try out various jobs in a rather controlled setting, 2) they allow aspects of "jobs" to be brought into school and classroom settings, (3) they are more like real work than are interest or aptitude tests and hence, may be more motivating to students, and (4) they can be used to assess a variety of traits including interests, aptitudes, and work habits. Additionally, work samples require minimum academic skills, and provide direct and immediate feedback to students (Swanson & Watson, 1982). Disadvantages of work samples include the following: (1) they emphasize quality and quantity of production rather than personality factors, (2) they provide a superficial assessment of interest and aptitude in that the conditions (environment) surrounding performance of the job are usually not replicated by the work sample, (3) they are expensive and time-consuming to utilize, and (4) they often lack acceptable psychometric properties; as such, there is no assurance that work samples accurately predict performance in specific jobs (Levinson, 1993).

Situational Assessment

Situational assessment techniques are designed to assess a student's interests, aptitudes, or work habits in a real or simulated work situation. Information about the student is gathered from peers and supervisors via use of observation, interviews, and rating scales. For example, a student who is interested in food service occupations may be placed under the supervision of a school cafeteria worker, work in the school cafeteria, and be observed and evaluated. Situational assessment techniques have numerous advantages. They closely resemble real work and as such may be particularly motivating to students. However, they are extremely time-consuming, difficult to establish, and tend to be rather expensive to operate. Additionally, situational assessment strategies usually require extensive coordination and cooperation with employers and instructors.

Structuring Assessments for Transition Planning

Several factors should be considered when structuring assessments for the purpose of transition planning. First, assessments should be structured with career development theory in mind, and all assessment data should be interpreted in light of this developmental theory. One cannot develop or implement a valid transition assessment program without an understanding of what is developmentally appropriate vocational behavior to expect of an individual at any given point in time. To design and implement a school-based transition assessment program, one must understand career development theory, and use such knowledge in deciding what traits will be assessed in a particular individual at any given grade or age level. Similarly, career development theory allow assessment results to be placed in perspective, and will allow users of the assessment data to generate developmentally appropriate recommendations for the student who has been assessed.

Second, assessment should be an ongoing process rather than a "once upon a time" occurrence. In that career development is a continuous process, and assessment should be linked to developmental objectives, it naturally follows that assessment should be a somewhat continuous process as well.

Consistent with this, many vocational and transition assessment programs based in the schools are multilevel programs. At each level, the assessment process has different purposes (based upon what is developmentally appropriate to assess at a particular point in time), uses a variety of assessment techniques and strategies, and is designed to gather many types of information. Different professionals are responsible for several aspects of the assessment, and assessment responsibilities are assigned based upon a professional's knowledge and expertise. Programs usually consist of either two or three levels of assessment. As summarized by Anderson, Hohenshil, Buckland-Heer and Levinson (1990), *level 1* assessments begin during the elementary school years, focus upon an individual's needs, values, interests, abilities, interpersonal skills, and decision-making skills, utilize vocational and career exploration activities, and have the goal of building self-awareness. *Level 2* assessments generally occur during the middle school or junior high school years, focus more specifically on an assessment of vocational interests, vocational aptitudes, work habits and career maturity, utilize interviews, observations, and standardized norm-referenced assessment instruments, and have the goal of continuing to encourage career exploration and assisting individuals in making tentative choices regarding educational and career goals. A *level 3* assessment generally occurs during the high school years, often employs more experientially-based assessment devices like work samples and situational assessment, and focuses upon the specific training one needs to obtain post-school education or employment. Level 3 assessments are also designed to determine what skills an individual may need in order to live independently in the community.

In structuring assessments for transition planning, it is sometimes helpful to integrate the assessment process with the special education reevaluation process that is mandated for all students with disabilities. This was alluded to earlier. As Levinson & Capps (1985) have noted, integrating the special education reevaluation process and assessment for transition planning has several advantages. First, it provides for a rather time and cost efficient assessment process. Rather than having the same school personnel gather the same information at two different points in time for two different purposes, the interfacing of the vocational and transition assessment and special education reevaluation processes reduces redundant information gathering, and conserves personnel time (resulting in cost savings). Second, the special education reevaluation process provides a framework for the multidisciplinary cooperation that must exist in transition planning. Third, integrating the vocational assessment and special education reevaluation processes insures a holistic and comprehensive assessment of the student. That is, assessment for transition planning will not be completed in isolation, but will be combined with psychological, educational, social, medical, and other data to provide a holistic picture of the student. An assessment that focused only upon the student's vocational functioning (and ignored other aspects of the student's functioning) would be very narrow in scope, and prone to error. Combining the two processes insures comprehensiveness, and insures the development of a transition plan based upon all aspects of the student's functioning.

SUMMARY

The assessment of individual student needs is a necessary first step in transition planning. Assessment has the purpose of identifying an individual's strengths and weaknesses, and is used to identify what skills a student may need to acquire in order to make a successful transition. Given that all transition planning and instruction is based upon assessment, a thorough and valid assessment of a student's needs is perhaps the most important part of the transition process. That is, if an adequate or inaccurate assessment of a student is conducted, skills the student lacks that are critical to successful transition may never be included in the student's transition plan, and may never be acquired by the student prior to leaving school.

Assessment that is conducted for the purpose of transition planning should be based on a multitrait-multimethod approach to assessment in which different transition team members collect similar information from a student using different assessment techniques and strategies. Similarly, errors in assessment can be reduced by recognizing assumptions inherent in the assessment process, interpreting assessment data in light of situational and background factors, and utilizing only assessment strategies and techniques which are reliable and valid. Lastly, assessments should utilize a variety of assessment techniques, focus upon skills which are "functional" for the student, and address intellectual/cognitive, academic/educational, personality/social skills, vocational interests/aptitudes, career maturity/self-advocacy, and life skills. The following chapters in this book address these areas.

REFERENCES

Anderson, W.T., Hohenshil, T.H. Buckland-Heer, K. & Levinson, E.M. (1990). Best practices in vocational assessment of students with disabilities. In A. Thomas & J. Grimes (Eds.) *Best practices in school psychology-II.* Washington, DC: National Association of School Psychologists.

Gay, L.R. (1987). *Educational research: Competencies for analysis and application,* 3rd ed. Columbus, OH: Merrill.

Isaacson, L.E. (1986). *Career information in counseling and career development,* 4th ed. Boston, MA: Allyn and Bacon, Inc

Keyser, D.J. & Sweetland, R.C. (Eds.) (1984-85). *Test critiques* (Vol 1-4). Kansas City: Test Corporation of America.

Levinson, E.M. (1993). *Transdisciplinary vocational assessment: Issues in school-based programs.* Brandon, VT: Clinical Psychology Publishing Co.

Levinson, E.M. & Capps, C.F. (1985). Vocational assessment and special education triennial reevaluation is at the secondary school level. *Psychology in the Schools, 22,* 283–292.

Mitchell, J.V. (Ed.) (1985). *The ninth mental measurement yearbook.* Lincoln: University of Nebraska, Buros Institute of Mental Measurement.

Reschly, D. (1990). Best practices in intellectual assessment. In A. Thomas & J. Grimes (Eds.) *Best practices in school psychology II.* Washington, DC: National Association of School Psychologists.

Salvia, J. & Ysseldyke, J.E. (1991). *Assessment,* 5th ed. Boston, MA: Houghton-Mifflin.

Sax, G. (1980). *Principles of educational and psychological measurement and evaluation,* 2nd ed. Belmont, CA: Wadsworth.

Sattler, J. (1988). *Assessment of children.* San Diego: CA: Jerome Sattler.

Sears, S. (1982). A definition of career guidance terms: A National Vocational Guidance Association perspective. *Vocational Guidance Quarterly, 31,* 137–143.

Super, D.E. (1942). *The dynamics of vocational adjustment.* New York: Harper.

U.S. Department of Education, Office of Special Education and Rehabilitative Services (1990). *Twelfth annual report to Congress on the implementation of the Education of the Handicapped Act.* Washington, DC: U.S. Government Printing Office.

VEWAA-CARF (1978). *Vocational evaluation and work adjustment standards with interpretation guidelines and VEWAA glossary.* Menomonie, WI: University of Wisconsin-Stout Vocational Rehabilitation Institute, Materials Development Center.

Wehman, P., Kregel, J. & Barcus, J.M. (1985). From school to work: A vocational transition model or handicapped students. *Exceptional Children, 52* (1), 25–37.

Chapter 2

TRANSITION ASSESSMENT: FOCUS ON COGNITIVE INTELLECTUAL ABILITY

Daniel Cane and Mark Nevill

INTRODUCTION: COGNITIVE ASSESSMENT IN TRANSITION

The concept of intelligence or IQ and its relationship to vocational transition is not well understood. Yet, IQ readily is associated with occupational status. In fact, the concept of "intelligence" itself has been the subject of a great deal of controversy over many decades. Society has readily identified it with success in school and in occupational endeavors. Education and military systems, for example, have been major consumers of intelligence measures and have found that intelligence is related to outcome criteria, such as educational and occupational success. However, specific cognitive profiles based on outdated individually administered intelligence tests have not provided transition assessment teams with direction on which to base recommendations. Recent advances in scientific statistical research, however, have resulted in increasingly validated instruments that measure multiple-cognitive ability and offer additional promise. As such, this chapter will begin with a brief review of the history of intelligence testing, and its relationship to occupational status.

INTELLIGENCE AND OCCUPATIONAL STATUS: AN HISTORICAL PERSPECTIVE

Spearman's "g" Theory

Spearman's "g" factor theory of general intelligence was originally devised to assess an individual's capacity for complex mental work, i.e., reasoning, comprehension, and hypothesis testing (Thorndike, 1997; Ortiz, Flanagan, & McGrew, 1999; Sattler, 2001; Wade & Travris, 1987). In 1904, Spearman based his revolutionary factor theory upon a newly discovered factor analytic statistical method (Thorndike, 1997). He believed that the general intelligence ability (g) represented a majority of cognitive tasks that an individual is likely to perform. Spearman's theory was often misrepresented as a single factor theory (Ortiz et al., 1999; Thorndike, 1997). Interestingly, Spearman later included smaller factors in addition to the overall "g" score (Ortiz et al., 1999). According to Jerome Sattler (2001), these smaller factors ". . . are less complex, emphasizing recognition, recall, speed, visual-motor abilities, and motor abilities (e.g., maze speed, crossing out numbers, counting groups of dots, simple addition, and tapping speed)" (p. 138). What followed the theory was an attempt at measuring intelligence through an objective and unbiased method. The 1916 Stanford-Binet Intelligence Test, Lewis Terman's version of the Binet-Simon Scale, was based on the g factor of intelligence. It provided the standard in America for classifying individuals (Sattler, 2001; Thorndike, 1997). The test provided a single composite intelligence score (IQ), resulting in a prolific acceptance of the objective measure (Ortiz et al., 1999).

Theories of Intelligence Evolve

Efforts ensued to advance intelligence theory with empirical data for improved individual intelligence measurement. Theories of intelligence were precursors to methods of measurement even though a mismatch occurred in development. Measurement typically followed behind progression in psychometric theory, resulting in gaps between theory and test development (McGrew & Flanagan, 1998; Ortiz et al., 1999). Raymond Cattell's dichotomous theory spearheaded the theoretical movement. His dichotomous theory categorized intelligence into fluid (Gf) and crystallized (Gc) domains (McGrew & Flanagan, 1998; Sattler, 2001). Fluid intelligence relates to non-verbal tasks that involve new learning capacities and mental operations, where as crystallized intelligence is associated with the acquisition of skills and stores of knowledge (Sattler, 2001). Many attempts were undertaken to interpret and integrate the dichotomous model into test development and practice (McGrew & Flanagan, 1998; Ortiz et al., 1999). The Wechsler series of intelligence test instruments, including Wechsler Intelligence Scale for Children (WISC) and Wechsler Adult Intelligence Scale (WAIS), are the most popular test instruments to incorporate a dichotomous orientation. It measures verbal and non-verbal (performance) abilities (Ortiz et al., 1999; Alfonso et al., 2000). David Wechsler's original measurement methods utilized aspects of the Army Alpha and Army Beta, tests that were initial group intelligence tests utilized in the military (Sattler, 2001). He also combined clinical, practical, and empirical findings to finalize his intelligence test (Ortiz et al., 1999). Another dichotomous type of intelligence test is the Kaufman Assessment Battery for Children (K-ABC; Kaufman & Kaufman, 1983), which measures simultaneous and successive processing (Ortiz et al., 1999). These areas involve perceiving and acting upon information in "wholes" or in "sequence," respectively (Sattler, 2001).

The third wave of intelligence theory progression occurred with an attempt at a "multiple" intelligence theoretical orientation (McGrew & Flanagan, 1998). Utilizing multiple factor analysis, Thurstone identified seven factors of intelligence (Sattler, 2001), which became a source of great debate in the 1930s (Thorndike, 1997). These factors included Space, Perceptual Speed, Number, Verbal Meaning, Word Fluency, Memory, and Inductive Reasoning (Sattler, 2001). Initially, Thurstone, theorized that the seven factors did not relate to a g score; however, later research confirmed that the identified factors were moderately correlated were moderate (Sattler, 2001). As such, he suggested that intelligence possesses a certain amount of systematic organization (Sattler, 2001).

A majority of current intelligence test instruments including the Standford-Binet: IV (SB-IV, Thorndike, Hagen, & Sattler, 1986), Differential Abilities Scale (DAS; Elliot, 1990), Wechsler Intelligence Scale for Children–Third Edition and Wechsler Adult Intelligence Scale–Third Edition (WISC-III & WAIS-III; Wechsler, 1990, 1997) have fallen short in assessing identified multiple cognitive domains (McGrew &

Flanagan, 1998; Ortiz et al., 1999). Additionally, the original Woodcock-Johnson Psycho-educational Battery was also considered an "incomplete" instrument due to adhering to the original Gf-Gc (crystallized and fluid intelligence) theory (WJ; Woodcock & Johnson, 1977) (McGrew & Flanagan, 1998; Ortiz et al., 1999). The successive and simultaneous information processing model from the Kaufman series of intelligence tests were incorporated into the Cognitive Assessment System (CAS; Naglieri & Das, 1997) (McGrew & Flanagan, 1998). The addition of attention and planning were included to fulfill the PASS (hence the acronym) theory of cognitive processing or information processing approach (McGrew & Flanagan, 1998). Most intelligence tests mentioned were not developed to match an operational definition of a strong theory (McGrew & Flanagan, 1998; Ortiz et al., 1999). Additionally, the above measures do not reflect a current empirically-based theory and do not provide a complete coverage of known "multiple" cognitive domains (McGrew & Flanagan, 1998; Ortiz et al., 1999).

Despite advancements in intelligence theory, measurement methods were slow to match evolving complex statistical research and development. Although a positive relationship between g and achievement has been established, the match between intelligence test profiles and academic achievement has been found to have little value within a multifactored school based assessment (Reschly & Grimes, 1995; Reschly, 1997).

Role of Intelligence in the Military

Supported by the United States Government, the military was another consumer of intelligence measurement in America. It was known at the time that general intelligence, g, served as a quantifiable method of mental measurement. Due to the need for efficient and objective-based personnel decisions, IQ paved the way for categorizing individuals into various military duties or occupational assignments.

The military first used a mental ability measure, the Army Alpha, in World War I. It was the first of two group administered ability measures that screened and classified approximately 1.7 million draftees (Thorndike, 1997). The results of the tests provided the military with direction regarding the assignment of occupational duties. The prototype for this test was a group administered intelligence test that was constructed by one of Lewis Terman's graduate students at Stanford

University, Arthur Otis (Thorndike, 1997). However, there was a flaw with the measurement because it failed to represent abilities of non-English speaking recruits. This resulted in a non-verbal type of instrument, the Army Beta, being developed (Thorndike, 1997).

Terman conceived of the intelligence quotient as an indicator of the inherited or genetic make-up of an individual that is not malleable, but rather as stagnant and fixed (Thorndike, 1997). As a result, based on the use of these tests, inaccurate interpretations and recommendations were prepared on the basis of questionable validity. Based upon low scores men were discouraged to apply for officers' positions (Wade & Travris, 1987).

Army's Classifications According to IQ

Despite obvious erroneous assumptions regarding IQ measures, broad themes emerged regarding occupational assignment groupings. In World War I, draftees' civilian occupations directly related to their intelligence standard scores, resulting in a corresponding rank order (Dawis, 1994). Those in professional occupations scored highest, and were followed by scores from those in white-collar positions. Those in unskilled positions scored lowest. The same findings occurred with World War II draftees on the Army General Classification Test (AGCT) (Dawis, 1994).

Dawis (1994) analyzed means (Averages) and score ranges from the Army Alpha, AGCT, and General Aptitude Test. He discovered that since implementation in the 1920s, the rank order of occupational categories according to their respective mean score remained fairly constant. The data also suggested that the amount of training or education one possessed was closely associated with the intelligence-occupation ranking (Dawis, 1994). Higher-level occupations demanded higher ability entrance standards as well as complex training programs. Lower level occupations did not require as much skill development, and were therefore associated with low training needs (Dawis, 1994). However, general themes within the data revealed that intelligence alone was an inadequate predictor. In addition to IQ, it appeared that occupational assignments were associated with educational experiences. Although themes emerged in the military's use of mental measurements, the connection between intelligence, education and occupational assignments was still unclear.

Intelligence and Occupational Status

The dynamic relationship between intelligence and experiences such as educational opportunities and exposure, continued to be studied. Although highly criticized, the concept of IQ survived because of its relationship with occupational and educational attainment. However, in retrospect, it was determined that education had a significant impact upon occupational ranking. Thus, the relation between IQ and academic achievement as a combined variable led to the increased predictive potential of occupational attainment.

Herrnstein and Murray (1994) revisited the phenomenon of intelligence and class structure in their book, *The Bell Curve.* Specifically, they sought to explain the degree of influence that intelligence or cognitive ability had on life outcomes, i.e., occupational, social, and economic outcomes. In this controversial book, Herrnstein and Murray analyzed occupational and cognitive data from the National Longitudinal Survey of Youth from 1979 to 1994 to offer explanations for societal stratification. Herrnstein and Murray (1994) discovered that when people sought advanced education, high IQ individuals gravitated toward occupations that required high IQs. Around the mid-century mark, Herrnstein and Murray (1994) observed that "bright" individuals were dispersed throughout occupational levels, which changed as the century drew near. They commented that high IQ becomes increasingly necessary as the difficulty level rises in the occupation. On the contrary, lower IQ was loosely associated with an increase in the potential for social or adjustment problems. When factoring out race, gender, SES, and education levels, Herrnstein and Murray (1994) found that IQ predicted social problems in society.

Intelligence and Use in Schools

In response to the practical utility of IQ tests within the school setting, Braden (1995) recommended that school psychologists should continue to administer IQ tests. Although he believes that IQ provides useful information, he concluded that when presented alone IQ measurement can overlook pertinent information. It is quite feasible that this narrow, one-dimensional means of assessment could disregard specific academically meaningful data that, in turn, could shape instructional practices. Therefore, a multifactor assessment creates the best outcome because the school team is better able to accumulate relevant information in order to determine how much weight IQ or other measures should have in educational decision-making, specifically in regard to academic instruction or vocational planning (Levinson, 1993; Levinson, 1998b; Oakland, 1995; Reschley & Grimes, 1995).

Current Trends in Transition and Cognitive Assessment

Intelligence, Achievement and Occupations

Researchers have long attempted to use data from cognitive assessments to predict functioning in a wide range of human activities. While IQ scores have been used in multiple studies, the lack of empirical research devoted to the application of cognitive assessment in transition evaluations is surprising. One strong area of research is the investigation of the relationship between IQ and academic achievement. Studies suggest correlations between intelligence and educational attainment range from .20 to .70, while a correlation of .50 is considered the most accurate and supports a moderate positive relationship between intelligence and academic achievement (Morris and Levinson, 1993; Oakland 1995). While a moderate positive relationship exists, intelligence cannot be viewed in isolation. This is especially true when cognitive assessment information is to be used by transition planning teams for exceptional students.

Oakland (1995) investigated the relationship between reading comprehension and intelligence. As expected, students with higher levels of intelligence scored better on tests of reading comprehension. However, the variability within the IQ groupings provided significant overlap among groups. As a result, some individuals within the lower IQ groups actually outperformed their higher IQ peers. Oakland (1995) supported the use of intelligence tests for a variety of purposes, but firmly indicated the need for a multifactored approach to assessment. Many variables impact academic achievement besides an individual's level of intelligence. As an example, levels of intelligence are not good predictors of college graduation for incoming students (Morris and Levinson, 1993).

Oakland (1995) states:

> one task . . . is to broaden our understanding of aptitudes, not by discarding general intelligence, but by going beyond it to identify qualities that impact

> achievement, and then to discover methods that enable students to know and utilize their aptitudes well while either working to improve those that are deficient or finding means to minimize their impact on important life outcomes. (p. 24)

While not discounting the presence of the general ability factor, Oakland (1995) found intelligence to be much more complex. He conceptualized intelligence as being represented in three different forms. The genotype form, or a persons potential based on biology and environment, the phenotype form, or the ability or skill visible such as memory or reasoning skill; and a tested form that is exhibited and measured under standardized conditions. Measures of intelligence have been used interchangeably with measures of aptitude with the belief that one predicts the other (Oakland, 1995, McClelland, 1994).

Variables such as personality, temperament, and personal decisions play important roles in successful vocational functioning. McClelland (1994) disputes the notion that academic aptitude predicts successful performance and higher-level jobs. He supported this position by illustrating the correlation of years of schooling on occupational status (r = .60). McClelland (1994) states "Thus, if you partial out the effect of education, the relation of scholastic aptitude to life outcomes (e. g., occupational level, income) are effectively reduced to zero (p. 66)."

It continues to be a common practice for employers to evaluate potential employees based on educational credentials. The research literature fails to support a high degree of correlation between intelligence and vocational\occupational performance (Morris and Levinson, 1995). Researchers interested in the predictive ability of intelligence tests to job performance try to identify how much variability can be explained by comparing the measure of the test (i.e., IQ) with outcomes designed to measure job performance (i.e., length of employment, supervisor ratings, production etc.).

> Across a large number of studies, the average validity coefficient between psychometric ability-test scores and job performance is about 0.2. The square of this value indicates that only about 4 percent of the variability in job performance can be attributed to variability in psychometric ability test scores. Obviously, although 4 percent is better than nothing, it is far from the ideal of accounting for a full 100 percent of the variability in job performance. How, then, does this result square with the view that psychometric ability tests have substantial validity for all jobs. (p. 1159)

Some researchers argue that the correlation of 0.2 is an overestimation of the variability predicted by IQ tests, while others maintain that it is an underestimation. Wagner and Loukides (1994) found that the true predictive validity falls between four and 25 percent. The utility of ability testing for job placement is wholly dependent on the job type. If the job being applied for requires little skill then the screening measure requires little specificity and many will be chosen for the position. It is when the occupation or job opening requires a select composite of skills that ability testing truly becomes useful and cost efficient (Wagner and Loukides, 1994). The reverse would seem true when working with an exceptional population within the context of transition planning. The degree of specificity required is not because of a highly unique job, but because of the incredibly unique make-up of every student that passes through a schools' transition team. It is the team's responsibility to assess the student's unique blend of skills and abilities, in order to identify potential occupational/vocational opportunities.

While it appears possible to sort individuals by intelligence across different occupations, the delineation of individuals within a job or occupational class has not been successful (Morris and Levinson, 1995). Dawis (1994) states that the variability of IQ between occupations is often so minor as to be of no consequence. The only way to group intelligence in such a way as to provide meaning is to form groupings such as high, medium, and low. The research is clear that individuals with higher levels of intellectual ability tend to amass more years of formal education. Jobs lower in status require less training. As the complexity of occupations increases so do the training demands and entry requirements. The need for greater verbal and numerical skills also increases. Measures of intelligence have been viewed as the best indicators of these abilities (Dawis, 1994). Higher status jobs are clearly linked to formal education (Morris and Levinson, 1995; Herrnstein and Murray, 1994), and success in formal education is associated with IQ.

McClelland (1994) is an advocate of competency-based testing. McClelland (1994) indicates that measures of aptitude can deny access to jobs for individuals who possess the work-based competencies to be successful. Exceptional students transitioning to the world of work have similar types of difficulties. He relates the plight of a group of African American women who functioned academically at approximately the sixth-grade level. They were being supported in their jobs by a federal program that supported disadvantaged workers. Their supervisors indicated that they were doing good work and wanted to transfer them into the county system. These women were unable to attain an acceptable score on the General Aptitude Test Battery and therefore were unable to transfer into the county system. In order to circumvent this glitch in the system, McClelland was contracted to construct a competency-based evaluation that would prove these women capable of working at a high enough level to be transferred from the subsidized work program to county employment. Once completed and transferred, the women in this case were ranked as "outstanding" or "typical" by supervisors (McClelland 1994, p. 67). The main competencies established for successful work within their area were "they must be able to relate to people and they must be able to perform certain clerical tasks accurately, such as processing benefits" (p. 68).

While Dawis (1994) would agree that educational / aptitude requirements create a minimum competency, Wagner and Loukides, (1994) respond by reminding us of the not too recent past when only those with wealth or connections were able to avail themselves of educational opportunities. The testing requirement inherent in the civil service system, as an example, protects citizens from the cronyism and nepotism of the past. This study continues to illustrate that while there is a clear relationship between intelligence and academic achievement, the relationship between intelligence or academic achievement and successful job performance is much less clear.

Think of an individual who shows some outstanding skill; for example, a student who is on the dean's list and the recipient of every type of honor. What may also come to mind when you remember this person are his or her poor social skills, or general lack of common sense. At this point, the concept of practical intelligence comes to bear. Researchers have long been aware of the distinction between academic intelligence and tacit or practical intelligence. Sternberg, Wagner, Williams, and Horvath (1995) differentiate tacit knowledge from academic intelligence as follows:

> An academically intelligent individual is characterized by their facile acquisition of formal academic knowledge, the knowledge sampled by the ubiquitous intelligence tests and related aptitude tests. Conversely, the hallmark of the practically intelligent individual is their facile acquisition and use of tacit knowledge. Tacit knowledge refers to the action-oriented knowledge acquired without direct come from others that allows individuals to achieve goals they personally value. (p. 916)

Sternberg et al. (1995) cites the work of Horn and Cattell (1996) in discussing the developmental progression of cognitive abilities in adulthood. According to Catell-Horn Gf-Gc theory, fluid abilities are utilized to deal with novel situations and events. Crystallized intelligence is the summation of our learning through school and cultural experiences. Speaking in terms of cognitive development, research demonstrates that fluid intelligence declines through adulthood, whereas levels of crystallized intelligence are maintained. Sternberg et al. (1995) indicate that fluid abilities increase from ages 20 to 30 and remain stable until approximately age 50 and then decline. Performances on everyday problem-solving tasks and measures of crystallized intelligence increase through age 70.

Measurement of tacit knowledge or practical intelligence is quite different from standard tests of intelligence. Often times 15 to 20 hypothetical questions or scenarios are presented to individuals in the context of a work environment. Scoring consists of assigning rank orders to individual responses based on the quality of the response. Research results indicate that measures regarding tacit knowledge are good predictors of job performance, accounting for an additional 32 percent of the variance not accounted for by intelligence testing (Sternberg et al., 1995).

Occupational Performance and Exceptional Students

Research on job performance and exceptional populations does provide basic information useful to individuals involved in the transition planning process. When dealing with an exceptional population, nonverbal reasoning scores are often better predictors of vocational training success and success in lower level jobs (Levinson, 1995). Students with Mental Retardation who possess relative strengths of verbal reasoning in combination with appropriate social and behavioral skills, are more likely to maintain their job placements. Higher IQ is also related to an individual's need for training time. Those with higher IQs are able to acquire work routines at a much faster pace, reducing the employers investment in training and increasing the chance of successful job placement (Levinson, 1995).

Ree, Carretta, and Teachout (1995) studied a sample of 3,428 air force officers in pilot training school to investigate the causal relationships between general cognitive ability and prior job knowledge on job knowledge acquisition and work sample performance. Past research (Dye, Reck and McDaniel, 1993) cited in Ree et al. (1995) demonstrated that measures of job knowledge can predict job performance. Results of the Ree et al. (1995) study showed that outcomes were mediated by job knowledge, not by general measures of "g." Wagner (1997) builds on the work of Ree et al., (1995) and furthers their findings to exceptional populations. One of the reasons that individuals with higher levels of intelligence are more successful in postsecondary settings is their ability to acquire job skills at a faster pace than their lower IQ peers. The research reviewed explains that it is specific knowledge about a job that predicts success. Intelligence predicts training success and, of course, training time. Hence, Wagner (1997) recommends providing lower IQ students with job specific training before placement occurs.

Ree and Earles (1991) conducted a study to investigate the predictive power of specific abilities as compared to a measure of general intelligence or "g." Past research (Hunter, 1986 & Jenson, 1984) indicated that there was little utility in using specific ability measures to predict job-training success. Ree and Earles (1991) hypothesize that prior research found little difference between measures of specific abilities and measures of general intelligence because the general ability test and specific ability tests measured the same underlying construct. The Armed Services Vocational Battery (ASVB) was administered to a sample of 78,041 Air Force enlistees over a four-year period. The outcome measure was a final grade received by the enlistee in one of 82 possible training programs. Results found a significant interaction with specific abilities being slightly more predictive than general measures of intelligence. However, the significant results were believed to be an artifact of the unusually large sample size. Ree and Earles (1991) concluded that the level of significance was too small to be truly predictive. It was concluded that measures of general intelligence were most predictive of training success.

Faas and D'Alonzo (1991) reviewed the transition literature and found that as many as 50 percent of learning disabled students fail to succeed in the transition to postsecondary employment. This study was conducted in order to evaluate the predictive value of intelligence test scores, specifically, the WAIS-R, on the level of job success. Job success was measured by length of employment. Results indicated that the WAIS-R comprehension cluster was the best predictor of a positive transition from school to work. This factor score measures an individual's ability to comprehend language and respond in an appropriate manner, to memory for factual information, and vocabulary development. Faas and D'Alonzo (1991) suggest that students with oral comprehension problems be provided with strategies that focus on improving their ability to comprehend both oral and written communication. Simulating the variety of activities and situations inherent in different types of employment settings may assist in providing a schema for exceptional students to build upon. Students need the skills to deal with situations where they do not understand instructions. Social skills training may be necessary for exceptional students to appropriately communicate their questions or concerns (Faas and D'Alonzo, 1991).

School Psychologists and Use of Cognitive Assessment in Transition

Current literature shows that the involvement of school psychologists in transition-related services is quite low, which is surprising when the skills of school psychologists are examined in relation to the needs of transition planning teams. While this chapter is meant to be helpful for all members of a transdisciplinary transition team, school psychologists will be the team member obtaining and interpreting cognitive assessment data, so a review of trends in current service delivery appears appropriate. Levinson (1988) reports statistics quantifying the amount of time school psychologists spend in vocational transition planning. The sample utilized in the study consisted of 636 Pennsylvania school psychologists whose names were obtained from the Department of Education. Of the 636 packets 67 percent or 426 completed protocols were returned. Results indicated that 34.1 percent of the responding psychologists had spent some portion of their time involved with vocational assessment activities, 39.3 percent had performed limited vocational counseling, and 41 percent have been involved in consultative services with vocational education teachers. Only 12.7 percent participated directly in developing any type of curriculum or vocational transition program development. Psychologists dually certified and working as guidance counselors appeared to be more involved with transition planning services (Levinson, 1988).

Levinson (1990) has discussed some of the issues that impede involvement of school psychologists in transition planning services for exceptional children. First, school psychologists do not feel adequately trained in the area of vocational assessment and transition planning.

Training in this area has been directed at guidance counselor and not school psychologists. Second, constraints inherent in the traditional "gatekeeper" role in the area of special education services restricts the amount of time school psychologists can devote to transition services. Additionally, some school psychologists feel that vocational services are outside their realm of responsibility and believe that these services should be provided by vocationally-oriented educators. Relatedly, school district administrations sometimes limit school psychologists' participation as they view their involvement in transition as being outside the traditional role of school psychologists (Levinson, 1990).

Despite these constraints, the National Association of School Psychologists has historically supported the role of a School Psychologist in vocational and transition activities as stated in the following standards for practice, "4.3.3.2 school psychologists design direct service programs to enhance cognitive, affective, social, and vocational development (p. 1169)," and "4.2.6 school psychologists are knowledgeable about community agencies and resources. They provide liaison and consulting services to the community and agencies regarding psychological, mental health and educational issues "(National Association of School Psychologists, 1995, p. 1168).

Psychologists complete comprehensive psychoeducational evaluations as a matter of course. Levinson (1995) describes the components of a comprehensive vocational assessment as encompassing measures of intelligence, achievement, social development, personality development, adaptive functioning, individual interests, and personal aptitudes. Areas of additional evaluation include memory, attention and executive functions (Levinson, 1998). In developing a comprehensive vocational evaluation, practitioners must be technically selective in their choice of assessment instruments. Research conducted by Alfonso, LaRocca, Oakland and Spanakos (2000) reports that the Wechsler series of intelligence tests are by far the most popular instrument utilized in cognition training courses. The Stanford-Binet is as a close second. Nevertheless, school psychologists must be mindful of the measurement used and be aware of current developments in the area of cognitive assessment. A more in-depth discussion of future trends in assessment will be offered in the final section of this chapter.

As time constraints are a well-known barrier to the participation of school psychologist in transition planning, Devinney, Kamnetz, Chan, and Hattori, (1998) provide many positive outcomes associated with the use of intellectual assessments for individuals needing initial transition or rehabilitative services. Intelligence data can provide transition teams with sound baseline information from which to begin developing appropriate transition goals. It is often the case that after years of paper reevaluations that data relating to the individual's level of intelligence and individual strengths and weaknesses is quite old and inappropriate for team use. In order for transition teams to have the required data to develop appropriate transition goals, the information must be available to teams very early within the transition planning process so that adequate time is available to remediate deficiencies.

To summarize, research suggests that the relationship between intelligence and occupational status is mediated by academic achievement (McClelland, 1994). When research results are applied to exceptional populations similar trends emerge. The literature supports three findings. First, exceptional students with higher levels of verbal ability perform much better in vocational/occupational training programs. High levels of verbal or crystallized IQ are also associated with tacit or practical intelligence. Second, individuals with stronger levels of fluid intelligence perform better in lower level jobs and in vocational versus academic training programs. Third, vocational maturity is positively associated with higher levels of intelligence.

It becomes painfully apparent that psychologists do not know nearly enough when a student with poor verbal intelligence presents themselves to a transition team for assistance. In addition to this unfortunate scenario is the student's delayed level of vocational maturity. Not only is the student often unsure of their strengths and weaknesses, so are those who hope to assist the student through the transition from school to work. While Scott and Truex's (1994) innovative attempt to link cognitive assessment data to jobs is a step in the right direction, the instrumentation utilized to assess individual cognitive functioning lacks the specificity to differentiate among subtle cognitive abilities (Wagner & Loukides, 1994). The need for greater specificity in cognitive assessment may be answered by Cattell-Horn-Carroll (CHC) contemporary theory of intelligence.

Future Directions in Transition and Cognitive Assessment

Over the course of 30 years, the Horn-Cattel Gf-Gc dichotomous theory has evolved into a ten-factor intelligence theory (Horn and Noll;

1997; McGrew & Flanagan, 1998). A more contemporary version of the Horn-Cattell Gf-Gc model developed following the discovery of inadequacies in the original theoretical framework (Horn and Noll; 1997). Emphasis is not placed upon a single g factor, rather on a conceptualization of human cognitive abilities. Systematic research and evidence resulted in the identification of seven additional domains of intelligence, including Visual Processing (Gv), Auditory Processing (Ga), Short-term Memory (Gsm), Long-term Memory (Glr), Processing Speed (Gs), Decision Speed (Gt), and Quantitative Knowledge (Gc) (Horn & Noll, 1997; McGrew & Flanagan, 1998). As far as theory and practice is concerned, the Woodcock-Johnson-Revised (WJ-R; Woodcock & Johnson, 1989) was designed with the eight known Gf-Gc broad abilities. John Horn and John Carroll served as consultants for the WJ-R. Carroll's (1993) advanced factor analytic studies discovered additional broad cognitive abilities. Based upon additional data, McGrew and Flanagan (1998) reported, ". . . the WJ-R does not have the breadth and depth of coverage of all broad Gf-Gc abilities" (p. 6).

Beyond Cognitive Theory

Empirical research in cognitive abilities progressed with advancements in statistical methods. John Carroll (1993) reviewed 465 factor analytic research studies from the last 50 to 60 years. Carroll's (1993) research literature was selected from English and non-English speaking countries; including the United States, Canada, Great Britain, Australia, France, Germany, Japan, Spain, and Russia/USSR. Serial factor analysis from original data resulted in a hierarchical classification of broad and narrow abilities. Carroll entitled his empirically-based theory, the three-stratum theory, which represents first, second, and third order classifications of cognitive differences (Carroll, 1997). The highest stratum is the general intelligence factor, i.e., "g." Eight broad factors were also identified at the broad "stratum II" level: fluid intelligence, crystallized intelligence, general memory and learning, broad visual perception, broad auditory perception, broad retrieval capacity, broad cognitive speediness, and processing speed (i.e., decision speed). Although Carroll (1993) did not consider his theory complete, it advanced what was known about the structure and organization of cognitive abilities. Carroll (1997) believed that his theory would evolve to include newfound abilities that could be added.

An intelligence theory that is closest to the three-stratum theory is Cattell-Horn's updated Gf-Gc theory, which Carroll (1993) describes as a "true hierarchical model covering all major domains of intellectual functioning" (p. 62).

Cattell-Horn-Carroll (CHC) Theory of Cognitive Abilities

Despite similarities between the three-stratum theory and the updated Horn-Cattell Gf-Gc theory, four differences are evident based upon confirmatory review (McGrew, 1997). The first apparent difference is Horn's disregard for g and its encompassing of broad abilities (Horn & Noll, 1997). In contrast, Carroll (1993) finds that general intelligence has varying degrees of relationship with broad abilities. The association with g or Stratum III is represented by the descending arrangement of broad abilities under Stratum II. Gf and Gc have the strongest association, while Broad Cognitive Speediness (Gs) and Decision/Reaction Time/Speed (Gt) have the weakest association (McGrew, 1997; McGrew & Flanagan, 1998). Secondly, the Horn-Cattell model identified a separate broad reading and writing (Grw) ability, whereas Carroll subsumed reading and writing within crystallized intelligence (McGrew, 1997; McGrew & Flanagan, 1998). The three-stratum theory classified phonological awareness as a crystallized narrow ability (McGrew, 1997). As a critical element of reading and writing development, phonological awareness refers to the awareness of the sound structure of language, such as rhyming (Mather & Woodcock, 2001). Horn considered phonological awareness to be a part of auditory perception (Ga) (McGrew & Flanagan, 1998). Third, Carroll categorized quantitative ability (Gq) under fluid intelligence, despite a separate broad ability for quantitative under Gq in Horn's theory (McGrew, 1997). Finally, delineations between aspects of memory are drawn largely from Horn's model (McGrew, 1997). Short-term memory is distinguished from storage and retrieval capacities. Carroll classified them together under a single factor.

In an attempt to integrate The Horn-Cattell and Carroll models for test development and interpretation, additional investigations were performed. McGrew (1997) performed a confirmatory factor analysis to resolve differences between the two models and to operationally define narrow abilities that make up the broad ability domains. The resulting data formed the basis for a joint or "cross-battery" factor analysis of major intelligence test batteries (McGrew, 1997; McGrew & Flanagan, 1998). It was concluded that no intelligence battery was able to adequately assess the complete range of multiple broad Gf-Gc abilities included in CHC theory (McGrew, 1997; McGrew & Flanagan, 1998). Ultimately, McGrew (1997) sought to "provide a 'bridge' between the theoretical and empirical research on the factors of intelligence and the development and interpretation of psychoeducational assessment batteries" (p. 151).

Broad CHC Ability Definitions

In this section, definitions of the broad abilities included in CHC theory are presented. Narrow stratum descriptors are not provided due our primary emphasis upon broad cognitive domains that are relevant to Transdisciplinary team members. For further details regarding specific narrow stratum abilities, school psychologists and any other transdisciplinary transition team member may refer to *Essentials of Cross-Battery Assessment.* The letter codes representing each broad area are from the grouping codes that Carroll (1993) used in his cognitive descriptors. The definitions are drawn from Carroll (1993), McGrew (1997), McGrew and Flanagan (1998), Flanagan and Ortiz (2001), and Mather and Woodcock (2001).

Fluid Intelligence (Gf) refers to one's ability to reason, form concepts, and problem solve when faced with novel tasks or information. It also includes inductive and deductive reasoning procedures.

Crystallized Intelligence (Gc) encompasses one's accumulation and application of knowledge from cultural experiences, i.e., education and general life experiences. However, it is not synonymous with achievement. Gc includes factual information, comprehension, concepts, as well as process reasoning, i.e., application of previously learned information.

Quantitative Knowledge (Gq) Refers to one's storage and application procedures of math knowledge over time. This ability is necessary for using quantitative information and manipulating numerical symbols, as opposed to reasoning through math-related problems with inductive and deductive reasoning.

Reading and Writing Ability (Grw) refers to storage of accumulated reading and writing development. It includes reading decoding, spelling, reading comprehension, and writing skill. Broad achievement measures assess these areas.

Short-Term Memory (Gsm) is the ability to efficiently hold information in immediate awareness and utilize what is held within a few seconds. The use of Long-Term Storage and retrieval capacities determines whether or not information in Short-Term Memory is either lost or stored in Gc, Gq, or Grw.

Visual Processing (Gv) refers to the ability to perceive and manipulate visual shapes and to analyze (break down) and synthesize (build-up) visual patterns. It also includes visual storage and retrieval capacities.

Auditory Processing (Ga) is an individual's cognitive capacity to analyze and synthesize auditory input. It encompasses auditory perception or discrimination of speech patterns and phonological awareness and processing. Additionally, tonal discrimination and tracking of auditory patterns in time are part of Ga.

Long-Term Storage and Retrieval (Glr) is the ability to efficiently store new or old information in long-term memory and retrieve it in time, minutes to months, through associations. It does not involve stored content domains such as Gc, Gq, and Grw.

Processing speed (Gs) involves fluently and automatically performing less complex cognitive tasks when pressure to sustain attention and concentration is evident.

Decision Reaction Time or Speed (Gt) is the immediate reaction, within seconds, to tasks or information, such as deciding and then providing correct answers to moderately difficult problems.

CHC and Practice

In adhering to ethical guidelines and best practice, it is imperative that intellectual or cognitive assessment comprehensively measures all relevant areas of an individual's functioning (Reschly & Grimes, 1995). A standard individually administered intelligence test, such as a Wechsler Intelligence Scale for Children – III or Standford-Binet Intelligence Scale: IV, is unable to measure all known cognitive areas (Reschly, 1997). Genshaft and Gerner (1999) argue that the reason intelligence assessment has been criticized is that practice continues to utilize inadequate assessment measures that do not assess the broad range of cognitive functioning.

The development of a "Cross-Battery Assessment" approach that incorporates CHC theory is a possible solution (McGrew & Flanagan, 1998; Flanagan & Ortiz, 2001). This method recommends selecting portions of individually administered tests to create a customized assessment. The Cross-Battery approach is designed to improve psychoeducational assessment practice by describing unique cognitive abilities that may be related to achievement and occupational outcomes (McGrew & Flanagan, 1998). Though it is beyond the scope of this chapter to provide comprehensive description of this approach, further details can be found in *Essentials of Cross-Battery Assessment,* written by Flanagan and Ortiz and published in 2001. A review of Cross-Battery procedures by Genshaft and Gerner (1998), found that it "provides a heuristic, conceptual, and procedural framework that can help school psychologists form better judgments about the complexity of a student's cognitive capabilities, not just their ability-achievement discrepancy" (p. 25). CHC theory-driven practice procedures outlined by Flanagan & Ortiz (2001) allows for a defensible method of carrying out supplemental assessments in a systematic and scientific manner (Gerner, 2001). Gerner (2001) commented that the psychometric sophistication of linking CHC theory to practice has far reaching advancements in how cognitive assessment is carried out, such as test development, practice of school psychology, personnel selection, and educational assessment.

The CHC comprehensive Cross-Battery (C-CB) assessment is consistent with best practice in intellectual assessment; nevertheless, the C-CB is not without weaknesses. Most importantly, C-CB lacks an internal norm group (Flanagan & Ortiz, 2001; Sattler, 2001). In other words, the administration of subtests from two or more different test batteries leads to a comparison using different norming populations. Consequently, errors may occur in interpretation.

To counter internal norming problems, Flanagan and Ortiz (2001) offered several methods of statistical manipulation necessary in minimizing error. The first is converting standard scores to a common metric, and the second is to incorporate confidence bands within each score to account for error or uncertainty. Additionally, emphasis and interpretation can be based upon broad ability domains to reduce error. Should two measures that make up the broad ability vary significantly, then the representation of the broad ability will be minimized.

Computer-based spreadsheets to assist in interpretation can be downloaded from the internet at http://www.iapsych.com.

It is unrealistic to cover all CHC narrow ability domains because of the time involved in measuring, up until now, 70 identified narrow stratum abilities. However, the recently published Woodcock-Johnson–III Tests of Cognitive Ability and Achievement (WJ III COG/ACH; Woodcock et al., 2001) was based upon CHC and include two to three measures of different narrow abilities under each broad stratum. Flanagan and Ortiz (2001) reported that the WJ III is the most theoretically and psychometrically sound test of cognitive ability on the market. Despite this, Flanagan and Ortiz (2001) caution that "nonetheless, the fact remains that no single battery will ever measure the full range of CHC constructs" (p. 286). Test selection based upon referral questions necessitates the types of instruments used, especially with impaired and culturally diverse individuals (Flanagan and Ortiz, 2001).

CHC Cognitive Abilities and Outcome Variables

Prior research has found moderately significant relationships between intelligence and vocational functioning (Levinson, 1993; Morris & Levinson, 1995). However, much of the research upon which these conclusions were based included intelligence measures that lacked a strong theoretical framework (McGrew, 1997). To understand the relationship between CHC specific abilities and occupational success, McGrew and Flanagan (1998) reclassified original research studies according to CHC terminology and drew the following logical:

> First, Gv abilities appear to contribute to success in a wide variety of occupations. Most of the occupations listed under Gv (e.g., architect, artist, carpenter, engineer, photographer, pilot, sculptor) are positions that appear to require routine use of a number of narrow abilities subsumed under Gv-for example, Visualization (VZ), Spatial Relations (SR), and Visual Memory (MV). Second, success in occupations in the broad fields of science and mathematics (e.g., engineer, mathematician, scientist) may require high Gf and Gq abilities. Third, most of the occupations listed under Gc seem to be professions that require much formal education (e.g., accountant, lawyer, poet, scholar, scientist). Fourth, Ga abilities appear to be related almost exclusively to performance in the music professions. Finally, the listing of clerk, typist, and proofreader under Gs most likely reflects the need for individuals to make rapid visual perceptual discriminations (e.g., Perceptual Speed-P) when performing in these occupations. (p. 45–46)

It is certainly plausible that transdisciplinary transition team members may be able to derive some sound hypotheses regarding appropriate occupational goals based upon an analysis of a CHC profile of strengths and weaknesses.

Understanding the dynamics of an individual's cognitive abilities, personality traits, and interest levels can be a daunting and complex task. Utilizing Carroll's three-stratum theory as a framework, Ackerman and Heggestad (1997) shed some light on this complex concern through their extensive review of cognitive ability and interest relationships and meta-analysis of over 2,000 cognitive ability-personality correlations from previous studies. Flanagan and McGrew (1998) reclassified ability descriptions into CHC terminology and summarized the results of the study:

> A review indicates that the abilities of Gf, Gc, and Gsm displayed the largest number of significant positive and negative correlations with a number of personality and interest traits. For example, the results summarized suggest that individuals who are high in Gf abilities may also display relatively high Realistic and Investigative interests together with low Enterprising interests. Furthermore, individuals who are high in Gf abilities may display a preference for new experiences (i.e., Openness to Experiences) and low Test Anxiety and Alienation. Of particular interest are the three intelligence-personality-interest "trait complexities" identified by Ackerman and Heggestad (1997). For example, an "intellectual/cultural" trait complex is presented that suggests relations between and among the abilities of Gc and Glr; Artistic and Investigative interests; and the personality traits of Openness to Experiences, Absorption, and Typical Intellectual Engagement. These observations are intriguing, but additional research is necessary to determine the practical utility of this and other intelligence-personality-interest trait complexes. (pp. 47–48)

Readers should note that "Realistic," "Investigative," "Artistic," and "Enterprising" interests are based upon John Holland's Theory of Vocational Personalities and Work Environments which is discussed in subsequent chapters.

McGrew and Flanagan (1998) recognized the lack of practical implications of these findings. However, the study moves research toward a multifactored and multitrait method of examining the complexity of human trait interactions that is consistent with best practice in transition assessment (Levinson, 1995, 1998; Reschly & Grimes, 1995). The development of meaningful and practical recommendations from sound research can increase team confidence in connecting specific abilities to vocational directions, thus reducing chance or inappropriate planning.

The development of intelligence measurement was to provide insight into the learning capacities of individuals. In America, group intelligence measurement was readily accepted as an efficient personnel management method in the military. During times of peace, testing became part of the private sector in the areas of industry and education. Although unclear, the relationship between intelligence and occupational attainment has intrigued society. It was found that intelligence in general allowed for improved training success. However, it was not predictive of job performance. When applied to exceptional populations similar trends emerged.

While cognitive measurements are valuable in general, research has validated a lack of specificity that prevents transition teams from successfully matching a student's unique abilities to jobs. However, the development of CHC theory offers new promise and provides school psychologists and other transition team members with a complete theoretical model that can be used to guide the use of cognitive assessment data for transition planning.

APPENDIX

Instrumentation Section

Wechsler Intelligence Scale–Third Edition (WISC-III; Wechsler, 1990)

Publisher: The Psychological Corporation

Publication Year: 1991

Ages: 6–16 years

Available Norms:
- 6-0 to 16-11-30

Standardization Sample:
- 2,200 children
- Matched to 1988 census data
- Stratified by age, race, ethnicity, geographic region, and parental education (SES).
- 100 boys, 100 girls in each of 11 age groups
- Norms available at four-month intervals

Scores:
- Standard Scores (Mean of 100 and Standard Deviation of 15)
- Test–Age Equivalents

Reliability:
- Excellent
- Full, Verbal, and Performance Scale IQ scores have internal consistency reliability coefficients of .89 or above.
- Test-Retest Reliability is Full Scale = .94, Verbal Scale = .87, and Performance Scale = .94
- Sattler (2001) reported test-retest reliability coefficients indicate that the WISC III provides stable IQs for full scale and Verbal scale, but less stable Scaled Score for Performance IQ.
- Validity: Criterion Validity with WISC III correlates at .72 with other intelligence measures.
- Construct Validity with the WISC III revealed debates in the literature regarding factor structure of the WISC III and whether it measures three or four factors.

Wechsler Adult Intelligence – Third Edition (WAIS-III; Wechsler, 1997)

Publisher: The Psychological Corporation

Publication Year: 1997

Ages: 16–0 to 74–11

Standardization Sample:

- 2,450
- Matched to census data
- Stratified by age, race, ethnicity, geographic region, and parental education (SES).
- 13 age groups: 100 men, 100 females in groups 16 to 64
- Ages female weighted per census
  - 65–69 90 Men 110 Females
  - 70–74 88 Men 112 Females
  - 75–79 83 Men 117 Females
  - 80–84 54 Men 96 Females

Scores:

- Standard Scores (Mean of 100 and Standard Deviation of 15)
- Scaled Scores (Mean of 10 and Standard Deviation of 3)

Reliability:

- Excellent
- Full, Verbal, and Performance Scale IQ scores have internal consistency reliability coefficients of .93 or above.
- Test-Retest Reliability across four age groups is Full Scale = .91 to .96, Verbal Scale = .91 to 97, and Performance Scale = .83 to .93

Validity:

- Concurrent Validity for the WAIS III Full Scale correlates at r = .88 with other tests of IQ.
- Sattler (2001) indicated Construct Validity support for Verbal, Performance, and Full Scale Scores.

Standford-Binet Intelligence Scale: Fourth Edition (SB: IV; Thorndike et al., 1986)

Publisher: Riverside Publishing Company

Publication Year: 1986

Ages: 2–Adult

Available Norms:

Age Range	*Interval Coverage*
2–6	4 month intervals
6–12	6 month intervals
12–18	one year intervals
18–23–11	6 month intervals

Standardization Sample:
- 5, 013 in 17 age groups
- Matched to 1980 census data
- Stratified by age, race/ethnicity, gender, geographic region, community size and parental education (SES).

Scores:
- Standard Scores (Mean of 100 and Standard Deviation of 16)
- Subtest Standard Scores (Mean of 50 and Standard Deviation of 8)

Factor Analysis:
- Sattler (2001) recommended reporting factor scores.
- Ages 2 to 6 have a two factor structure
  Verbal Comprehension
  Non-verbal Reasoning/Visualization
- Ages 7 to Adult have a three factor structure
  Verbal Comprehension
  Non-verbal Reasoning/Visualization
  Memory

Reliability:
- Excellent
- Composite score has internal consistency reliability coefficients of .95 to .99.
- Sattler (2001) reported excellent test-retest reliability with 5 year olds (r = .91) and 8 year olds (r = .90) samples.

Validity:
- Criterion Validity indicates correlations with other IQ tests from .44 to .78.
- Sattler (2001) reported acceptable Construct Validity

Differential Ability Scale (DAS; Elliot, 1990)

Publisher: The Psychological Corporation

Publication Year: 1990

Ages: 2-6 to 17-11 years

Available Norms:
- Eight groups
  Age Blocks in Norm Table:
  3 month blocks (Age 2-6 to 7-11)
  6 month blocks (Age 8-0 to 17-11)

Standardization Sample:
- 3,475
- Representative of 1987-89 demographic data
- Stratified by age, sex, ethnicity, geographic region, educational preschool enrollment and parental education (SES).

Scores:
- Standard and Composite Scores (Mean of 100 and Standard Deviation of 15)
- Subtest T-Scores (Mean of 50 and Standard Deviation of 10)
- General Conceptual Ability (GCA)
  Lower-Order Composites:
  Upper Preschool (Age 3-6 to 6-11)
  Verbal Ability
  Non-verbal Ability
  School Age
  Verbal Ability
  Non-verbal Reasoning Ability
  Spatial Ability
- Score Information:
  Range of Standard Scores for Total Test Composite
  Lower Preschool (Age 2-6 to 3-5): 31 to 169
  Upper Preschool (Age 3-6 to 5-11): 25 to 175
  School-Age (6-0 to 5-11): 25 to 174

Reliability:
- Internal consistency reliability coefficients of .95 for school age level.
  - GIA Lower .90
  - GIA Upper .94

Validity:
- Criterion Validity- mean coefficient of .76 with other IQ tests.
- Sattler (2001) reported acceptable Construct Validity

Kaufman Adolescent and Adult Intelligence Test (KAIT; Kaufman & Kaufman, 1993)

Publisher: American Guidance Service

Publication Year: 1993

Ages: 11-0 to 85+ years

Standardization Sample:

- 2,000 individuals
- Representative of 1990 census data
  West = Overrepresented
  Northeast = Underrepresented
- Stratified by gender, ethnicity, geographic region, and parental or examinee education (SES).

Scores:

- Standard Scores (Mean of 100 and Standard Deviation of 15)
- Subtest Scores (Mean of 10 and Standard Deviation of 3)
- Four Area Scores:
  Fluid, Crystallized, and Composite Scores

Reliability:

- Internal consistency reliability coefficients:
  Fluid: r = .95
  Crystallized and Full Scale: r = .97
  Subtests: median r = .89
- Test-Retest
  Composite: median r = .94

Validity:

- Sattler (2001) reported that the KAIT demonstrates adequate construct and concurrent validity. The factor analytic support is evident for crystallized and fluid IQ factors. The correlations of .55 to .85 are adequate with other tests of intelligence.

Cognitive Assessment System (CAS; Naglieri & Das, 1997)

Publisher: The Riverside Company

Publication Year: 1997

Ages: 5–17 years

Standardization Sample:

- 2,200
- Representative of 1990 census data
- Stratified by age, gender, race, ethnicity, geographic region, community setting, classroom placement, educational classification, and parental education (SES).

Scores:

- Standard Scores (Mean of 100 and Standard Deviation of 15)
- Full-Scale
- Four Area Scores:
  Planning, Attention, Simultaneous Processing, and Successive Processing

Reliability:

- Internal consistency reliability coefficients:
  Subtests: median r = .82
  Scales: median r = .90
  Composites: median r = .87
- Test-Retest
  Subtests: median r = .73
  Composite: median r = .82

Validity:

- Sattler (2001) reported that the CAS displays inconsistent construct validity for the four factor structure. CAS correlates with the WISC III at a correlation of .69 and the WJ-R at a median r = .49.

Woodcock-Johnson III Tests of Cognitive Abilities (WJ III COG; Woodcock et al, 2001)

Publisher: The Riverside Company

Publication Year: 2001

Ages: 2–90+ years

Standardization Sample:
- 8,818
- 1,143 preschool, 4,784 school age, 1,165 college students, 1,843 adults
- Based upon census projections for 2001
- Stratified by gender, race, Hispanic origin, census region, community size, type of school, type of college/university, education of adults, and occupational status (adult sample).

Scores:
- Computer scored
- No manual option for scoring
- Standard Scores (Mean of 100 and Standard Deviation of 15)
- Percentile Ranks
- Co-normed with Woodcock-Johnson III Tests of Achievement
- Relative Proficiency Index

Reliability:
- Internal consistency reliability coefficients are at .97 or above.
- Test-Retest coefficients ranged from .71 to .92.

Validity:
- Construct validity is demonstrated through factor analytic support from CHC (Cattell-Horn-Carroll) intelligence theory.
- Concurrent validity is satisfactory with a median r = .67 with other intelligence tests.

Factor Analysis:
- Development is based upon CHC theory.
  Comprehension–Knowledge
  Long-Term Retrieval
  Visual-Spatial Thinking
  Auditory Processing
  Fluid Reasoning
  Process Speed
  Short-Term Memory
- The WJ III Tests of Achievement covers Quantitative Knowledge and Reading-Writing Ability

REFERENCES

Alfonso, V. C., LaRocca, R., Oakland, T. D., & Spanakos, A. (2000). The course on individual cognitive assessment. *School Psychology Review, 29*(1), 52--64.

Braden, J. P. (1995). For whom "The Bell" Tolls: Why *The Bell Curve* is important for school psychologists. *School Psychology Review, 24*(1), 27–35.

Brown, W. H. (1995). Using the Wechsler adult intelligence scale–revised to predict vocational aptitudes of adolescents with learning disabilities. *Dissertation Abstracts International, 56*(2A), 491.

Carroll, J. B.(1993). *Human cognitive abilities: A survey of factor-analytic studies.* New York: Cambridge University Press.

Carroll, J. B. (1997). The three stratum theory of cognitive abilities. In D. P. Flanagan, J. L. Genshaft, & P. L. Harrison (Eds.), *Contemporary Intellectual Assessment,* (pp. 122–130). New York: Guilford Press.

Cummings, R. W. & Maddux, C. D. (1987). Holland personality types among learning disabled and nonlearning disabled high school students. *Exceptional Children, 54*(2), 167–170.

Devinney, D.J., Kamnetz, B., Chan, F., & Hattori, K. (1998) . Wechsler short forms in vocational and evaluation settings. *Vocational Evaluation and Work Adjustment Bulletin. 44,* 4–9.

Dawis, R. V. (1994). Occupations. In R. J. Sternberg (Eds.), *Encyclopedia of Human Intelligence* (pp. 781–785). New York: Macmillan.

Dye A.P., Reck, M., & McDaniel, M (1993). The validity of job knowledge measures. *International Journal of Selection and Measurement, 1,* 153–162.

Elliot, C. D. (1990). *Differential Ability Scales.* San Antonio, TX: Psychological Corporation.

Faas, L. A. & D'Alonzo, B. J. (1990). WAIS-R scores as predictors of employment success and failure among adults with learning disabilities. *Journal of Learning Disabilities, 23*(5), 311–316.

Flanagan, D. P. & Ortiz, S. (2001). *Essentials of Cross-Battery Assessment.* New York: John Wiley & Sons.

Genshaft, J. L. & Gerner, M. E. (1998). Gf-Gc cross-battery assessment: Implications for school psychologists. *Communique, 26*(*8*), 24–27.

Gerner, M. E. (2001). Multiple Intelligences in Theory and Practice: Towards an International Model of Cognitive Ability Testing. Submitted for Publication.

Herrnstein, R. J., & Murray, C. (1994). *The bell curve: Intelligence and class structure in American life.* New York: Free Press.

Horn, J. L. & Noll, J. (1997). Human cognitive capabilities: Gf-Gc theory. In D. P. Flanagan, J. L. Genshaft, & P. L. Harrison (Eds.), *Contemporary Intellectual Assessment,* (pp. 53–92). New York: Guilford Press.

Kaufman, A. S., & Kaufman, N. L. (1993). *Kaufman Assessment Battery for Children.* Circle Pines, MN: American Guidance Service.

Levinson, E. M., (1987). Incorporating a vocational component into a school psychological evaluation: A case example. *Psychology In the Schools, 24,* 254–263.

Levinson, E. M. (1998a). Correlates of vocational practice among school psychologists. *Psychology in the Schools. 25,* 297–305.
Levinson, E. M. (1998b). *Transition: Facilitating the Postschool Adjustment of Students with Disabilities.* Boulder, CO: Westview Press.
Levinson, E. M. (1990). Vocational assessment involvement and use of the self directed search by school psychologists. *Psychology in the Schools, 27,* 217–227.
Levinson, E. M. (1993). *Transdisciplinary vocational assessment: Issues in school-based programs.* Brandon, VT: Clinical Psychology Publishing Co., Inc.
Levinson, E.M. (1994). Current vocational assessment models for students with disabilities. *Journal of Counseling & Development, 73*(1), 94–109.
Levinson, E. M. (1995). Vocational assessment in the schools. In A. Thomas and J. Grimes (Eds.), *Best Practice in School Psychology III,* (pp. 741–751). National Association of School Psychologist: Washington, DC.
Mather, N., & Woodcock, R. W. (2001). *Examiner's Manual. Woodcock-Johnson III Tests of Cognitive Abilities.* Itasca, IL: Riverside Publishing.
McGrew & Flanagan, D. (1998). *The Intelligence Test Desk Reference: Gf-Gc Cross Battery Assessment.* Boston: Allyn & Bacon.
Morris, T. W. & Levinson, E.M. (1995). Relationship between intelligence and occupational adjustment and functioning: A literature review. *Journal of Counseling & Development, 73*(5), 503–515. May/June.
Naglieri, J. A, & Das, J. P. (1997). *Cognitive Assessment System.* Itasca, IL: Riverside.
National Association of School Psychologists, (1995).Standards for the provision of school psychological services. In A. Thomas and J. Grimes (Eds.), *Best Practice in School Psychology III,* (pp. 1161–1172). National Association of School Psychologist: Washington, DC.
Oakland, T. (1995). The Bell Curve: Some implications for the discipline of school psychology and practices of school psychology. *School Psychology Review, 24*(1), 20–26.
Ortiz, S. O., Flanagan, D. P., & McGrew, K. S. (1999). Assessment in school psychology: Past, Present and Future. *Communique, 28*(2), 30–31.
Ree, M. J. & Earles, J. A. (1991). Predicting training success: not much more than g. *Personnel Psychology, 44*(2), 321–333.
Ree, J. R., Carretta, T.R., & Teachout, M.S. (1995). Role of ability and prior job knowledge in complex training performance. *Journal of Applied Psychology, 80*(6), 721–730.
Reschly, D. J. & Grimes, J. P. (1995). Intellectual Assessment. In A. Thomas and J. Grimes (Eds.), Best Practice in School Psychology III, (pp. 763–772). National Association of School Psychologist: Washington, DC.
Reschly, D. J. (1997). Diagnostic and treatment utility of intelligence tests. In D. P. Flanagan, J. L. Genshaft, & P. L. Harrison (Eds.), *Contemporary Intellectual Assessment,* (pp. 437–453). New York: Guilford Press.
Scott, M. E. & Truex, M. H. (1994). A procedure use of Wechsler Intelligence Scale for Children-Revised (WISC-R): Scores for more successful vocational placement of slow learning and developmentally delayed secondary students. *Journal for Vocational and Special Needs Education, 16*(3), 33–37.

Sternberg, R.J., Wagner, R.K., Williams, W. M. & Horvath, J.A. (1995). Testing common sense. *American Psychologist, 50*(11), 912–927.

Thorndike, R. M. (1997). The early history of intelligence testing. In D. P. Flanagan, J. L. Genshaft, & P. L. Harrison (Eds.), *Contemporary Intellectual Assessment,* (pp. 3–16). New York: Guilford Press.

Thorndike, R. L., Hagen, E. P., & Sattler, J. M. (1986). *Stanford-Binet Intelligence Scale: Guide for administering and scoring the Fourth Edition.* Chicago: Riverside.

Wade, C. & Travris, C. (1987). *Psychology.* New York: Harper Row.

Wagner, R. K., & Loukides, Z. (1994). Intelligence in the workforce . In R. J. Sternberg (Eds.), *Encyclopedia of Human Intelligence* (pp. 1158–1164). New York: Macmillan.

Wagner, R. K. (1997). Intelligence, training and employment. *American Psychologist, 52*(10), 1059–1069.

Weschler, D. (1991). *Wechsler Intelligence Scale for Children–Third Edition.* San Antonio, TX: Psychological Corporation.

Weschler, D. (1997). *Manual for the Wechsler Adult Intelligence Scale–Third Edition.* San Antonio, TX: Psychological Corporation.

Woodcock, R. W. & Johnson, M. B. (1977). Woodcock-Johnson Psycho-Educational Battery. Chicago: Riverside.

Chapter 3

TRANSITION ASSESSMENT: FOCUS ON ACADEMIC ACHIEVEMENT

Deborah A. Houck

INTRODUCTION: TRANSITION ASSESSMENT: FOCUS ON ACADEMIC ACHIEVEMENT

This chapter discusses the assessment of academic achievement as it relates to transition and vocational planning for students with disabilities. Methods and purposes of academic assessment are explored and current issues in achievement testing are reviewed. Best practices for assessing academic achievement are offered. And, the relevance of academic assessment for disabled students, and its implications for a transdisciplinary approach to transition planning, are discussed. A brief review of instruments and suggestions for multidimensional assessment are also included.

An important consideration in the development of transition services for students with disabilities is the academic skills that they will need for life after high school. In terms of proficiency in the areas of reading, mathematics, and writing, expectations will vary considerably for college-bound students, students planning to enroll in post-secondary training programs, or those entering the world of work. To this end, our choice of assessment instruments should be guided by the student's specific post-school plan. By using this approach, a link can be established between what the student knows now, what he needs to know for the future, and what instruction needs to occur in order to bridge the gap.

ACADEMIC ACHIEVEMENT

Definition and Historic Perspective

Academic skills are those skills most traditionally linked with schools and learning. Broadly speaking, these skills encompass the areas of reading, mathematics, writing, and communication and are learned as a result of direct instruction. In contrast to theories of intelligence, there is very little controversy as to what is meant by academic skills. They are the skills that parents expect their children to learn when they go to school in order to become functioning adults. And they are the basic skills employers expect their employees to have. Surveys of employers consistently report that literacy and numerative skills are important for all types of jobs (Holzer, 1997); and relatedly, weaknesses in reading, spelling, writing and math are regarded as barriers to employment (Biller, 1988). Of course, colleges and universities also expect their students to display high levels of academic achievement, as evidenced by their emphasis on SAT and ACT scores. Academic skills are the foundation of educational instruction; teachers have been teaching and assessing these skills for decades.

Methods of Academic Assessment

Assessment of academic skills can take many shapes and forms, ranging from highly informal, flexible methods to highly standardized, structured methods. Teachers have always created their own tests for measuring their students' progress and skills, and continue to do so today. But, with the advent of public education and education of the masses in the mid nineteenth century, the concept of large group testing and standardized assessment of academic skills became increasingly popular (Sexton, Kelley & Aldridge, 1998). These types of tests, often referred to as "achievement tests," are attractive to school districts because they are cost-effective, reliable, objective, and easy to administer/score.

Today, mass testing, using standardized achievement batteries, is an integral component of public instruction, from elementary school through high school. This chapter will review a variety of current methods and instruments used to assess academic skills, and discuss their relevance for students with disabilities.

Purposes of Academic Assessment

Just as the concept of academic skills is not new, neither is the concept of test taking, or assessment of these skills. Why are academic tests important? They are important because they provide specific information about a student's current level of performance across the academic domains. This information is valuable to both student and teacher in terms of measuring progress and in determining future instruction. In its most basic form, the purpose of academic assessment is to determine whether a student has mastered the concepts that were taught. Over time, academic assessment has come to serve other purposes as well, and a myriad of tests have been devised to measure students' academic achievement over the last 100 years. Currently, the purposes, or uses of academic assessment generally fall into two categories–as a measure of group achievement or as a measure of individual achievement.

As a Measure of Classroom Achievement

One purpose of academic testing is to measure the overall progress of an entire group of students. Tests can provide feedback to the teacher regarding the acquisition of skills for the class as a whole, and direct the development of appropriate instruction. If the majority of students have not mastered certain concepts, the teacher can reteach the content or design alternative ways to present the material.

Academic assessment is also used to document the progress of students. Students' mastery of skills or concepts can be charted as they move through the curriculum and yearly test scores are recorded in students' cumulative files.

Relatedly, academic assessment provides accountability. Students' performance on tests can show parents, school boards, and the community that the teacher is teaching and that the students are learning. It is important to note, however, that this seemingly simple concept has evoked a firestorm of controversy regarding the use of standardized achievement tests (also referred to as "high-stakes tests") for this purpose. With accountability in mind, these test scores are being used to draw comparisons among school districts, as a determinant for allocation of funds, and as a benchmark for awarding salary supplements to teachers (Sexton, et al., 1998; Jones, 1999; Barton, 1999).

As a Measure of Individual Achievement

Academic assessment can also be used on an individual basis, as feedback to both the student and teacher regarding the student's profile of skill acquisition. The teacher can determine the individual student's specific strengths and weaknesses, and then modify instruction or provide remediation if necessary.

Academic assessment is also useful in determining if a student has, or is developing the skills needed for future instruction, training, or the world of work. For example, in high school a student needs to have mastered the skills in Algebra I before registering for Algebra 2 or Geometry. Some vocational training programs, and many trade and technical schools have certain entry requirements. And certainly, college boards require certain coursework and entrance exam scores for admission. In the world of work, even entry-level jobs often require a certain level of proficiency in basic academic skills.

Academic assessment is used to document individual progress. Ongoing tests and measurements can provide a record of a student's mastery of skills over time. In fact, for students with disabilities, continual assessment is essential for developing, modifying and implementing appropriate Individualized Education Plans (IEPs), and adapting instruction to meet the students' needs. For example, if assessment reveals deficiencies in academic skills necessary for a particular training program, this information can be used to design compensatory instructional methods (such as audiotapes of the textbook for poor readers) for the student (Levinson, 1998).

Academic assessment can also be used as a predictor of success in college, training programs or on the job. Research indicates that academic achievement correlates with success in vocational education programs, educational attainment and occupational status (Levinson, 1998). Among college-bound students with disabilities, Levinson &

Ohler (1998) list as some of the academic predictors of success: completion of an academically-oriented curriculum; success in English class; and a 2.5 grade average. This is not surprising given the heavy emphasis on reading, writing, and math skills at the college level.

Finally, the most controversial use of achievement tests in education today is the use of these tests scores to make promotion/retention and graduation decisions for individual students. Spurred by efforts to raise expectations and academic standards for students, Jones (1999) reports that most states have adopted or are developing these "high-stakes tests" to be used as a basis for grade-to-grade promotion and receipt of a high school diploma. While most people would agree that assessment of academic skills is an essential part of the educational process, there is considerable debate about how it should be measured (Brown, 1983).

Opponents of high-stakes tests and standardized achievement tests charge that the exams water down the course content and reduce classwork to rote memorization (Shafer, 2001). Kohn (2001) exclaims that ". . . schools under intense pressure to show better test results have allowed those tests to cannibalize the curriculum," and goes so far as to list 15 ways teachers and parents can protest the use of these tests, including boycotts. As Sexton et al. (1998) sum it up,

> Tests were considered efficient, scientific tools to bring order to an otherwise messy enterprise. Unfortunately, standardized test results are increasingly being used to sort and classify students in ways that discriminate and limit their access to continued education opportunities, as in the case with test score-based graduation requirements. It is this primary desire to address both equity and efficiency in American education that seemingly undergirds the tension in standardized testing. (p. 259)

Relevance of Academic Achievement for Students with Disabilities

In light of the debate regarding the use or misuse of achievement tests, what relevance or impact does this have on students with disabilities? It seems obvious, by virtue of their documented academic difficulties that they might struggle with standardized achievement tests. As a result, students with disabilities are particularly vulnerable to and affected by these types of mandates. Nonetheless, these mandates–the application of minimum competencies to students with disabilities–have been challenged in a number of court cases, and have generally been held to be valid (Rothstein, 2000).

Clearly, achievement tests adversely impact certain groups of students. Research studies consistently report the lags in test scores for the poor, the disabled, the minority and the traditionally disaffected populations (Shafer, 2001; Kohn, 2001; Sexton et al., 1998). And in reaction to schools purposefully excluding students with disabilities from standardized testing so the school's overall tests scores would not be lowered, the 1997 reauthorization of the Individuals with Disabilities Education Act (IDEA) specifically speaks to the assessment of disabled students (Sexton et al., 1998).

Despite protest and debate, standardized tests are accepted as significant indicators of school success for individuals, teachers, and school districts (Haertel & Calfee, 1983). Consequently, achievement tests and academic assessment will continue to play an important role in determining a student's progress or failure in the foreseeable future. As pointed out by Levinson (1995) and others, this impacts students with disabilities for the following reasons: students with disabilities are at greater risk for academic failure; academic failure is linked to the dropout rate; and not surprisingly, students with disabilities have higher dropout rates; additionally, students with disabilities have higher rates of unemployment and underemployment.

Implications

Current prevailing patterns of falling employment and wages for the less educated and rising employment and earnings for the more educated worker, cited by Holzer (1997), make this a critical issue for keeping our disabled students in school. A significant number of learning disabled students (27% to 29%) drop out of school with minimal academic skills and very little vocational training (Patton & Blalock, 1996).

The need to stem the dropout rate for student disabilities is clear; the most observable measure of job success is the number of years of school and the educational degrees that an individual has earned. Relatedly, the gap between the earnings of high school and college graduates rose from 13 to 43 percent from 1982 to 1992. In fact, data show that the large majority of job applicants today hold a high school diploma; therefore, the lack of one sends a strong negative signal to prospective employers (Holzer, 1997).

The implications of academic failure for students with learning disabilities are obvious. As a result, appropriate academic instruction is essential to decrease the likelihood of failure and increase students' opportunities for success. Appropriate assessment facilitates effective academic instruction. In response to contentions that high-stakes tests are too narrow in scope and have a negative impact on instruction, there is a movement toward alternative assessments, including performance-based instructional techniques that promote critical thinking and problem solving skills (Miller & Legg, 1993). This concept applies to disabled and non-disabled students alike. The point is not to abandon testing, but to make it appropriate and relevant to the student's individual needs.

Faced with the statistics and rates of failure previously cited, it appears that the most effective thing we can do for students with disabilities is to begin, sooner rather than later, the process of planning for their transition needs. We need to carefully and comprehensively assess their skills, plan appropriate instruction, and determine the services that each student will require to make a *successful* transition to life after high school.

Current Trends in Transition Assessment: Focus on Academic Achievement

A Process for Transition Planning

Transition planning is not an event, but an ongoing, evolving *process,* that develops as the student moves through the middle and high school years. The process might look something like this:

1. Define/determine post-school plan
2. Define academic skills/competencies required for chosen path
3. Assess current academic skills
4. Design instructional strategies to bridge the gap between requisite and current skills.

Define/Determine Post-School Plan

What is the student's plan after high school? Determine whether the student aspires to a four-year college, a two-year college, a trade or technical school, an apprenticeship program, military service, vocational training, or the work force.

Define the Academic Skills/Competencies Required

What are the requisite skills for the chosen path? Colleges typically require the highest level of academic achievement. Though colleges and universities are expected to make some accommodations for disabled students, the college student is still expected to pass college entrance exams, read, write, compute, and communicate at a fairly high level of competence.

For many other students with disabilities, institutions of higher learning will not be realistic, and their preparation for life after high school will require some type of vocational training rather than an emphasis on academics (Rothstein, 2000). Patton and Blalock (1996) report that the majority of learning disabled students do not go on to college; therefore, remediation in basic reading and math skills may not be appropriate. Instead, academic instruction should focus on the kinds of skills needed in vocational education, training programs, and employment settings.

For these tracks, the expectations for academic skills can vary greatly. While jobs that require a college diploma generally require a higher degree of academic- related skills, Holzer (1997) reports that even blue-collar and service jobs require extensive ". . . daily customer contact, reading and writing, arithmetic, general work experience or specific work experience." He reports that only about 5 percent of jobs in his multicity employer survey did not require these skills. And interestingly, the greatest rise in need for basic academic skills has occurred among the blue-collar, service jobs that previously placed less of a demand of these types of skills (Holzer 1997).

The only way to properly define the skills needed for each choice is to thoroughly examine the curricula for the training program, or to conduct a task analysis for specific jobs or occupations. Vocational teachers and career counselors have expertise in this area. Also, Levinson (1993) and Clark, Patton & Moulton (2000) offer a variety of instruments to facilitate assessment of setting requirements.

Assess Student's Academic Skills

Several points must be considered when assessing the student's academic skills. Most importantly, the method of assessment must relate to the purpose of the assessment. Different types of assessment yield different data, and assessment results must be relevant to the individual's needs and assessment data must relate to the student's post-school goal. The emphasis must be placed on assessing the most relevant skills for each individual. As noted by Levinson (1998), the academic skills that are necessary for successful functioning and that should be targeted for assessment vary from one student to another, depend on many factors, and are especially influenced by the severity of a student's disability.

Finally, assessment data drive instructional strategies. Therefore, in order to be meaningful and relevant, assessment data should have direct implications for classroom instruction, program design, curriculum planning, and additional assessment requirements (Clark, 1996).

Design Instructional Strategies to Bridge the Gap Between Requisite and Current Skills

Appropriate assessment of the student's present level of performance as well as a clear understanding of the required academic skills for the postsecondary goal will provide both student and teacher with the information necessary to create a plan, define objectives, and design instructional strategies to meet the student's goal.

Methods of Academic Assessment

We are all familiar with the ubiquitous, non-standardized teacher-made tests which come in all shapes and sizes and are given throughout thousands of classrooms every day. There is also a myriad of achievement tests that are considered standardized. Standardized tests differ from teacher-made tests in that they share certain critical features, such as construction of items that are field-tested, analyzed and revised, standardized procedures for administration and scoring, and clearly prescribed methods for score interpretation (Brown 1983). They can be norm-referenced or criterion-referenced and constructed for individual or group administration. Rothstein (2000) cautions that an understanding of the limitations of such tests with respect to measuring the abilities of students with disabilities is necessary. Standardized tests, supplemented with informal assessment procedures, complement each other to form a foundation for making decisions about a student. The use of a multimethod approach can provide a wealth of data regarding the student (Sattler, 1988). The most common types of academic tests are described below.

Norm-Referenced

In norm-referenced testing, the student's performance is compared with the performance of a specific group or sample of students. This can be a nationwide sample, state or even a local sample. Examples of group, norm-referenced tests include: the Iowa Tests of Basic Skills, California Achievement Tests and the Stanford Achievement Tests. There are also many individually administered norm-referenced tests, some of which are listed in the Review of Instrumentation that concludes this chapter. These are used especially in the assessment of learning-disabled students and to determine eligibility for special education as defined by law. Bergin, Hudson, Chryst & Reseter (1992) note some limitations of standardized measures: they are not sensitive to small changes in achievement; they are not reflective of the classroom curriculum; and they may not measure the content that students actually experience.

Criterion-Referenced

With criterion-referenced testing, there is a pool of items for the content area being measured which are sometimes arranged in a hierarchy of difficulty. The student's performance is compared to a criterion point to determine level of mastery in reference to the set of items. Minimum competency tests are an example of a criterion-referenced test. Scores are interpreted in terms of each student's mastery of content rather than compared to the performance of others. How other students perform is irrelevant; all students could pass or fail a criterion-referenced test (Brown 1983). Some examples of criterion-referenced tests are listed in the Review of Instrumentation at the end of this chapter.

Curriculum Based

Another type of academic assessment is curriculum based, meaning that students are assessed using their day-to-day curriculum as the context. This would encompass informal, teacher-made tests but also includes more formalized, systematic methods referred to in the literature as Curriculum-Based Measurement (CBM) and Curriculum Based-Assessment (CBA). Both CBM and CBA allow the teacher to align assessment with what is actually being taught, using the curriculum's scope and sequence. Assessment results can then be related directly to instructional planning and interventions. Numerous studies have supported the effectiveness of CBM. Shinn (1995) noted that special education students' achievement outcomes improved significantly using CBM, and the method allows for validation and modification of individual interventions.

Informal Assessments

The last type of assessment includes the less formal, less standardized methods, such as portfolios, checklists, inventories, observations, and demonstrations. These assessment techniques are often best for evaluating functional academic and literacy skills. Functional academics encompass basic academic skills that are taught with the context of real-life activities, including the workplace, that are experientially based and applicable and meaningful for daily living. Patton and Blalock (1996) report functional competency as the "ability to live independently through use of skills in reading, writing, and math." The National Literacy Act of 1991 defines literacy as "an individual's ability to read, write, and speak in English, compute and solve problems at levels of proficiency necessary to function on the job and in society, to achieve one's goals, and to develop one's knowledge and potential" (Mislevy, 1997).

While there are specific instruments designed to assess these skills, they're frequently not referred to as "tests." They can take the form of checklists, inventories, observations, work samples, and demonstration of skills. Vocational and special education programs may use a "portfolio-based assessment approach" to measure the level of work readiness skills of the students. The end result is a compilation of the student's skills across several domains which can give teachers and employers a sense of what individuals can accomplish. Rabinowitz & McLaughlin (1998) review one commercially packaged portfolio-based assessment tool called the Career Preparation Assessment (CPA) by WestEd that assesses at the personal and interpersonal skills, thinking and problem-solving abilities, communication skills, and employment and technological literacy of individuals. Other measures of this type are listed at the end of this chapter in the Review of Instrumentation.

Future Directions in Transition Assessment: Focus on Academic Achievement

A Multimethod, Multidimensional Approach

Given a review of the purposes and methods of academic assessment, the need for a multimethod, multidimensional approach seems clear. Since the concept of "testing" is so strongly associated with standardized achievement tests, it is important that all members of the transdisciplinary team–school psychologists, parents, teachers, administrators, counselors, community agencies–become aware that other methods (probably more legitimate to the purpose) exist and should be used. Patton and Blalock (1996) recommend that academic assessment techniques include curriculum-based assessment as well as formal and informal assessment instruments, and suggest that practitioners be made aware of the validated instruments that currently exist. The points made by opponents of high-stakes testing are equally applicable to students with disabilities as to non-disabled students: students cannot be measured by a single test score; instead, multiple measures, authentic, performance and curriculum-based assessments and portfolios, can be used to demonstrate the totality of a student's knowledge and growth (Shafer, 2001; Ediger, 2000; Barton, 1999; Perrone, 1991).

Suggested Methods of Assessment Based on Post-High School Plan

Using a continuum of test methods, from highly standardized to high individualized, selection of instruments is based on the purpose of assessment as related to the student's post-high school plan (See Figure 3.1.).

Norm-referenced tests and Criterion-referenced tests might best assess the academic skills of a college-bound student. Scores on a stan-

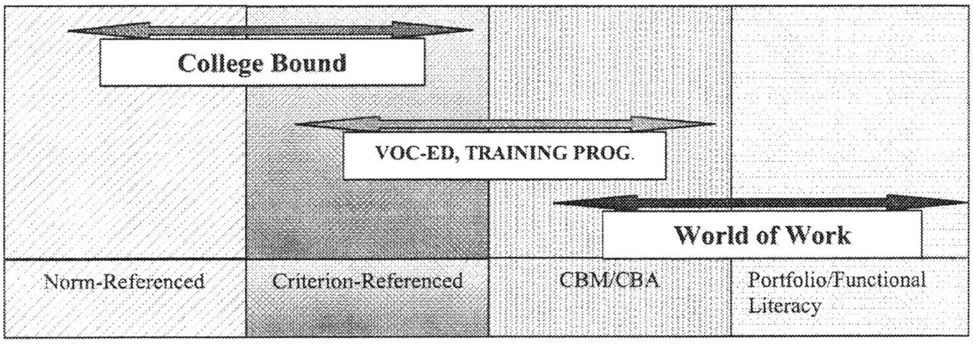

Figure 3.1. Suggested Methods of Assessment Based on Post-High School Plan.

dardized achievement battery reflecting the student's profile of strengths and weaknesses may be helpful in selecting a college and a major field of study (Brown, 1983).

Criterion-referenced tests of Curriculum-Based Measurement might be used for students going on to vocational training programs and CBA or portfolio-based assessments might be used to measure the academic skills of students entering the work force.

Suggested Methods of Assessment Based on Severity of Disabilities

Again, on the continuum of assessment, Figure 3.2 suggests methods of assessment based on the severity of the student's disability.

The relevance of the norm group depends upon the degree to which the sample population is comparable to the group with which you wish to compare the students (Kapes, Mastie and Whitfield, 1994). In other words, the less the student resembles the norm or the average student, the less appropriate and less helpful it is to use tests that compare that student to a large group or even to another student.

Suggested Methods of Assessment Based on Population Size and/or Types of Skills

On the continuum of assessment, Figure 3.3 illustrates the selection of instruments based on the population skills and/or types of skills to be assessed.

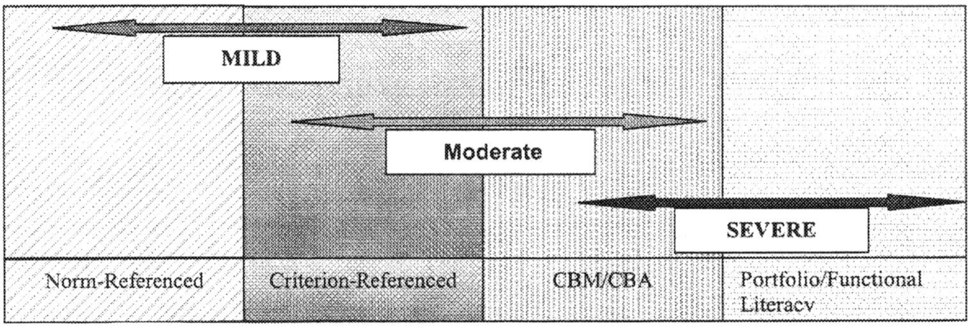

Figure 3.2. Suggested Methods of Assessment Based on Severity of Disabilities.

For large group or global skills, Norm-referenced tests and Criterion-referenced tests are considered to be the most efficient method. To measure more specific academic skills or to assess the skills of a particular group of students, then Criterion-referenced tests or curriculum-based measures would yield more meaningful data.

And finally, to assess very specific or isolated academic skills for an individual student, use less formal, more task-oriented, job-related types of assessment as they relate to functional literacy or functional academics.

CONCLUSION

Used appropriately, academic assessment can be an effective tool for determining students' current level of academic skills in identifying what skills they still need to attain their goals, and in developing instructional strategies to bridge the gap. Assessment of academic achievement is just one important component of transition planning for students with disabilities. It can serve many purposes, and there are many methods for assessing the continuum of students' academic skills. Therefore, it is crucial to link the type with its intended purpose. Additionally, assessment should be conducted by a team of professionals, utilizing different methods, techniques, and a transdisciplinary approach (Levinson & Ohler 1998).

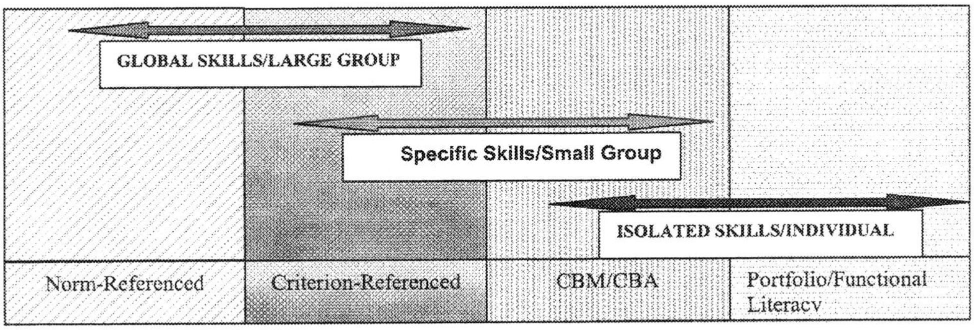

Figure 3.3. Suggested Methods of Assessment Based on Population size and/or Types of Skills.

Review of Instrumentation

This section is included to give the reader a sample of the academic assessments available for transition planning, and is by no means meant to be exclusive or exhaustive (national and/or state norm-referenced, standardized, group tests are not included in this list as they are administered by the school district, in a mass-testing format). When choosing standardized instruments, it is important to consider the psychometric properties of the test, including reliability and validity, the norming sample, its limitations, its appropriateness for its intended use, and administrator qualifications.

Norm-Referenced, Individually-Administered Achievement Tests

Wechsler Individual Achievement Test–Second Edition (WIAT-II)

The Psychological Corporation (2001)

- Assesses a wide variety of academic skills, including: oral expression, listening comprehension, written expression, basic reading skills, reading comprehension, mathematics calculation, mathematics reasoning
- Ages: 5 yrs. to 19 yrs. 11 mos.
- Administration time: 30 to 60 minutes
- Reliability: .94 to .97 (split-half)
- Validity: .43 to .80 (correlation with CTBS, ITBS)

- Administrator: school psychologist, educational diagnostician, special education teacher

Woodcock-Johnson III Tests of Achievement (WJ III ACH)
Woodcock, McGrew & Mather (2001)
Riverside Publishing

- Assesses broad areas of curricular achievement: reading, mathematics, written language, oral expression, listening comprehension, academic knowledge, academic fluency
- Ages: preschool to geriatric
- Administration time: 30 to 90 minutes
- Reliability: .90s (test/retest)
- Validity: .65 to .79 (correlation with WIAT, KTEA)
- Administrator: school psychologist, educational diagnostician, special education teacher

Kaufman Functional Academic Skills Test (K-FAST)
Kaufman & Kaufman (2000)
American Guidance Service

- A brief, individually administered test to determine performance in reading and mathematics as applied to daily life situations
- Ages: 15 through 85+
- Administration time: 15 to 25 minutes
- Reliability: .84 to .94 (internal consistency, test-retest)
- Validity: Conormed w/KAIT, K-BIT and K-SNAP
- Administrator: special education teacher, regular education teacher, vocational teacher, guidance counselor

Woodcock Reading Mastery Tests–Revised/Normative Update (WRMT-R/NU)
Richard W. Woodcock (1998)
American Guidance Service, Inc.

- A comprehensive battery of tests measuring several important aspects of reading including: readiness, basic skills, and reading comprehension
- Ages: 5-0 through 75+
- Administration time: 10 to 30 minutes per cluster
- Reliability: .98 (split-half)

- Validity: .78 to .92 (correlation with ITBS, PIAT, WJ-R, grades 5-12)
- Administrator: school psychologist, educational diagnostician, special education teacher

KeyMath Revised: A Diagnostic Inventory of Essential Mathematics
Austin J. Connolly (1998)
American Guidance Service, Inc.

- A comprehensive assessment of a student's understanding and application of important mathematical concepts and skills
- Ages: 5 through 22
- Administration time: 35 to 50 minutes
- Reliability: .90s (split-half, alt. Form)
- Validity: .66 to .76 (correlation with ITBS, CTBS)
- Administrator: school psychologist, educational diagnostician, special education teacher

Test of Written Language–Third Edition (TOWL-3)
Hammill & Larsen (1996)
American Guidance Service, Inc.

- A measure of written language skills, including essay analysis (spontaneous) and traditional test (contrived) format; can be administered to groups
- Ages: 7–6 through 17-11
- Administration time: 90 minutes
- Reliability: .60 to .92 (internal consistency)
- Validity: .46 to .55 (for composites, correlated w/CSSA)
- Administrator: educational diagnostician, special education teacher, regular education Teacher, guidance counselor

Criterion-Referenced, Individually-Administered Achievement Tests

Basic Achievement Skills Individual Screener (BASIS)
The Psychological Corporation (1983)

- An individually administered achievement test designed to provide *both* norm-referenced and criterion-referenced information for reading, mathematics, and spelling

- Grades: 1 through 12, post-high school
- Administration time: less than 1 hour
- Reliability: not reported
- Validity: .30 to .72
- Administrator: educational diagnostician, special education teacher, regular education teacher, guidance counselor

Brigance Diagnostic Inventory of Essential Skills
Albert H. Brigance (1981)
Curriculum Associates, Inc.

- Assessment of commonly identified minimal competencies in academic skills, (including reading and language arts, math, and study skills) and life skills
- Grades: 6 through adult education
- Administration time: varies
- Reliability: not reported
- Validity: not reported
- Administrator: special education teacher, regular education teacher, vocational teacher

Developmental Assessment for Students w/Severe Disabilities–2nd Ed. (DASH-2)
Dykes & Erin (1999)
Pro-Ed

- A comprehensive assessment and programming system that aid in identification of discrete changes in behaviors, includes a basic academic Pinpoint Scale related to concept formation, basic reading, and number skills
- Ages: individuals of all ages functioning within birth to 7 years
- Reliability: not reported
- Validity: not reported
- Administrator: school psychologist, special education teacher, vocational teacher

Classroom Reading Inventory–8th Edition (CRI-8)
Nicholas Silvaroli (1997)
McGraw-Hill

- Attempts to identify a student's reading skills and/or abilities in word recognition, comprehension, spelling, and listening capacity

- Ages: elementary through adult
- Administration time: 30 minutes
- Reliability/Validity: not reported, (based on Fry Readability Formula)
- Administrator: school psychologist, educational diagnostician, special education teacher, regular education teacher, vocational teacher, guidance counselor

Informal Assessments of Academic Skills

Informal Assessments for Transition Planning
Clark, Patton & Moulton (2000)
Pro-Ed, Inc.

- 1st Section–describes background information and how it can be used for transition planning
- 2nd Section–Comprehensive Informal Inventory of Knowledge and Skills for Transition, relates to 46 competency statements of the *Transition Planning Inventory* (TPI) and contains more than 600 additional competency statements
- 3rd Section–Selected Informal Assessment Instruments, contains reproducible examples of a variety of instruments that can be used for further assessment
- Ages: school-aged
- Administrator: special education teacher, regular education teacher, vocational teacher, guidance counselor

Career Planner's Portfolio–A School-to-Work Assessment Tool
Robert G. Forest (1997)
Curriculum Associates, Inc.

- Discovering Yourself–self assessment; reviews written by others concerning personal characteristics; comparisons of positive qualities in self and others
- Getting the Most Out of Your Education–students collect data to build a solid career-knowledge base; record completed course work; record extracurricular and volunteer activities
- Obtaining Your Career Choice–students develop a job-search plan; read classified ads; write a resume; write a cover letter; contact and use references

- Teacher Information Guide–contains reproducible activities for each portfolio area; list of resources to aid in building a career development program

REFERENCES

Barton, P. (1999). *Too much testing of the wrong kind.* Princeton, NJ: Educational Testing Service.

Bergin, Hudson, Chryst & Reseter (1992). An after school intervention program for educationally disadvantaged young children. *The Urban Review, 23* (3), 203–217.

Biller, E. F. (1988). *Understanding adolescents and young adults with learning disabilities: a focus on employability and career placement.* Springfield, IL: Charles C. Thomas.

Brigance, A.H. (1981) *Brigance inventory of essential skills.* North Billerica, MA: Curriculum Associates.

Brown, F. G. (1983). *Principles of educational and psychological testing,* 3rd ed. Fort Worth: Harcourt Brace Jovanovich.

Clark, G. M. (1996). Transition planning assessment for secondary level students with learning disabilities. *Journal of Learning Disabilities, 29* (1), 79–93.

Clark, G. M., Patton, J. R.& Moulton, R. (2000). *Informal assessments for transition planning.* Austin, TX: Pro-Ed.

Connolly, A. J. (1988). *KeyMath–Revised: A diagnostic inventory of essential mathematics.* Circle Pines, MN: American Guidance Service.

Dykes, M. K. & Erin, J. N. (1999) *A developmental assessment for students with severe disabilities–Second edition.* North Billerica, MA: Curriculum Associates.

Ediger, M. (2000). Purposes in learner assessment. *Journal of Instructional Psychology, 27* (4), 244–250.

Forest, R.G. (1997). *Career planner's portfolio: A school to work assessment tool.* North Billerica, MA: Curriculum Associates.

Haertel, E. & Calfee, R. (1983). Thinking about what to test. *Journal of Educational Measurement, 20,* 119–131.

Hammill, D.D. & Larsen, S.C. (1996). *Test of written language–Third edition.* Austin, TX: Pro-Ed.

Holzer, H. J. (1997). Is there a gap between employer skill needs and the skills of the work force? In A. Lesgold, M. Feuer & A. Black (Eds.). *Transitions in work and learning: Implications for assessment.* Washington, DC: National Academy Press.

Jones, L.V. (1999, April) *The assessment of student achievement: The hundred years war.* Paper presented at the Annual Meeting of the American Educational Research Association, Montreal, Quebec, Canada.

Kapes, J. T., Mastie, M. M. & Whitfield, E.A. (Eds.). 1994). *A counselor's guide to career assessment instruments,* 3rd ed. Alexandria, VA: The National Career Development Association.

Kaufman, A.S. & Kaufman, N.L. (2000). *Kaufman functional academic skills test.* Circle Pines, MN: American Guidance Service.

Kohn, A. (2001). Fighting the tests: A practical guide to rescuing our schools. *Phi Delta Kappan, 82* (5), 348–358.
Levinson, E. M. (1993). *Transdisciplinary vocational assessment: Issues in school-based programs.* Brandon, VT: Clinical Psychology.
Levinson, E. M. (1995). Best practices in vocational assessment in the schools. In A. Thomas & J. Grimes (Eds.), *Best practices in school psychology.* Washington, DC: National Association of School Psychologists.
Levinson, E. M. (1998). *Facilitating the post-school adjustment of students with disabilities.* Boulder: Westview Press.
Levinson, E. M. & Ohler, D. L. (1998). Transition from high school to college for student with learning disabilities: needs, assessment & services. *High School Journal, 82* (1), 62–70.
Mislevy, R. J. (1997). Postmodern test theory. In A. Lesgold, M. Feuer & A. Black (Eds.). *Transitions in work and learning: Implications for assessment.* Washington, DC: National Academy Press.
Miller, M. D. & Legg, S.M. (1993). Alternative assessment in a high-stakes environment. *Educational Measurement: Issues and Practice, 12* (2), 9–16.
Patton, J. R. & Blalock, G. (Eds.) (1996). *Transition and students with learning disabilities.* Austin, TX: Pro-Ed.
Perrone, V. (1991). On standardized testing. *Childhood Education, 67,* 131–142.
Rabinowitz, S. & McLaughlin, D. (1998). Show and tell (measuring student skills through career preparation assessment). *Techniques, 73* (3), 24–26.
Rothstein, L. F. (2000). *Special education law,* 3rd ed. New York: Addison Wesley Longman.
Sattler, J. M. (1988) *Assessment of children* (revised and updated 3rd ed.). San Diego: Jerome M. Sattler, Publisher.
Sexton, D., Kelley, M., Aldridge, J. (1998). Continuing tensions in education. *Childhood Education, 24* (5) 258–261.
Shafer, G. (2001). Tests that fail democracy. *Humanist, 61* (2) 14–20.
Shinn, M.R. (1995). Best practices in curriculum-based measurement and its use in a problem-solving model. In A. Thomas & J. Grimes (Eds.), *Best practices in school psychology.* Washington, DC: National Association of School Psychologists.
Silvaroli, N.J. (1997). *Classroom reading inventory, 8th edition.* Boston, MA: McGraw-Hill.
Woodcock, R.W. (1998). *Woodcock reading mastery tests–Revised.* Circle Pines, MN: American Guidance Service.
Woodcock, R. W., McGrew, K.S., & Mather, N. (2001). *The Woodcock-Johnson III.* Itasca, IL: Riverside.

Chapter 4

TRANSITION ASSESSMENT: FOCUS ON PERSONALITY AND SOCIAL SKILLS

Kelley E. Keith and Kirsten L. Stiffler

INTRODUCTION: TRANSITION ASSESSMENT: FOCUS ON PERSONALITY AND SOCIAL SKILLS

It has been proposed that vocational choice is a function of personality (Levinson, 1993). In addition, job-related social skills have been found to determine vocational success (Elksnin & Elksnin, 1998). Therefore, it is important to recognize these domains as vital components of the transition assessment and planning processes.

Throughout this book, various domains of assessment are discussed by our colleagues that are pertinent to transition planning. It is emphasized throughout this text that specific domains influence success in transition. However, in order for an individual to succeed in the work force, it is important to acknowledge both personality traits and social skills that may impact performance. While one may demonstrate sound cognitive abilities or competencies in job-related tasks, personality or social skills and deficits may inhibit one's ability to function effectively in an occupational setting. For example, a family physician with vast amounts of medical knowledge, but who displays impulsivity and poor communication skills, may not perform proficiently in the medical field.

While this chapter will focus on how personality and social skills relate to functioning in the work force and post-secondary educational settings, it is important to also evaluate how these domains influence other aspects of one' life such as peer/marital relations, family interactions, leisure activities, and other interests. As such, this chapter will be organized around three sections. First, we will introduce personality and social skills assessment and describe implications for transition and vocational planning. Secondly, we will present information on "best practices" in assessment of this domain. Finally, a review of instrumentation will be presented.

Defining Personality

According to Allen (2000), personality has several facets: individual differences, behavioral dimensions, and traits. People differ in a variety of ways based on personality traits, which are often based on psychological characteristics related to many adjectives we use to describe others such as "shy," "friendly," "mean," "outgoing," "passive," and so on. Each of these traits is related to a behavioral dimension, which is defined as a continuum of behavior, with extremes and opposite extremes, and characteristics somewhere in between (Allen, 2000).

In the past, personality has been linked to career choice, suggesting that various functions of an individual's personality are directly related to the type of occupation one will choose. For example, those who choose passive jobs with low level demands and low levels of control possess the same type of personality traits (Karasek & Theorell, 1990). It has also been suggested that personality may have a mediating effect on the impact of many occupational stressors (Landy, 1992). Therefore, personality is one important area to assess when developing a transition plan, especially for those students with disabilities.

Personality can be described as a relatively permanent set of traits or characteristics that are relatively stable over time (Baron & Greenberg, 1990). Personality includes things like interests, skills, and values. More specifically, the work personality, as Power (2000) indicated, is defined as a set of interrelated motives, coping skills, and defense strategies that people use in the work environment. These strategies are based on the interests, skills, and behaviors that allow a person to adhere to work rules in a particular work setting (Power, 2000).

Personality in the Work Force

Personality theory has generated a variety of vocational applications, especially for students with disabilities. Students with learning or behavioral difficulties often have unrealistic expectations or job aspirations. School professionals such as teachers, guidance counselors, school psychologists, and other administrators can assist these students by conducting proper psychoeducational evaluations related to aptitude, interests, intellectual abilities, achievement, and personality/ social skills. By conducting such evaluations, professionals can better recognize strengths and weaknesses within these areas and use this information for transition planning.

Holland's Theory of Vocational Personalities and Work Environments

John Holland's theory of vocational personalities and work environments (Holland, 1966, 1973, 1985a) currently serves as one of the most popular and well-known trait-factor theories that addresses the relationship between personality and occupational choice. According to Levinson (1993), it is applied in numerous high school and college vocational guidance centers. Holland's theory is classified as a trait-factor and consists of the following key premises:

1. Each person is "keyed" to one or several "correct" occupations.
2. If left alone, people have a natural tendency to gravitate toward the "right" occupational choice.
3. Vocational counseling can make the process of occupational choice more efficient and effective.
4. The "key" can and should be learned during early adolescence.
5. The right occupational choice has a great impact on educational decisions.
6. The final occupational goal should be known early and should determine decisions related to and leading toward this goal. (pp. 33–34)

Along with considering Holland's work to be a trait-factor theory of career development, his theory may also be considered a personality theory that has a wide variety of vocational applications. According to Levinson (1993), Holland's work "is based upon some common sense and frequently applied vocational stereotypes that have been validated by research. These vocational stereotypes are what allow us to form impressions of people and to ascribe characteristics to people when we know nothing about them except the kind of work they do" (p. 34).

Holland proposes that individuals choose occupations that are consistent with their personalities and people with similar personalities select similar occupations. Therefore, the choice of an occupation is simply the expression of one's personality. Holland also suggests that the extent to which an individual's personality matches the demands and requirements of his/her job influences the extent to which the person performs the job well, experiences satisfaction with his/her job, and remains in an occupation for a long period of time.

Four basic assumptions of Holland's theory. Holland's theory of vocational personalities and work environments is based upon four basic assumptions. They are as follows:

Assumption #1–Most individuals can be categorized as possessing one of six major personality orientations in our culture. Personality orientations include realistic, investigative, artistic, social, enterprising, or conventional.

Assumption #2–There are six model work environments that correspond to each of the six personality types.

Assumption #3–Work environments are sought out by individuals in an attempt to express attitudes and values, exercise skills and abilities, and take on agreeable roles and problems.

Assumption #4–An interaction between work environment and personality determines behavior.

In his presentation of the six personality orientations, Holland emphasizes that no one personality orientation can adequately describe any one person, but that a combination of the six orientations better depicts the complexity of an individual's personality. It is, however, suggested that most individuals resemble one personality type more so than others. Holland's six major personality orientations are described below:

Realistic–These individuals demonstrate manual, manipulative, technical, and mechanical skills and prefer activities that utilize machines and tools to solve problems. They are observed to not engage in therapeutic or educational activities or possess strong interpersonal or verbal skills. The realistic personality type is characterized by valuing concrete things and expressing opinions.

Investigative–Investigative types display intelligent, analytical, independent, rational, and scholarly skills. They express an interest in systematic and creative investigation activities that examine biological, physical, and cultural phenomena. Mathematical and scientific skills are acquired while leadership and interpersonal skills are not exhibited strengths.

Artistic–This personality orientation is characterized by originality, creativity, autonomy, and non-conformity. While these individuals prefer unstructured, independent, and unsystematic activities that require the manipulation of physical, human, or verbal materials to create products or art forms, they evidence an aversion to routine, systematic, and highly organized activities. Artistic types acquire skills in art, dance, music, drama, or writing and demonstrate deficits in office-related and clerical skills.

Social–Social types express an interest in interacting with others for the purpose of training, enlightening, curing, or helping others. In turn, strong verbal and interpersonal skills are demonstrated. These individuals display an aversion to activities that require the utilization of tools and machines and also develop deficits in technical and manual competencies. Social types are observed to generally be cooperative, sociable, helpful, patient, generous, warm, empathetic, kind, idealistic, and understanding.

Enterprising–These individuals tend to be aggressive, ambitious, talkative, energetic, assertive, and domineering. They value wealth, status, and power and prefer activities that entail the manipulation of others for obtaining economic gain or achieving organizational goals. They tend to not prefer observational, scientific, or symbolic activities and demonstrate deficits in scientific competencies. Enterprising types exhibit interpersonal, leadership, and persuasive competencies.

Conventional–Conventional types tend to prefer clerical and office-related types of activities including organizing, business machine operating, and filing. They develop clerical, business-system, and computational competencies, however artistic skills are demonstrated deficits. Conventional individuals tend to be careful, orderly, precise, efficient, obedient, unimaginative, practical, and inflexible and prefer highly organized and structured activities that require the systematic manipulation of data.

Holland also proposes six model work environments that correspond to each of the six personality types. Each environment presents specific demands and requirements to the individual. Work environments also reinforce certain basic traits in people and withhold reinforcement of other traits. A brief description of these work environments follows:

Realistic–(Ex. Farm, machine shop, construction shop). These work environments often require physical exertion and the use of machines and tools. They also present concrete, physical tasks that require manipulative, mechanical, and manual skills.

Investigative–(Ex. University research laboratory). These work environments value and reinforce intelligence, scholarship, and scientific accomplishments. They require the utilization of higher level, abstract, and creative thought to solve problems related to scientific, mathematical, and symbolic phenomena.

Artistic–(Ex. Concert hall, theater, dance studio, recording studio). These work environments value and reinforce originality, creativity, autonomy, independence, and freedom. They present demands and requirements of an unstructured nature usually involving the imaginative and creative use or production of art forms.

Social–(Ex. Health centers, social service agencies, churches, schools). The employees within these work environments value and reinforce compassion, empathy, cooperation, understanding, and concern. Work settings require extensive interpersonal and social contact to help and teach others.

Enterprising–(Ex. Real estate office, political office, car dealership). This work environment values aggressiveness, influence, persuasiveness, and ambition. It also reinforces wealth, status, and/or power. Individuals in these environments are presented with demands that require the manipulation of others to attain organizational-related goals or self-interest.

Conventional–(Ex. Accounting firm, post office, business office). These work environments present tasks that are typically repetitive and routine. They require little interpersonal contact, however explicit, systematic organization and ordering of mathematical and verbal data is typically expected. Persistence, efficiency, compliance, orderliness, and conscientiousness are valued and reinforced here.

Holland suggests that individuals who demonstrate similar skills, interests, and values all seek out similar kinds of work environments. These environments will allow persons to become involved in activities in which they express interest and also utilize specific skills to complete tasks. Individuals will search for environments in which their attitudes and values are shared and reinforced by others.

Finally, Holland suggests that vocational outcomes, (i.e., job performance, job satisfaction, and length of service) can be predicted by assessing "congruence," or comparing a person's personality with the type of work environment he/she will be entering. If, and when, an individual enters an environment that provides opportunities, reinforcers, and demands that are compatible with his/her personality, congruence exists and the individual is likely to be satisfied and productive. Low levels of congruence, which is associated with dissatisfaction and low levels of productivity occurs when a person's preferences, values, and skills are incompatible with his/her work environment.

Holland proposes that a particular disposition is created by skills/interests that influence an individual to perceive, act, and think in different ways. In turn, personality orientations, which result from hereditary and environmental factors, are characterized by a set of beliefs, values, and attitudes that result in an individual coping in predictable ways. While no one personality orientation can solely describe any one person accurately, a combination of the six personality orientations best describes an individual's personality. In total, 720 personality profiles can be derived from the six personality orientations

Holland believes that some personality types are more similar and more closely related to one another than are other types. For example, enterprising and social types both tend to demonstrate interpersonal and sociability skills and, while their motives and values may differ greatly, they tend to be more similar to one another than are social and realistic types, for example.

Holland suggests that most people can be described more accurately by examining a combination of the six personality types. As such, he encourages the development of a three-letter code to describe personality. Instruments like Holland's Self-Directed Search, which will be discussed later in this chapter, can be used to develop these codes for individuals.

To better understand the relationship among personality orientations, Holland introduces the constructs of *consistency* and *differentiation*. *Consistency* refers to the degree of relatedness among the types that depict an individual's personality. Examination of Figure 4.1 illustrates the concept of *consistency*, whereby closer personality types positioned on the hexagon resemble one another to a greater degree than those further apart. *Differentiation* refers to the degree to which an individual's personality or particular work environment more closely resembles a single type, rather than multiple types. It is noted that personalities that comprise a relatively equal number of traits from several orientations are considered to be less differentiated than are personalities dominated by characteristics of one orientation.

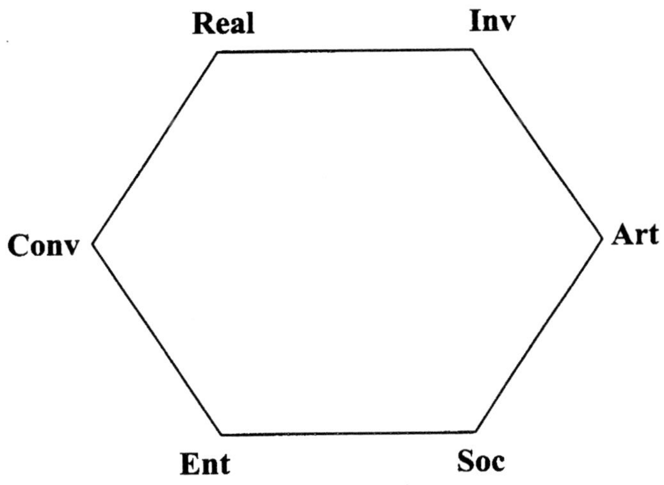

Figure 4.1. Holland's Hexagonal Model.

Hershenson's Theory of Career Development

Hershenson (1981) proposed a somewhat similar model of work adjustment in which the two principal elements are the person and the person's environment. Three domains develop over time within each person including: (1) the work personality; (2) work competencies; and (3) work goals. "Work personality" focuses on the self-concept and system of work motivation. This begins to develop during the preschool years and is largely influenced by a child's family. For example, the small child begins to see his parents go to work on a daily basis and becomes attuned with a daily routine, usually revolving around his parent's work schedule.

"Work competencies" focus on work habits, physical and mental skills related to jobs, and interpersonal or social skills in the work setting. This domain begins to develop during the elementary school years and continues to grow throughout high school. Competencies developed within children are influenced by success and failure experienced in the school setting and by teacher expectations, academic requirements, grades, and peer group expectations.

The domain of "work goals" focused on the transition from school to work or post-secondary schooling for adolescents or young adults. Familial experiences and peer groups influence students during this time. In addition, personal interests contribute to the development of "work goals."

These three domains develop and function throughout an individual's life, each acting independently and also serving to affect each other. This theory provides a comprehensive description of how children develop their personalities and social skills through unique experiences with family, peers, and academic demands. Based upon these influences, students develop a "work personality."

Defining Social Skills

Social skills are defined as discrete, learned behaviors displayed by individuals for the purpose of performing a task. Social skills are observable, measurable, and concrete in nature (Sheridan, Maughn, & Hungelmann, 1999) and are more easily observed than personality traits. Social skills are goal-directed behaviors that help people interact and function effectively in the workplace and in other settings. Research has suggested that social skills are setting-specific, meaning people display certain skills in varying situations (Elksnin & Elksnin, 1999). For example, a 17-year-old boy may use good listening and self-control skills in his eleventh grade trigonometry classroom. However, when he leaves school, he may disobey his parents and ignore his younger sister at home. It is noted that this is not abnormal as an individual is easily capable of knowing when to use certain social skills in a particular setting. Social skills should be flexible and responsive to the demands of society, the workplace, and other settings. However, students with disabilities may not be as flexible in adjusting to the utilization of appropriate social skills in various settings.

Social Skills in the Workplace

There are a variety of skills essential for utilization in the work setting including: (1) Communication skills such as listening and oral communication; (2) Adaptability skills including problem-solving strategies and creative thinking; (3) Developmental skills related to self-esteem, motivation, goal-setting, and career development; (4) Group effectiveness skills such as interpersonal skills, the ability to work on a team, and negotiating; and (5) Influencing skills involving organizational effectiveness and leadership skills (Carnavale, Gainer, & Meltzer, 1990). These are skills that most work environments require for one to be productive in job task completion and successful in the development of relationships with co-workers. They also assist people in cooperating, following directions, working independently, and accepting constructive criticism.

Many of these skills can be directly observed within the classroom setting by teachers, counselors, and psychologists. Even though the federal regulations require that transition planning should begin at age 14 for students with disabilities (Education of the Handicapped Act Amendments of 1990, P.L. 101-476, section 602), school professionals can begin observing social skills essential for employment at a much earlier age. Moreover, when students with deficits in social skills are identified in elementary or middle school, teachers or other school professionals can implement appropriate interventions such as social skills training programs and/or direct instruction of social skills.

Personality and Social Skills in Society, Friendships, and Leisure Activities

For the purpose of this chapter, we will be discussing how personality traits and social skills affect one's ability to function in a particular work environment or post-secondary setting. However, we must not forget the importance of functioning in society on a day-to-day basis with friends, family, and in recreational activities. Therefore, school professionals must not only recommend interventions and instructional programs to help assist the student in developing skills for future transitions, but for life in general.

Implications for Vocational Planning and Assessment

The relationship between personality and career development plays an integral role in vocational evaluation approaches, especially for students with disabilities. Personality and social skills affect occupational decision-making, successful work production, job performance, and satisfaction (Power, 2000). The results from personality assessments can be used to determine the traits and skills a student possesses, which helps professionals involved in the assessment examine the degree to which functioning in a particular vocational setting is realistic or not (Levinson, 1993). Evaluation procedures should focus on the behaviors necessary for productivity and success in the variety of settings in which the individual is likely to function once they exit school.

Current Trends in Transition Assessment: Focus on Personality and Social Skills

Goals for Assessment

There are several goals one expects to achieve when conducting personality and/or social skills assessment (Elksnin & Elksnin, 2000). First, professionals involved in transition planning and assessment need to determine a student's strengths and weaknesses. It is particularly important to determine social skills/personality strengths that may function as assets in the work force. We also need to determine social skills that need to be further developed and personality traits that may inhibit success in the work environment.

Second, occupational social skills, particularly those related to the career choice or postsecondary schooling plans of the student, must be examined. For example, if the student plans to attend a vocational technical school to study auto mechanics, a comprehensive list of the required social skills and personality traits that are conducive to what would be expected for an auto mechanic should be identified and assessed. The transition team should then examine the list and determine which skills or traits the student already possesses or lacks.

Third, professionals must determine if a discrepancy exists between the child's characteristics and the essential occupational skills. If a significant discrepancy exists, the involved professionals may encourage the student to explore other career options more closely related to the student's particular strengths and weaknesses.

However, before concluding that a student's personality profile will not fit a particular occupation, the team must determine the reason for the deficit, for some deficits are easily remedied. Is it an acquisition deficit or a performance deficit? The team must consider whether the student has not been exposed to a skill and, therefore, has not acquired it (acquisition deficit). On the other hand, the student may have developed the skill but performs the skill incorrectly (performance deficit).

Interventions such as direct instruction or social skills training programs may facilitate proper displays of a particular skill.

Areas to Assess

There are many factors that facilitate adjustments within the work setting and relationships between people (Power, 2000). The following are areas that should be evaluated to investigate these specific factors. They are as follows: (1) motivation, including the student's energy level and goal directedness; (2) self-concept, including self-esteem and self-efficacy; (3) adjustment to disability, including coping and self-advocacy skills; (4) strengths and needs, (5) values, such as importance placed on success, academic achievement, and working cooperatively with others; (6) mood/temperament; and (7) attitudes toward self and others. By examining all of these aspects of an individual's personality, one can get a clear picture of interests, beliefs, attitudes, values, and other characteristics that are typical for the student.

There are several behaviors to also consider when evaluating students for transition planning (Power, 2000). First, we must determine the student's emotional reactivity to certain factors such as working under stressful situations involving deadlines and handling pressure from others. If a student displays excessive anxiety when placed in these types of situations, he or she may not be suited for a job or career with such requirements.

Next, we should examine the student's response to authority or supervision. A student with oppositional tendencies or difficulties with obeying authority may not be compatible with a job or career that requires constant feedback or instruction from a supervisor. We must determine if the student can adjust appropriately to the demands of others as well.

Third, we must assess dependency to determine if a student enjoys working on his own or seeks the advice and support from others throughout the day while on the job. This factor can play a key role in determining exactly what type of job one is best suited for. For example, if a student prefers to work independently most of the time but plans to be a secretary upon graduation, a conflict may exist. Most commonly, secretaries are asked to answer phones, provide assistance to people coming in and out of an office throughout the day, and perform jobs to meet the needs of others. They do not experience much 'independence' or quiet time in the office. However, an accountant may work in a busy office firm, but may be behind closed doors most of the day, performing various duties for others, but under their own supervision. Therefore, if the student possesses good mathematical skills, which most secretaries do, the school professional may encourage the student to explore alternative career options that require less dependency and involvement with others.

Lastly, professionals should evaluate the student's understanding of their disability and the vocational implications of the disability. The student needs to be aware of how their specific disability can have an impact on how they perform tasks within the work setting.

In addition, the student should be encouraged to develop strong self-advocacy skills. After high school graduation, individuals with disabilities must be able to communicate effectively with supervisors or professors about their disability and the appropriate accommodations necessary for successful functioning. For example, an 18-year old college freshman with a learning disability in writing should have the self-advocacy skills to approach a professor and explain the types of writing difficulties they possess. Moreover, accommodations that have been helpful to them in previous years should be presented and discussed.

In order to conduct a comprehensive occupational personality and social skills assessment, a variety of approaches must be utilized (Elksnin & Elksnin, 1997). Evaluations must embrace a multifaceted approach, whereby information is provided by various contacts and an individual's social skills/personality is assessed in a variety of settings.

Tools Used to Assess Personality and Social Skills

Rating scales are one tool that is useful in assessing personality and social skills. Rating scales target generic personality/social skills traits that promote or inhibit successful employment, recognize occupational social skills considered essential by various educators/employers, and assist in identifying behaviors that may interfere with an individual acquiring and performing occupational social skills (i.e., withdrawal, attention problems, hyperactivity, etc.). They can assist the evaluator in gathering information from a variety of raters (i.e., peers, parents, teachers, employers, students) across a variety of settings (work, community, school) and also aid in determining discrepancies between skills that a student needs for successful employment and skills that the student has already acquired. When using rating scales, the evaluator should keep in mind that rater bias may occur, information about the cause of the social skills deficit will not be provided, and ratings may not correlate with observations (Elksnin & Elksnin, 1998).

A second evaluation tool that provides valuable information on personality traits/social skills is interviews. This assessment method allows the evaluator to obtain information related to occupational social skills and identify those skills essential for employment success. Interviews yield information that assists in determining discrepancies between skills that are required in the vocational setting and those skills that an individual cannot yet demonstrate. Specifically, during administration, the interviewer can observe a student's level of self-awareness and motivation (social competence), along with social skills demonstrated (i.e., eye contact, communication, etc.). Interviewing "close contacts" of the student can also aid in gathering information regarding the perceptions of others. It is noted that, when using this assessment method, reliable information may not be provided (due to opinions of others being expressed) and information may not be useful unless a structured interview is administered. The interview process may also be time-consuming (Elksknin & Elksnin, 1998).

A third assessment method that can be used to gather information on personality/social skills is behavioral observations. In observing a student's behavior, social strengths and weaknesses can be identified. This approach also aids in recording and graphing an individual's behavior in observable and measurable terms. While this evaluation technique is useful, it may be more time-consuming than other approaches and may not assist in assessing occupational social skills that occur infrequently (Elksnin & Elksnin, 1998).

A fourth assessment tool that may be used to assess personality and social skills strengths/weaknesses is role-play. This approach allows the evaluator to control the assessment situation and observe whether a specific skill has been acquired. In turn, skill performance can be evaluated. Elksnin and Elksnin (1998) provide information on how to conduct a successful role-play. First, the professional must break down or task analyze the occupational social skill into small steps. For example, if the professional wants the student to role-play "Asking a Supervisor for Help," the skill steps should be written down and should include the following steps: "wait for a good time," "approach the person," "explain what your problem is or ask your question," "listen when the person is talking to you," "ask for further explanation," "thank the person for his or her help," and "continue working" (p. 22). The professional should set up the situation that requires the use of the aforementioned skills and then observe whether or not the student displays all of the steps in a competent manner. Feedback should then be provided to the student regarding what their strengths are and what particular steps need to be improved upon. Role-play may be a beneficial assessment method to practice when time is limited, when observing a skill in the natural setting is not possible, or when a skill is performed infrequently. It may also be conducted during an interview.

One final assessment technique that may be beneficial in assessing occupational social skills/personality is curriculum-based vocational assessment. This method emphasizes direct observation of skill performance in the occupational/vocational setting. It assists in establishing criteria for acceptable performance and also aids in conducting an inventory of the work environment. By administering curriculum-based vocational assessment, vocational educators, employers, and co-workers can be interviewed and a determination regarding a student successfully meeting the criterion of a job can be developed (Elksnin & Elksnin, 1998).

Limitations of Assessing Personality/Social Skills

According to Levinson (1993), personality assessment is plagued by a variety of difficulties. The majority of personality assessment instruments provide little evidence of reliability or validity and also are standardized on unrepresentative populations (Salvia and Ysseldyke, 1991). It has been suggested that school personnel hesitate from utilizing instruments that measure personality traits. However, while many older personality assessment instruments are characterized by inadequate technical properties, more recent instruments such as the Behavior Assessment System for Children (Reynolds & Kamphaus, 1992) or the Self-Directed Search (Holland, 1985b) possess acceptable psychometric characteristics (Levinson, 1993).

One assessment method that should be used cautiously if at all is projective techniques. Due to their inadequate psychometric properties and subjective scoring procedures, school professionals should generally refrain from using such instruments. Professionals should only include those assessment devices that are characterized by acceptable reliability, validity, and standardization samples into their transdisciplinary evaluation (Levinson, 1993).

Future Directions in Transition Assessment: Focus on Personality and Social Skills A Review of Instruments

Personality Assessments

Brown (1990) has suggested that personality tests used to make vocational decisions fall into two broad categories. The first category, "clinical" tests, assesses maladjustment or psychopathology. The second category, tests that measure "normal" personality, examines one's values, motives, attitudes, and other characteristics. Both clinical and normal personality tests can be useful in investigating one's ability to function effectively within the work environment.

For the purpose of this chapter, two "clinical" personality tests and two "normal" personality tests will be presented and described based on their implications for vocational and transition assessment of school-aged students. "Clinical" tests will include the Behavior Assessment System for Children (BASC) and the Prout-Strohmer Assessment System (PSAS). "Normal" tests will include the Self-Directed Search (SDS) and the Sixteen Personality Factor Questionnaire (16 PF).

The Behavior Assessment System for Children (BASC).

The BASC (Reynolds & Kamphaus, 1992) is designed to assess personality, behavioral problems, and emotional disturbance in children ages four through 18. The BASC allows information from various sources to be compared and assists in the identification of emotional disturbances that may impact transition or vocational decisions/development.

Components of the BASC include the following: Teacher Rating Scales (TRS), Parent Rating Scales (PRS), Self-Report of Personality (SRP), Structured Developmental History (SDH), and Student Observation System (SOS). Administration time for the TRS and PRS is approximately 20 minutes, while required time to complete the SRP is approximately 30 minutes.

The PRS and TRS are composed of five composite scales including Adaptive Skills and Externalizing, Internalizing, School, and other problems. A Behavioral Symptoms Index score is also yielded. The SRP is composed of four composite scales including Personal Adjustment, Other Problems, and Clinical and School Maladjustment. An Emotional Symptoms Index score is also available. The SDH is an extensive background and history survey that can be completed during an interview by the clinician conducting the assessment. It may also be administered as a questionnaire to parents either in the school or home environment. Finally, the SOS is a direct observation recording method that assesses the classroom behavior of a child. The SOS can be completed by teachers or clinicians via the utilization of a momentary time-sampling technique.

The standardization sample for the BASC consists of children from 39 North American sites. Norming procedures considered maternal education, gender, age, race, geographic location, and special education placement. It is noted that both males and whites were overrepresented in the sample. Scores yielded on the BASC can be converted to T-scores and percentile ranks with a descriptive label applied (i.e., Clinically Significant, At-Risk, Average, etc). The test manual indicates that this instrument demonstrates adequate to excellent internal consistencies, test-retest and inter-rater reliabilities. The BASC has also been reported to exhibit adequate to good concurrent, construct, criterion, and content validity.

The Prout-Strohmer Assessment System (PSAS)

The PSAS (Prout & Strohmer, 1989) is a multimethod, multitrait system designed to assess behavioral and emotional problems of adolescents and adults, ages 14 years and up in the mildly mentally retarded and borderline intelligence ranges (IQs in the 55 to 83 range). The PSAS consists of two component parts, the Prout-Strohmer Personality Inventory (PSPI) and the Strohmer-Prout Behavior Rating Scale (SPBRS).

The PSPI is an individually administered, self-report instrument that takes approximately 30 minutes to complete. One-hundred sixty-two items, with a "yes/no" format are used to gain information from raters with at least a fourth grade reading. The PSPI is composed of six clinical scales: low self-esteem, thought/behavior disorder, anxiety, depression, impulse control, and total pathology. Two validity scales are also included: lie scale and response set indicator.

The SPBRS is a rating scale composed of 135 items that is completed by a rater who is familiar with the student. Administration time is approximately 15 minutes. Scores are yielded from 12 clinical scales: low self-esteem, somatic concerns, withdrawal, depression, anxiety, thought/behavior disorder, non-compliance, hyperactivity, distractibility, physical aggression, verbal aggression, and sexual maladjustment. Two global factors examining externalizing and internalizing disorders are also produced.

The PSPI and the SPBRS were normed on approximately 700 subjects from Canada and seven sites in the United States. The PSPI is reported to yield reliability coefficients ranging from .80 to .96, while the SPBRS possesses reliabilities ranging from .90 to .97. Validity studies have indicated that the PSPI and the Beck Depression Inventory demonstrate significant correlations. In addition, the PSPI and the SPBRS have both been correlated with clinical diagnoses, behavior plans, vocational placement, and vocational performance. Therefore, this instrument is useful to utilize in vocational planning and placement, along with planning for residential placement, treatment monitoring, and diagnostic assessment (as cited in Levinson, 1993).

The Self-Directed Search (SDS)

The SDS (Holland, 1985b) is a self-administered guide for students and adults needing career-planning assistance. This instrument assists students in exploring occupations and engaging in career planning. The SDS can be administered individually or in groups with an administration time of approximately 30 minutes.

Three forms of the SDS are available and are as follows: Form R, Form E, and Form CP. Form R consists of 118 items and can be administered to high school/college students and adults. Items require raters to assess their competencies and preferences for occupations and activities. A three-letter code describing their occupational personality is yielded. Raters can then utilize the *Occupations Finder*, a companion booklet of the SDS, to investigate over 1,300 occupations according to their occupational personality code.

Form E can be administered to students and adults with limited reading skills (at least a 4th grade reading level) and consists of 198 items that are similar to those included in Form R. The resulting occupational code consists of only two letters, instead of three, obtained from a simplified scoring system. Raters can investigate over 800 occupations in the *Jobs Finder* booklet that require a high school education or less. An interpretive booklet entitled *You and Your Job* is provided to aid the rater in understanding assessment results.

Form CP is an alternate version of Form R and can be administered to professional-level employees and adults in transition. The *Career Options Finder* booklet generates descriptions of over 1,300 occupations that require upper levels of education. The *Career Options Finder* also offers information on career exploration theory and the Holland system.

Scores yielded from the SDS are converted into an occupational personality code which is indicative of an individual possessing characteristics of two to three of the six personality orientations discussed earlier in this chapter including: Realistic, Enterprising, Investigative, Artistic, Social, and Conventional. It is noted that the SDS may be self-scored and self-interpreted, however, it is recommended that a trained professional, such as a counselor or school psychologist, supervise the student or adult who is engaging in the interpretive practice.

The SDS was normed separately for each form. The standardization sample for Form R consisted of 2,602 people, ages 17–65, while Form E's sample consisted of 719 people, ages 15–72. Finally, the standardization sample for Form CP consisted of 101 working adults, ages 19–61. It is noted that Forms E and CP have more restricted norm groups than Form R, which may impact psychometric stability.

The SDS manual indicates internal consistency reliability coefficients range between .69 and .94. Test-retest reliability ranges from .76 to .89 over four to 12 weeks. Evidence of adequate validity of the SDS exists and compatibility with other vocational interest inventories is reported. It is noted that the SDS lacks predictive validity, however, it possesses strong psychometric properties that can assist in vocational exploration and transition planning.

Sixteen Personality Factor Questionnaire (16 PF)

The 16 PF (Cattell, Eber, & Tatsuoka, 1970) is designed to assess 16 "source traits" in individuals in high school, college, and adulthood. The

16 PF consists of five forms including: A, B, C, D, & E. This instrument is characterized by a forced-choice format that yields scores of 16 bipolar primary factors including the following: concrete/abstract thinking, reserved/outgoing, not assertive/dominant, affected by feelings/emotionally stable, serious/enthusiastic, shy/venturesome, tough/tender minded, expedient/conscientious, practical/imaginative, forthright/shrewd, trusting/suspicious, self-assured/apprehensive, group dependent/self-sufficient, conservative/experimenting, relaxed/tense, and undisciplined/self-disciplined (as cited in Levinson, 1993).

The 16 PF is reported to possess test-retest reliabilities ranging from .45 to .93 for forms A and B, and .67 to .86 for forms C and D. Limited validity data are provided in the manual. The 16 PF has been found to compare favorably with other personality inventories (Bolton, 1978).

Social Skills Assessment

Social skills rating scales have been developed to obtain information from multiple raters (i.e., parents, teachers, etc.) that are familiar with a child's behavior in a variety of settings. Social skills assessments also enable the professional to gather information on a student's perception of his/her own behavioral capacities. These measures may consist of one or more subscales that assess different areas. Single-subscale instruments examine more narrowly defined behaviors, while multiple-subscale rating scales assess different domains of behavioral constructs.

Scores obtained from social skills rating scales may generate vocational applications in transition planning and vocational assessment. For example, social skills such as communication, technical competency, adaptability, interpersonal relations/teamwork, and motivation can be evaluated and applied to the exploration of vocational interests.

For the purpose of this chapter, three social skills instruments will be presented and discussed. These include the Social Skills Rating System (SSRS), the School Social Behavior Scales (SSBS), and the School Social Skills Rating Scale (SSSRS).

The Social Skills Rating System (SSRS)

The Social Skills Rating System (SSRS; Gresham & Elliot, 1990) provides a broad, inter-rater assessment of a student's social behaviors that can affect teacher-student relations, peer acceptance, and academic performance. It can be used to examine the frequency and importance of behaviors influencing preschool, elementary, and secondary aged students. The SSRS assists professionals in screening and classifying children suspected of having significant behavior problems and aids in the development of appropriate interventions for identified children.

The SSRS is one tool designed to identify students at risk for social behavior difficulties and poor academic performance. This instrument also categorizes behavior difficulties as either performance or acquisition deficits, concepts discussed earlier in this chapter. The SSRS also pinpoints social behavioral strengths.

There are three forms of the SSRS: teacher form, parent form, and student form. Each form yields three subscale composites including: (1) social skills, including cooperation, assertion, responsibility, empathy, and self-control; (2) problem behaviors, including externalizing problems (verbal or physical aggression, arguing, etc.), internalizing problems (sadness, loneliness, anxiety, low self-esteem), and hyperactivity (excessive movement, fidgeting, impulsive behavior); and (3) academic competence (performance in reading and math, motivation, parental support, and general cognitive functioning).

Completion of this instrument takes approximately 20 minutes by either the teacher, parent, or student. Raw scores are transferred into standard scores, percentile ranks, and Behavior Levels. The Behavior Levels allow for a comparison to the average student with "fewer," "average," and "more" displays of a particular behavior or skill.

The SSRS was standardized on a national sample of 4,170 children. It should be noted that the norms for the 11th (N=44) and 12th (N=80) grade populations were underrepresented compared to the rest of the norming sample (Demaray & Ruffalo, 1995). In addition, according to Demaray & Ruffalo (1995), the standardization sample overrepresents Whites and African American and underrepresents Hispanic Americans and other minorities.

The SSRS has good to excellent psychometric properties. Test-retest reliability coefficients range from .62 to .88 and internal consistency coefficients ranging from .73 to .95. Evidence for content and criterion validity was determined using good item development and correlations with the Child Behavior Checklist (CBCL) and the Social Behavior Assessment, respectively. Evidence for good construct validity is available as well.

The School Social Behavior Scales (SSBS)

The School Social Behavior Scales (SSBS; Merrell, 1993) was designed to measure school-based social competence and antisocial behavior patterns of school-aged children (K-12). It is a 65-item, norm-referenced rating scale that can be completed by teachers or other school professionals. Two major scales comprise this instrument: social competences and antisocial behavior. Each scale includes three subscales: Social Competence (interpersonal skills, self-management, and academic skills) and Antisocial Behavior (hostile-irritable, antisocial-aggressive, and disruptive-demanding). The SSBS is a screening tool used to identify students who are at risk for behavior difficulties and is utilized through a multimethod, multisource assessment battery. Classroom teachers can complete the SSBS in approximately five to ten minutes.

On the SSBS, raw scores are used to formulate standard scores, percentile ranks, and social functioning levels, which can indicate further behavior problems and evaluations. The manual provides means and standard deviations by grade and sex for the major scales and respective subscales.

The SSBS was normed on a standardization sample of 1,858 children, grades Kindergarten through twelfth. There are several limitations of the sample (Demaray & Ruffalo, 1995). Forty percent of the sample came from Oregon and Washington states. Therefore, the distribution is not representative of the country's population. Also, separate norms for males and females are not available.

The SSBS has adequate to excellent psychometric properties for all scales and subscales. Internal consistency is excellent, while test-retest reliability indicates adequate short-term stability over a three-week time period. Inter-rater reliability is also adequate. Evidence for adequate to excellent content, criterion, and construct validity is present.

The School Social Skills Rating Scale (SSSRS)

The SSSRS (Brown, Black, & Downs, 1984) is a 40-item criterion referenced rating scale that can be used with children in grades Kindergarten through twelfth. It is designed to examine strengths and weaknesses in school-related social behaviors. The SSRS has an administration time of approximately ten minutes and can be com-

Title/Publisher	***Grade Age***	***Features***	***Reading Level***	***Admin Time***	***Validity***	***Reliability***
Behavior Assessment System for Children/ American Guidance Services	4–18	Components: Teacher Rating Scales, Parent Rating Scales, Structured Developmental History, Student Observation System; Measures areas including adaptive/behavioral skills, externalizing/internalizing, school & other problems.	N/A	20–30 Mins.	Good	Adequate to Excellent
Self-Directed Search/ Psychological Assessment Resources	N/A	Forms: R(118 items), E (198 items), CP. Occupational personality code yielded that is used to investigate compatible occupations/vocational choices.	4th Grade	30 Mins.		
Prout-Strohmer Assessment System/Genium	14 & Up; IQ's 55–83.	2 Component Parts: Prout-Stohmer Personality Inventory and Strohmer-Prout Behavior Rating Scale. Assesses areas including self-esteem, behavior disorder, anxiety, etc.	4th Grade	PSPI: 30 Mins. SPBRS: 15 Mins.	Good	Good to Excellent
Sixteen Personality Factor Questionnaire (16 PF)/Institute for Personality & Ability Testing	High School through Adulthood	Forms: A-D. Measures 16 bipolar primary factors. Including areas like concrete/abstract thinking, shy/venturesome, practical/ imaginative, undisciplined/ self-disciplined.			Limited	Poor to Good

Social Skills Rating System/American Guidance Services	K–12th	Consists of Parent, Teacher, & Student Forms. Examines areas like social skills, problem behaviors, & academic competencies.	N/A	30 Mins.	Good to Excellent	Adequate to Excellent
School Social Behavior Scales/ Clinical Psychological Publishing Company	K–12th	Completed by teachers or parents. Assesses social competence and antisocial behavior.	N/A	10 Mins.	Adequate to Good	Adequate to Excellent
School Social Skills Rating Scale/Slosson Educational Publications	K–12th	Criterion-referenced test with well-written questions can be completed by adults involved with student. Questions examine adult & peer relations, school rules compliance, and classroom behavior.	N/A	10 Mins.	N/A	N/A

Figure 4.2.

pleted by any school professional involved with the child. Given that this instrument is a criterion-referenced and not norm-referenced instrument, the rater should be familiar with the scale and the student's accompanying curriculum.

This scale is comprised of a list of well-written, objective items, with four categories included: adult relations, peer relations, school rules, and classroom behavior. Due to the scale not being standardized on a normative sample, no standard scores or percentile ranks can be derived. The SSSRS has adequate to excellent inter-rater and test-retest reliabilities. The authors also present adequate evidence of content validity, but limited data to support criterion or construct validity.

The SSSRS does not enable professionals to make classification or diagnostic decisions. However, facilitation of problem conceptualization and planning/intervention can be developed from the information gathered by this tool. Therefore, information yielded from this instrument may be applied to transition and vocational planning.

REFERENCES

Allen, B. P. (2000). *Personality theories: Development, growth, and diversity,* 3rd ed. Boston, MA: Allyn & Bacon.

Baron, R. A. & Greenburg, J. (1990). *Behavior in organizations: Understanding and managing the human side of work,* 3rd ed. Boston, MA: Allyn & Bacon.

Bolton, B. F. (1978). A review of the 16 personality factor questionnaire. In O. K. Buros (Ed.), *The eighth mental measurements yearbook.* Highland Park, NJ: The Gryphon Press.

Brown, L. J., Black, D. D., & Downs, J. C. (1984). *School social skills rating scale.* New York: Slosson Educational Publications.

Carnavale, A. P., Gainer, L. J., & Meltzer, A. S. (1990). *Workplace basics: The essential skills employers want.* San Francisco, CA: Jossey-Bass.

Cattell, R. B., Eber, H., & Tatsuoka, M. (1970). *Sixteen personality factor questionnaire.* Champaign, IL: Institute for Personality and Ability Testing.

Demaray, M. K. & Ruffalo, S. L. (1995). Social skills assessment: A comparative evaluation of six published rating scales. *School Psychology Review.*

Elksnin, N. & Elksnin, L. E. (1998). *Teaching occupational social skills.* Austin, TX: ProEd.

Gresham, F. M. & Elliott, S. N. (1990). *The social skills rating system.* Circle Pines, MN: American Guidance Service

Hershenson, D. B. (1981). Work adjustment, disability, and the three r's of vocational rehabilitation: A conceptual model. *Rehabilitation Counseling Bulletin, 25,* 91–97.

Holland, J. L. (1966). *The psychology of vocational choice.* Waltham, MA: Blaisdell.
Holland, J. L. (1973). Some practical remedies for providing vocational guidance for everyone. *Center for the Study of Social Organization of Schools,* 163.
Holland, J. L. (1985a). *A theory of vocational personalities and work environments.* Englewood Cliffs, NJ: Prentice-Hall.
Holland, J. L. (1985b). *The self-directed search professional manual.* Odessa, FL: Psychological Assessment Resources.
Karasek, R. & Theorell, T. (1990). *Healthy work: Stress, productivity, and the reconstruction of working life.* New York: Basic Books.
Landy, F. J. (1992). Work design and stress. In G. P. Keita & S. L. Sauter (Eds.), *Work and well being: An agenda for the 1990'* (pp. 119–158). Washington DC: American Psychological Association.
Levinson, E. M. (1993). *Transdisciplinary vocational assessment: Issues in school-based programs.* Brandon, VT: Clinical Psychology Publishing Company, Inc.
Merrell, K. W. (1993). *School social behavior scales.* Brandon, VT: Clinical Psychology Publishing Company, Inc.
Power, P. W. (2000). *A guide to vocational assessment,* 3rd ed Austin, TX: Pro-Ed.
Prout, T & Strohmer, D. (1989). *Prout-Strohmer assessment system.* Schnectady, NY: Genium.
Reynolds, C. R. & Kamphaus, R. W. (1992). *Behavior assessment system for children.* Circle Pines, MN: American Guidance Service.
Salvia, J. & Ysseldyke, J. E. (1991). *Assessment,* 5th ed. Boston: Houghton-Mifflin.
Sheridan, S. M., Maughn, D. P., & Hungelmann, A. (1999). A contextualized framework for social skills assessment, intervention, and generalization. *School Psychology Review, 28* (1), pp. 84–104.

Chapter 5

TRANSITION ASSESSMENT: FOCUS ON VOCATIONAL INTERESTS AND APTITUDES

MEGAN COSTANZA AND NICHOLE LEHMAN

INTRODUCTION

Career exploration involves activities that attempt to relate knowledge of ones' self to the external world (Blustein, 1993). In the educational environment this means providing students with information about their aptitudes, interests, and values and attempting to match that information to characteristics of specific postsecondary education programs or occupations. While aptitudes and interests are important components in career development and planning, these are areas of self-knowledge that develop over time.

Interests can be defined as "those things a person does for fun or enjoys" (Reardon, Lenz, Sampson, & Peterson, 2000). Interests are largely related to the enjoyment or satisfaction that an individual will experience with his or her career. While many individuals choose a profession or career based on their interests or what they think they would enjoy, this does not guarantee that they will succeed in their endeavors. Although interests do play a critical role in the job satisfaction an individual will experience, aptitude is also a key component that impacts the amount of success an individual will find in his or her profession. Aptitudes, which are defined as "the specific capacities or abilities required of an individual in order to facilitate the learning of some task or job duty" (United States Department of Labor, as cited in Altson & McCowan, 1994), are highly related to the success one may find in a given profession. Both interests and aptitudes are essential in transition planning from school to work or college.

Current Trends in Transition Assessment: Focus on Vocational Interests and Aptitudes

John Holland's Theory of Vocational Personalities and Work Environments

As discussed in the previous chapter, John Holland's theory of vocational personalities and work environments is widely considered one of the most influential career development theories and occupational taxonomies in vocational assessment (Tracey & Rounds, 1993). Holland's theory is widely accepted in the area of vocational psychology and has greatly influenced career counseling approaches and the organization of occupational information in high school and college career counseling programs. Central to Holland's theory is the idea that both people and work environments can be meaningfully classified into six types: realistic (R), investigative (I), artistic (A), social (S), enterprising (E), and conventional (C: RIASEC). Holland's RIASEC model has considerably impacted vocational-interest assessment and the classification of occupations. Many interest inventories use Holland's model as a means of integrating both individual vocational interests and occupations.

According to Holland's theory, the relationship among the six personalities and work environments can be depicted in a hexagonal model. With this model structure, the types (RIASEC) that are proximate to each other are considered to be more similar than those that are more distant. Holland's hexagonal model provides an easily grasped means of understanding and integrating interest and occupational information with respect to the similarity of types and occupations, and allows predictions to be made about optimal person-environment match. For instance, people with interests more closely located on the hexagon should demonstrate greater stability in interests and vocations than those with less proximate interests. In addition, individuals who have a better fit or congruence between their interests and the occupational environment are likely to have better vocational outcomes, such as fewer job changes and greater vocational achievement and satisfaction, than people who have a lower degree of interest-occupation fit.

As a means of assisting counselors and employers in helping individuals find their best "fit" with interests and work environments, Holland designed the Self-Directed Search (1985). This assessment tool assists in identifying an individual's interests and personality type, and is discussed later in this chapter. In addition, Holland developed the *Dictionary of Holland Occupational Titles* (Gottfredson, Holland, & Ogawa, 1982), which categorizes most occupations by Holland type. Therefore, a student can take an interest inventory, such as the Self-Directed Search, that provides a Holland code representative of his or her personality, and use the *Dictionary* to identify occupations congruent with his or her personality.

Ann Roe's Theory of Career Choice

Roe based her theory of career choice partially on Maslow's needs-based theory of motivation. She believed that unconscious needs as well as genetic influences and early childhood experiences, such as emotional climate in the home, parenting styles, and parent-child interactions influenced personality development and career choice. Roe further believed that the type of home environment the child is exposed to will determine the orientation the child takes towards people. These orientations then lead persons to migrate into certain occupations that are consistent with the orientation developed (Levinson, 1993).

Occupations are grouped into eight fields that reflect the primary focus of the activities: Service, Business Contact, Organization, Technology, Outdoor, Science, General Culture, and Arts and Entertainment. The relationship between these levels or fields is represented by a circular arrangement that is based on the intensity and nature of the interpersonal relationships involved in the occupational activities. As with Holland's theory, Roe's model also suggests that adjacent fields are more alike than non-adjacent fields. Roe also suggests, however, that within each area, occupations can be categorized by one of six levels based on the degree of responsibility, capacity, and skill. The levels include: Professional and managerial 1 (independent responsibility), Professional and managerial 2, Semiprofessional and small business, Skilled, Semiskilled, and Unskilled. By combining occupational groups with training, skills, and other job function demands, the counselor and student can more easily recognize appropriate matches between interests and work environments (Levinson, 1993).

Interpretations have been suggested for the dimensions underlying the two dimension model structures used by both Roe and Holland. Recognition of these dimensions is beneficial for professionals who are involved with transition planning. By being aware of the characteristics associated with each dimension, professionals can better match students' vocational interests with optimal work environments. The first accepted and empirically validated dimension is *people vs. things* (Gati, 1991). The second dimension supported by research is commonly referred to as *data* versus *ideas*. According to Prediger (1982), the *data* pole of *data-ideas*, which is represented by both Enterprising and Conventional interests, is characterized by a preference for impersonal, ordered tasks, whereas the *ideas* pole, represented by Investigative and Artistic interests, is characterized by a preference for intrapersonal tasks involving abstraction, curiosity, and originality. The *people-things* dimension is represented by Realistic interests at the *things* pole and Social interests at the *people* pole. The *people* pole is characterized by a preference for interpersonal tasks such as persuading, directing, and caring for others, whereas, the *things* pole is characterized by a preference for impersonal tasks involving machinery and working with one's hands. While it is beneficial for counselors to recognize the characteristics associated with each dimension, it is also important that counselors, psychologists, or other professionals are aware of the influences on interests, which guide individuals towards a particular dimension. These will be discussed next.

Influences on Interests

Age of Student

As with all likes and dislikes, career interests also develop over time and the rate of development largely varies among individuals. The process of an individual's development largely influences the stability of particular career or vocational interests. While assessment of a student's career interests is essential in transition planning, the level of vocational development should also be considered to determine the stability of their interests. Vocational developmental theorists report that children's career interests are generally unstable in childhood and early adolescence. During this time, children's career interests are largely influenced by their families, peers, and experiences in recreational and educational settings. However, theorists indicate that when students reach their middle teens, interests appear to stabilize and play a significant factor in vocational decisions and planning (Levinson, 1993).

While most theorists agree that career interests and choices tend to stabilize in mid-adolescence, their views on how children's career development progresses varies. Gottfredson (1981) viewed career decision making as a four-stage process where children begin to restrict their occupational aspirations as they acquire a better and more accurate understanding of themselves and the work world (Wahl & Blackhurst, 2000). Based on Gottfredson's theory, children's occupational decisions are based on age-specific themes that the child is experiencing. The theory states that children, between the ages of three and five, make career decisions based on themes of size and power. Children who are between six and eight years of age base career aspirations on sex roles, while social valuation begins to influence the career decisions of children aged nine to 12. Gottfredson reported that it is not until students are 14 or older that they begin to make career choices based on their unique personal characteristics.

Another theorist who has provided significant research in the field of vocational development is Donald Super. He defined vocational development as the existence of five major stages: Growth, Exploration, Establishment, Maintenance, and Decline (Levinson, 1993). The Growth and Exploration stages are the two most relevant to interest development and transition planning. The Growth stage, which includes children from birth to approximately 14 years of age, involves gaining awareness of the self as well as the world of work. The Growth Stage is composed of three substages: Fantasy, Interest, and Capacity. During the Fantasy substage (birth to 10 years of age), children define their career choices based on their fantasy play. It is during the Interest substage (11 to 12 years of age) that children begin to gain an awareness of their likes and dislikes and become aware of their interests. While their career interests are not stable, their interests begin to become more reality based. During the Capacity substage (13 to 14 years of age) adolescents begin to become more aware of their particular strengths and weaknesses and their aptitudes may begin to influence their career choices. In other words, students begin to shift from asking, "What do I like to do?" to "What can I do well?" This may be a time that students need support if they realize that they may not be able to succeed at some of their occupational interests. This type of awareness may lead to some students becoming discouraged and anxious, which may negatively influence their education and future career development (Seligman, 1980). Further discussion regarding realistic expectations will be presented later in this chapter.

Many researchers have evaluated children's occupational interests and choices during the Growth stage. Research completed by Trice and King (as cited in Wahl & Blackhurst, 2000) found that career preferences are evident as early as kindergarten. Ring (as cited in Wahl & Blackhurst, 2000) reported that tentative college plans may be formed as early as elementary school. Similarly, research has found that 97 percent of children in second grade reported that they had thought about what they would like to be when they grew up (Siegel, as cited in Wahl & Blackhurst, 2000). Research has also found that by the time a child is 12 years of age or in sixth grade, they have tentative career choices and can explain reasons for these choices (Herr & Cramer, as cited in Seligman, 1980). Seligman (1980) reported that while interests expressed by children during the Growth stage may change, the process of career development and exploration during this stage is essential for children.

The Exploration stage, which includes individuals from 15 to 24 years of age, is a developmental stage when individuals begin to explore various vocational options and begin to implement a vocational choice (Levinson, 1993). The three substages of the Exploration stage are: Tentative, Transition, and Trial. The Tentative substage (15 to 17 years of age) is when the individual begins to develop tentative but realistic career goals based on his or her interests and aptitudes. It is during the Transition substage (18 to 21 years of age) that the individual specifies a career choice and begins to acquire the necessary skills for employment in that career. The Trial substage (22 to 24 years of age) involves the individual acquiring a job and beginning to evaluate his or her satisfaction, or suitability, with the particular vocation.

While Super's theory is a developmental theory that specifies age ranges, individuals differ significantly in regard to the age at which they progress through each stage. Therefore, it is important to determine each student's vocational developmental level when considering student interests in planning for transition from school to work or college. The level of a student's self-awareness, which Super suggests develops between the ages of 13 to 14 years, will influence the stability of career interests that the student is able to express.

Personal Needs for Job Satisfaction

Identifying a student's interests not only helps to identify occupations that the individual might enjoy, but also helps to predict the satisfaction that that individual may find in a particular career. Research completed by Gottfredson and Holland (1990) indicated that work environments that allow the expression of a person's interests and competencies result in increased job satisfaction. Similarly, Henderson (2000) found in her research that individuals who were reportedly happy at work demonstrated a commitment to follow their interests.

Along with evaluating an individual's interests when developing a transition plan, particular attention needs to be focused on the work-related needs of the individual. The Minnesota Theory of Work Adjustment, while not intended to be a theory of career development, suggests that job satisfaction is influenced by the relationship between the work environment and the ability of that environment to fulfill the individual's work-related needs (Levinson, 1993). The theory suggests that the individual's satisfaction with his or her career is largely influenced by the extent to which the occupation meets these work-related needs. The theory also suggests that each individual has different levels of importance for specific needs and each job provides reinforcement for different needs. Unlike interests that tend to remain stable after adolescence, work-related needs change depending on the individual's development. Therefore, a job that may be satisfying to an individual trying to advance in his or her career, may not be satisfying later in life when his or her needs begin to focus more on security, for example. So while it may appear that an individual's interests are unstable, it may actually be that the individual's work-related needs are changing. This change may likely result in the individual beginning to search for new employment. Research has identified at least 20 different work-related needs that influence job satisfaction (Levinson, 1993):

1. *Ability utilization*–The need to use one's abilities.

2. *Achievement*–The need to feel accomplished with one's performance.
3. *Activity*–The need to be active or to stay busy.
4. *Advancement*–The need to advance in one's present occupation.
5. *Authority*–The need to be in charge or to tell others what to do.
6. *Company policies and practice*–The need to feel comfortable with company policies and practices.
7. *Compensation*–The need for individuals to feel that they are being valued and compensated for the work put into their occupation.
8. *Co-workers*–The need to get along with others in the work environment.
9. *Creativity*–The need to explore and try one's ideas.
10. *Independence*–The need to work independently and to perform without supervision.
11. *Moral values*–The need to feel that one's work is not against moral values.
12. *Recognition*–The need to be recognized for one's work.
13. *Responsibility*–The need to feel that one can be trusted with using his or her own judgment.
14. *Security*–The need to feel secure with one's position or job.
15. *Social service*–The need to feel that one's work is benefiting others.
16. *Social status*–The need to feel respected by others.
17. *Supervision-Human relations*–The need to get along with one's supervisor or superiors.
18. *Supervision-Technical*–The need for quality technical supervision regarding job specifics.
19. *Variety*–The need to have a variety of experiences.
20. *Working conditions*–The need to feel comfortable with one's working environment.

Gender

Career aspirations of young women and men appear to be influenced in part by personal attitudes regarding appropriate female/male behaviors. These attitudes of expecting a set of distinct behaviors and responsibilities within a group reflect gender role stereotyping. With this in mind, it is not surprising to find research that suggests students' preferences and interests for jobs are influenced by gender stereotypes relating to occupations. For instance, Cook (1994) found that gender influences how individuals perceive various roles and role priorities. Likewise, Johnson's (1995) analysis of vocational aspirations of college students also validated gender as an underlying dimension of job preference.

Investigation of adolescents' attitudes toward gender roles of occupations revealed that gender also plays a factor in the type of working environments preferred by adolescents (Tuck, Wolfe, & Adair, 1994). Lent, Brown, and Hackett (1994) suggested that learning experiences, including gender-role socialization, influence self-referent beliefs, which then give rise to interests. Interests, in turn, influence career choice goals (e.g., intended occupation) and actions (e.g., declaring a major), both of which vary in gender traditionality. Similarly, Tokar and Jome's (1998) research with male undergraduate and graduate students supported the mediational role of vocational interests in the relation between masculinity and traditionality of career choice. Likewise, they also found partial support for the influence that masculine gender roles have in predicting vocational interests.

Prestige

While research has indicated that gender and gender-stereotypes influence vocational interests and job preference, these findings might also be interpreted as being related to occupational prestige, which is often confounded with an occupation's sex-type. That is, male-intensive occupations tend to be associated with higher prestige than are female-intensive occupations. Recent research has supported the belief that prestige is an important aspect to consider when assessing vocational interests and occupations. Einarsdottir and Rounds (2000) studied the influence of occupational sex-type or prestige on individuals' vocational interests. Their research revealed that individuals differed in their preference of prestige level associated with an occupation. Just as individuals differ in how much they like working with people versus things, they also vary in regard to the degree of prestige they seek within an occupation. As such, responses on interest inventories might reflect that some people prefer more highly prestigious occupations while others prefer moderate- or low-prestige occupations. For example, Tracey and Rounds (1996) found that prestige, or social status of occupations is likely to influence the responses on vocational interest items. The importance of occupational prestige was also supported in a study by Leong (1991), who found that Asian American students placed greater emphasis on extrinsic (e.g., income, status, and prestige) and security values when compared to Caucasians. In general, it appears that interests incorporate elements of both sex-type and prestige; therefore, these three variables cannot be viewed as completely separate and independent when conducting an interest assessment.

Ethnicity

The increasing diversity among students requires an understanding of the role of racial and cultural influences on career development. There are particular areas to address when using interests measures with students who represent an ethnic minority. The student's socialization and acculturation within a minority culture can affect vocational interests and career choices. Minority children may frequently embrace values that differ from those of the dominant culture. These values may include the importance placed on interpersonal relationships and helping behavior versus task achievements. Likewise, emphasis may be placed on the goals and needs of a group or family rather than the individual. It is important, however, to remember that two people from the same race may share some values, attitudes, or beliefs but may also have very different cultural make-ups. Therefore, assumptions about cultural stereotypes should not be made. Rather, focus should be placed on guiding the individual student toward the educational program or work environment that best matches his or her interests.

Family Influences

Research suggests that one's family also plays a significant role on students' career interests and choices. For instance, it is not unusual for children to take over family businesses or for families to consist of generations of doctors, lawyers, farmers, or teachers. Kinnier, Brigman, and Noble (1990) reported that career decision making and family dynamics are related and that children tend to identify with the adult workers in their lives (Wahl & Blackhurst, 2000). Theorists, such as

Gottfredson (1981), have also indicated that socially accepted career choices, that are determined from the individual's family, are the last to be discarded when an individual is making career choices. Research completed by Reisman and Banuelo (1984) found that children from families without an adult working had less developed occupational fantasies when compared to children who had at least one parent working. However, research has also indicated that while parent occupations influence the career choices of children, the child's perception of the parent's satisfaction with a particular occupation also influences the child's aspirations (Trice & Tillapaugh, 1991).

Research has found that while children's occupational aspirations are highly related to the occupations held by their parents, the mother's occupation tends to have a greater influence (Trice & Knapp, 1992). Wahl and Blackhurst (2000) speculated that this may be influenced by children having more first-hand knowledge about their mother's occupations due to children being more likely to attend work with their mothers and being more likely to have an awareness of what their mothers do for a living (Trice & Knapp, 1992).

Similarly, research completed by Tuck, Rolfe, and Adair (1994) found that mothers have a large influence on their sons' and daughters' attitudes towards work-related roles in relationships and the division of labor. They found that mothers who had a primary commitment to caregiving had children with more conservative attitudes toward employment than did mothers who had "careers" in which either they managed employees or owned a business. These mothers tended to make a significant commitment to their "career," often requiring their families to restructure the delineation of household tasks. As a result, children in these households tended to experience not only a mother with a commitment to a career but also more of an egalitarian distribution of labor. Tuck, et al. (1994) also examined Holland's interest categories and their relation to adolescents' egalitarian attitudes. Their research found that adolescents with "social," "artistic," and "enterprising" personalities tended to show more indications of egalitarian attitudes toward work roles than those with "investigative" personalities.

Recent research in the field of career interests and family influences have primarily focused on the role that families play on females' career choices. Steele and Barling (1996) completed research that specifically assessed the impact of maternal and paternal roles on daughters' vocational interests. While the mother's role satisfaction and gender-role ideology influenced the daughter's vocational interests and gender-role identity, their research did not support fathers' effects on daughters' career interests. On the other hand, Hoffman, Hofacker, and Goldsmith (1992) found that fathers did influence their daughter's career interests. Their research indicated that the emotional closeness that daughters experienced with their fathers positively influenced their consideration of non-traditional careers. Similarly, Blustein, Walbridge, Friedlander, and Palladino (1991) reported that women's level of attachment to both parents, as well as their experiences with independence through conflict, was related to increased career commitment and less likelihood of foreclosure on a career choice.

Research has also examined the balance of work and family and its impact on career interests and college majors. Savage and Fouad (1994) reported on two studies that indicated women might choose traditional careers in order to manage the double-shift lifestyle of working and caring for the family. They also reported that the career interests in social fields, such as education, are closely associated with the traditional manner of integrating work and family.

Methods of Assessing Interests

Super (1949) identified three types of interests: expressed, manifest, and tested. Along with each type interest having specific characteristics, there are also different types of assessments that can be used to identify an individual's vocational interests.

Interviews

Expressed interests are verbal statements of liking a stimulus, object, activity, task, or occupation. These types of interests can be identified through the use of clinical interviews where the student is asked about what they do and do not enjoy. As Super's developmental theory indicates, by the time students enter early adolescence, they are beginning to identify and express their interests. Research has been inconsistent on whether interests inventories or interviews are the most effective and predictive measures of vocational choice. Research by Salomone (1996) found that while counselors may be more inclined to use interest inventories, verbal expression of interests or aspirations is a better predictor of future vocational choice. On the other hand, Spokane (1991) reported that interest inventories are the most effective and desired strategy. Regardless of the measure, it is important to gain as much input available about the student's interests, desires, and concerns when planning for transition. Using multiple assessment methods and using data from both interest inventories and interviews will likely result in the most reliable and valid data.

Observations

Manifest interests are reflected by an individual's behaviors when participating in various activities, occupations, or tasks. These interests are evident by the activities in which an individual voluntarily engages. Information regarding these types of interests is gained through direct observation and clinical interviews.

Standardized Tests

Tested or inventoried interests are those interests identified through standardized, objective measures. While interest inventories were originally developed in the 1940s, they continue to be widely used today (Reardon, Lenz, Sampson, & Peterson, 2000). While interest inventories are the most widely used types of measurement, they should not be used alone. Observations and interviews should also be used to determine the most appropriate occupational choice for students.

There are two widely used methods of developing interest inventories. One commonly used method involves comparing the individual's strength of interest in various activities to those activities that are commonly found in various careers. These types of "activity-similar" measurements assess the individual's likes and dislikes of particular *activities* commonly found in specific occupations. Particular occupations are then determined to meet the individuals' preferences based on their enjoyment of various activities associated with the occupations (Levinson, 1993; Power, 2000).

The other method commonly used to assess interests is the "people-similar" approach where the individual's interests, or likes and dislikes, are compared to the interests of satisfied individuals in specific occupations. From this information, occupations of interest are identified based on a pattern of interests found to be similar to professionals in specific occupations (Levinson, 1993).

The purpose of interest inventories is to help to predict job choices that will hopefully result in the job satisfaction. The predictive validity of interest inventories is determined by comparing vocational interests with later job choices and determining the rate of successful predictions. The validity of interest inventories is also assessed by correlating the scores on one interest inventory to the scores obtained from the same group of individuals on another interest inventory. This type of correlation is defined as concurrent validity. The reliability of interest inventories is also assessed through internal consistency measurements and also through test-retest procedures. While both approaches of assessing interests have relativity positive psychometric properties, the "people-similar" approach has been found to be particularly good (Levinson, 1993).

While there are many inventories available to assess interests, the choice of an appropriate interest inventory should not be based on availability alone. Along with being aware of the psychometric properties of an instrument, the practitioner should take into account the individual's needs and characteristics. The following are some of the suggestions recommended for practitioners when determining an appropriate measurement:

1. The evaluator's "choice" of interest inventories should be based on the kind of information provided by the instrument and not simply on the cost, availability, or time required for administration.
2. For students with emotional issues, interest inventories may not be the most appropriate measurement. Students with emotional disturbances tend to make negative responses and endorse more passive interests.
3. A consideration for selecting an interest inventory is the student's vocational goals and aspirations. For a student who wants to make fine distinctions within a general occupation area, the use of interest inventories may be of limited value. The use of interviews may be a more appropriate method to examine extrinsic needs, such as salary or education that the student may need to consider.
4. Educational level should also be considered when selecting an interest inventory. For example, instruments used in junior high school should be geared toward career exploration. Whereas, inventories used in high school should be more oriented toward decision-making regarding future education and employment.

5. The student's reading level should also be considered when selecting an interest inventory. The use of a non-reading instrument may be a more appropriate choice for students who have limited reading skills. While interest instruments have expanded to help professionals evaluate students with exceptionalities, there is recognition that more effective measures need to be developed for those individuals with physical and mental disabilities, those who have a very low reading ability, or those with a limited awareness about jobs or occupations.
6. The student's motivation to complete the interest inventory should be considered when interpreting the results. Prior counseling on the purpose and importance of the assessment should be provided to the student to increase motivation. (Hood & Johnson, 1997; Levinson, 1993; Power, 2000; Spitzer & Levinson, 1988)

Once information is collected and the appropriate interest inventory has been selected, interpreting information becomes the examiner's responsibility. Many experts in the field express concerns regarding inappropriate usage of interest inventories (Clark & Kolstoe, 1995). As previously discussed, individuals proceed gradually through career development with interests becoming more defined and realistic as the student matures. Often the ultimate focus of interest inventories is the product, or the test results, rather than the student's process of development. Practitioners need to be reminded to focus on the process of developing career interests when interpreting the results that are obtained from interest inventories, and use interest inventories to facilitate self-awareness.

The method used in developing a particular interest inventory, such as the people-similar vs. activity-similar approach, also needs to be considered when interpreting results (Levinson, 1993). Professionals also need to consider that past experiences exert a strong influence on the results of interest inventories (Levinson, 1993). If a student has no awareness or has no experience with a particular occupation, they are less likely to indicate interest in this occupation. Therefore, it is important when interpreting results to distinguish between lack of interest and lack of exposure to or experience with a particular occupation.

When interpreting results, it is also important to ensure that the needs of the student are assessed. As discussed earlier, the student's particular needs play an important role in whether they will be satisfied in a job. When interpreting interest inventory results, the student should be provided clear distinctions between external and internal needs (Levinson, 1993). Interest inventories measure intrinsic sources of satisfaction, but tend not to focus on extrinsic rewards that one may require from their occupation. Therefore, it is essential that extrinsic needs, such as salary, activity level, and variety of experiences, are identified and discussed in relation to the individual's intrinsic reinforcement that is identified through interest inventories.

Validity and reliability take on additional importance in cross-cultural testing in that the instrument must be validly translated, the items must have conceptual and linguistic equivalence, and the test, as well as the items, must be free from bias. It is also important that counselors are aware of the norm group to which the individual is compared and that the comparison is an appropriate one. Prince, Vemura, Chao, & Gonzales (as cited in Power, 2000) offer the following suggestions for using interest measures for those students representing a minority culture:

1. If the student's primary language is not English, the evaluator should explore administering a version of the inventory that corresponds to the individual's language.
2. The student's test-taking attitude and response style need to be explored. Individuals from different minority backgrounds may have certain expectations in mind when responding to an inventory.
3. When interpreting test results, the evaluator should be sensitive to the student's response, in that the response that may reflect cultural values and reinforce cultural stereotypes. It is also possible that the individual may have a restricted range of interests. If so, professionals should encourage the individual to broaden career considerations beyond those reflected by the measured interests.

Best Practices in Assessing Aptitudes

Aptitudes can be defined as "the specific capacities or abilities required of an individual in order to facilitate the learning of some tasks or job duty" (United States Department of Labor, as cited in Altson & McCowan, 1994). Frequently the terms intelligence, ability, achievement, and aptitude are used interchangeably. While aptitude tests provide information regarding an individual's cognitive strengths and weaknesses, these tests differ from the standardized ability and achievement tests that are frequently administered in schools. For instance, aptitude tests measure more specialized abilities than do intelligence tests. Aptitude tests aim to identify an ability or characteristic, mental or physical, native or acquired, that is believed to indicate an individual's potential for learning a particular skill or knowledge (Power, 2000). In other words, aptitude tests measure specific skills and proficiencies that are intended to predict how well one may perform on a job or in an educational or training program.

Some confusion also exists about the differences between aptitude and achievement tests. Anastasi (1982) believed that achievement tests measure the outcomes of standardized school experiences while aptitude tests measure a wider range of cumulative daily experiences. Aiken (1985) provided another defining characteristic in his belief that aptitude measurement focuses on the future whereas achievement measurement focuses on the past. In other words, achievement tests attempt to measure the outcome or amount of profit from specific training, education, or past experience, while aptitude tests attempt to measure capabilities that have been developed without conscious effort, allowing predictions to be made about future performance in certain situations.

Influences on Aptitudes

Just as age influences the development of interests, it also plays a factor in the expression of one's aptitude. Seligman (as cited in Levinson, 1993) suggests that aptitudes are relatively unstable in childhood and it is not until an individual reaches adolescence or adulthood that their aptitudes begin to stabilize. While aptitude assessments aim to determine the extent to which an individual has the potential or capacity to satisfy specific educational or occupational demands, they may not necessarily be predictive of success or performance. Factors such as motivation, personality characteristics, social skills, or past experiences may also influence performance on a task or activity (Levinson, 1993).

Methods of Assessing Aptitudes

Similar to the assessment of interests, aptitudes can be measured through the use of interviews, observations, and standardized instruments. While standardized tests are the most commonly used method of obtaining aptitude data, information obtained from interviews and observations provide pertinent information that can be used to assess a student's strengths and weaknesses. Not only does the information provided by interviews and observations give the transdisciplinary transition team additional material on which to base transition plans, the student is also observed in a more natural type of work or school environment.

As previously mentioned, standardized tests are the most widely used method of assessing student's aptitudes. Most of these multidimensional tests measure a common set of aptitudes. These aptitudes (Levinson, 1993) include the following:

General Learning Ability (G)–The ability to understand instructions and underlying principles; the ability to reason and make judgments. This measure closely relates to doing well in school and is often used to make predictions about level of success during postsecondary school.

Verbal (V)–The ability to understand the meaning of words and ideas associated with them and to use them effectively; ability to comprehend language, to understand the relationship between words, understand meanings of whole sentences and paragraphs; and ability to present information or ideas clearly.

Numerical (N)–The ability to perform arithmetic operations quickly and accurately.

Spatial (S)–The ability to comprehend forms in space and understand relationships of solid objects to a plane; ability to visualize objects of two or three dimensions; and ability to think visually of geometric forms.

Form Perception (P)–The ability to perceive pertinent detail in objects, in pictorial or graphic material; ability to make visual comparisons and discriminations and see slight differences in shapes and shadings of figures and width and length of lines.

Clerical Perception (Q)–The ability to perceive pertinent detail in verbal or tabular material; ability to observe differences in copy, to proofread words and numbers, and to avoid perceptual errors in arithmetic computation.

Motor Coordination (K)–The ability to coordinate eyes and hands or fingers rapidly and accurately in making precise movements with speed; ability to make a movement response accurately and quickly.

Finger Dexterity (F)–The ability to move the fingers and manipulate small objects with the fingers rapidly and accurately.

Manual Dexterity (M)–The ability to move the hands easily and skillfully; ability to work with the hands in placing and turning motions.

Future Directions in Transition Assessment: Focus on Vocational Interests and Aptitudes

While aptitude and interests are measured separately, both sources of information must be used together to improve the success of transition planning. The goal of transition planning is to identify high interest occupational areas in which the student demonstrates successful performance. In order to accomplish this goal, professionals need to incorporate both interest and aptitude data in the evaluation process. If professionals expend their energy on only one of these areas, they are likely to overlook essential areas in effective transition planning. Considering students' interests and aptitudes in transition planning will increase the likelihood of their happiness and success in a given occupation.

When combining interests and aptitudes, the professional must recognize the extraneous factors that may influence student's vocational choice. Such factors include unrealistic expectations and beliefs held by the student. While these factors may influence the student's career aspirations, the professional must work with the student to either accommodate for these factors or educate the student on alternative occupations that may coincide with their interests and aptitudes.

Realistic Expectations

As discussed previously in this chapter, many influences, from family issues to gender, play a factor in the development of career interests. Some students may "fixate" on one vocational objective or choice because of family, parental, or other influences in their environment (Power, 2000). Unfortunately, when working with students with exceptionalities, some of these objectives or interests may not coincide with their ability or aptitude. Therefore, it is the professional's role to help the student recognize the discrepancy between his or her career interest and ability. Professionals working with the student then need to work with the student in adjusting his or her occupational objectives to meet his or her interests while also building on his or her ability or aptitude. One way to do this is to identify jobs or different levels of the occupation in the student's interest area. This emphasis should be placed not only on the student's intrinsic needs, but also on his or her extrinsic needs (variety, advancement, salary, etc.). Education and time involved in training is also an issue that should be discussed with a student. In enterprising-related occupations, for example, the training to become a lawyer or to become a retail store manager varies significantly. However, both occupations involve leading and manipulating others to attain personal or organizational goals. Explanation of the duties and time involved with training for each profession may aid students in readjusting their own career expectations.

In addition to identifying the relationship between a student's interests and aptitudes, job availability and the expectancy of obtaining employment after schooling or training should also be considered in planning for transition to postsecondary school or work. Many students' expectations about employment after training may not be realistic based on statistics. Educating students prior to their entering the Transition substage of Super's model, at which point the individual specifies a career choice and begins to acquire the necessary skills for employment in that career, may help prevent frustration and discouragement.

Beliefs

While it is clear from research that interests and aptitudes play a significant factor in the job satisfaction and success an individual experiences with a particular occupation, one's beliefs are also an area that play a significant factor on occupational choice and satisfaction. Naylor and Krumboltz (1994) report that while aptitude theories emphasize suitability and interest theories emphasize preference, it is beliefs that inhibit or facilitate the expression of an aptitude or the realization of an interest. Regardless of an interest or aptitude measurement's objectivity, this data will eventually be compared to the individual's beliefs. Naylor and Krumboltz (1994) found that aptitudes, interests, and beliefs are independent entities and all three should be considered as independent sources of data in transition planning.

Research completed by Gottfredson and Holland (1990) also revealed the importance that beliefs play in job satisfaction. They found that the single most efficient predictor of job satisfaction was a measure of expected satisfaction in a given profession. Their research concluded that simply asking an individual if they will be satisfied with a job will generate predictions of subsequent job satisfaction.

Along with interviewing and listening to the student, The Career Beliefs Inventory (CBI) (Krumboltz, 1991) is an instrument that can be used to evaluate career beliefs. The CBI consists of 25 belief scales, which represent themes in beliefs about the individual in relation to work. These themes, such as career path flexibility (scale 15), are important in career decision-making.

BRIEF REVIEW OF INTEREST INVENTORIES AND APTITUDE ASSESSMENTS

Nonreading Interest Inventories

Wide Range Interest-Opinion Test

This instrument is a non-reading interest inventory in which the individual is shown triads of pictures and is asked to indicate, through pointing, the most and least preferred activity. This instrument can be used with individuals as young as five years of age and its' use is also appropriate for adults. The administration of this instrument can be completed individually or to a group in about 40 minutes. It can be hand- or machine-scored, with scores translated into 18 basic interest scales. There are also four scales that focus directly on response bias.

Reading Free Vocational Interest Inventory-Revised

The Reading Free Vocational Interest Inventory-Revised was developed to assess occupational interests of individuals who are 13 years or older and who are mentally retarded, learning disabled, or have some other disability. The instrument consists of 55 triads of pictorial depictions of occupations in a forced choice format. It can be administered to individuals or groups. Administration of this test takes approximately 20 minutes. This instrument is presented on a non-reusable booklet that can be hand-scored. This instrument covers 11 occupational areas, which range from skilled to unskilled.

Geist Picture Interest Inventory-Revised

This instrument was developed for individuals from eighth grade through adult who are culturally limited, educationally deprived, or have verbal disabilities. The GPII-R can be administered in about 20 to 40 minutes to an individual or group. It requires a fourth grade reading level for written questions; however, it may be read to individuals who are severely disabled. This instrument is divided into male and female booklets containing illustrations of occupations that are recognizable in most parts of the United States. Interest areas are scored into broad fields of interest, 11 for females and 12 for males. A motivational questionnaire is also included in the instrument to identify motivations behind each choice.

Reading-Based Interest Inventories

The Self-Directed Search (SDS)

The Self-Directed Search is based on Holland's theory of career development and is popular and frequently used. It can be self-administered and self-scored. It provides a self-interpretation guide for students and adults in need of assistance in career planning. It can be used with high school and college students as well as with adults. The SDS requires approximately 30 to 40 minutes to administer. Results provide students with three letter codes that correspond to Holland's theory of personality and career interests. The student is then able to identify careers that correspond with his or her personality/interest areas.

Career Key

The Career Key was originally developed in a paper-and-pencil version and later transferred to an online version. The Career Key is comparable to Holland's Self-Directed Search in that it assesses the six personality types proposed by Holland. Those who use the Career Key online version view a list of several occupations, identify those that are of interest, and read suggestions for furthering their career exploration (Jones, 1990). It requires approximately 20 to 30 minutes to administer. Psychometric properties for the online version are not currently available, though some recent studies have suggested that it possesses technical characteristics which are comparable to both the paper-pencil version and to the SDS (Levinson, Ohler & Zeman, 2002; Buchan & Levinson, 2003).

Occupational Aptitude Survey and Interest Schedule–Second Edition Interest Schedule (OASIS-2 IS)

The OASIS-2 IS is an instrument used to pair interests and aptitudes with occupational choices. It is used to assist students in eighth through twelfth grade to define their career interests and to match these interests with their aptitudes. It measures interests in 12 areas: artistic, scientific, nature, protective, mechanical, industrial, business detail, selling, accommodating, humanitarian, leading-influencing, and physical performing. The OASIS-2 IS can be administered to a group or individual in about 30 to 45 minutes.

Strong Interest Inventory (SII)

This instrument is one of the oldest and most scientifically developed instruments on the market today. The interpretation of the SII is based on Holland's theory of personality and career development. This instrument requires a sixth-grade reading level and scoring needs to be completed with a computer program. Interpretation is based on six general occupational themes, 23 basic interest scales, and 124 occupational scales. This instrument allows interpretation of data based on the gender of the individual. The total time to complete this instrument is 30 to 40 minutes.

Kuder Form DD Occupational Interest Survey–Revised

This instrument is intended to identify occupational and college major interests. It takes 30 to 40 minutes to administer and it must be machine scored. This instrument compares interests of the individual with interests commonly found in individuals in particular occupations or college majors. There are 119 occupational scales, 48 college major scales, 10 traditional Kuder interest scales, and eight experimental scales. The instrument provides norms for both men and women in occupational and college major scales.

Career Assessment Inventory–The Enhanced Version (CAI)

The CAI was originally developed to assess interests in individuals that were not intending to pursue postsecondary education. The new version of this instrument now includes measurements for individuals who seek professional careers. The CAI is patterned after the Strong Interest Inventory by including administrative indices, general theme scales, non-occupational scales, basic interest scales, and occupational scales. This instrument is organized based on Holland's Occupational Themes. Holland's six general themes are divided into 25 Basic Interest Area Scales (BIA). It is written at a sixth-grade reading level and it takes between 20 and 40 minutes to complete. The instrument is computer scored and mail-in scoring is available.

Aptitude Assessments

General Aptitude Test Battery (GATB)

The General Aptitude Test Battery (U.S. Department of Labor, 1983) is a group-administered test designed for use in vocational and occupational counseling. The battery is composed of eight paper-and-pencil tests and four apparatus tests. Together these 12 tests measure nine aptitudes: general learning ability, verbal aptitude, numerical aptitude, spatial aptitude, form perception, clerical perceptions, motor coordination, finger dexterity, and manual dexterity. Administration of the test takes two and a half to three hours. Raw scores are converted to standard scores that have a mean of 100 and a standard deviation of 20.

Through an extensive validation program, minimum cut-off scores have been established for aptitudes that are important for success in various occupations. These cut-off scores have been used to determine occupational ability patterns (OAPs) and Specific Aptitude Test Batteries (SATB) for which 66 work groups, that include thousands of occupations, were established. OAPs are cut-off scores on the few most important aptitudes for clusters of similar occupations. SATBs are cut-off scores that have been established for specific occupations. Occupational success is predicted for individuals who score above the cut-off score for all critical aptitudes associated with a particular occupation.

USES Nonreading Aptitude Test Battery

The USES Non-Reading Aptitude Test Battery (NATB; United States Employment Service Office, 1982) is an adaptation of the GATB for individuals with limited reading skills. Many of the mechanics and principles of use and interpretation are the same for the two test batteries. However, the NATB adds the following subtests to the nine subtests already included in the GATB: picture-word matching; oral vocabulary; coin matching; design completion; tool matching; three-dimensional space; form matching; coin series; name comparison: and mark making, placing, turning, assembling, and disassembling.

Occupational Aptitude Survey and Interest Schedule–Second Edition Aptitude Survey (OASIS-2 AS)

The OASIS –2 AS (Parker, 1991) can be administered, individually or in a group, to students in grades eight through 12. The instrument consists of five subtests: vocabulary; computation; spatial relations; word comparison; and missing marks. A sixth score, general ability, is obtained by summing the raw scores of the vocabulary and computation subtests. Specific time limits are placed on each subtest, with total administration time being approximately 35 minutes. The test can be hand- or machine- scored in which raw scores for each subtest are converted to percentiles and stanine scores.

The Differential Aptitude Test (DAT)

The fifth edition of the DAT Forms C and D (Bennett, Seashore, & Wesman, 1990) has two levels that measure the aptitudes of students in grades seven through 12, as well as adults. Level 1 is designed primarily for students in seventh to ninth grade, while level 2 is primarily used with students in tenth through twelfth grade. At both levels, two forms are available (Forms C and D) that are parallel in content and difficulty. Both levels of the DAT consist of the following scales: Verbal Reasoning; Numerical Reasoning, Abstract Reasoning, Perceptual Speed and Accuracy, Mechanical Reasoning; Space Relations, Spelling, and Language Usage. Nine scores are provided, one for each scale, and a composite score, the Scholastic Aptitude score, is derived from Verbal Reasoning and Numerical Reasoning. Scores are reported in percentile ranks, stanines, and scaled scores. Administration time for the complete battery takes approximately three hours. The test can be hand- or machine-scored. A computerized adaptive edition is also available.

Wang (1995) states, "that the DAT remains one of the most frequently used batteries is a tribute to its quality, credibility, and utility" (p.170).

Armed Services Vocational Aptitude Battery 18/19 Career Exploration Program

The Armed Services Vocational Aptitude Battery–18/19 (ASVAB; United States Department of Defense, 1992), is a multiple aptitude battery designed to be administered to individuals ages 16-23. The ASVAB consists of 334 items arranged in ten subtests, each of which yields a percentile rank score. The subtests are general science, arithmetic reasoning, word knowledge, paragraph comprehension, numerical operations, coding speed, auto and shop information, mathematics knowledge, mechanical comprehension, and electronics information. Three composite scores of verbal ability, math ability, and academic ability are also derived. Scores are reported in percentile ranks for same grade/sex, same grade/opposite sex, and same grade/combined sex. Administration of the test takes approximately three hours. An important consideration is that the test may only be administered by specially trained examiners from the Department of Defense or the U.S. Office of Personnel Management.

The newest version of the ASVAB contains a Career Exploration Program (CEP) that attempts to provide students with occupational guidance for both military and civilian careers. Using a chart referred to as OCCU-FIND, students combine their ASVAB scores with their educational goals and interests from Holland's Self-Directed Search (SDS). As a result, a list of military and civilian occupations that match student aptitudes and interests are provided.

SUMMARY

While this chapter recognizes that interests and aptitudes are an integral component in transition planning, these areas should not be assessed in isolation. Interests inventories and aptitude tests should be part of a multimethod approach to vocational and transition assessment. It is critical to also consider the student's cognitive ability, social skills, personality characteristics, career maturity as well as other factors

Interest Inventories

Title: Publisher	Grade/ Age	Features	Reading Level	Time	Adm. Validity	Reliability
Career Assessment Inventory-The Enhanced Version: National Computer Systems, Inc.	Junior high school and above	The CAI was originally developed to assess interests of individuals not attending college. The new version now is appropriate for those who seek professional careers. This instrument is patterned after the Strong Interest Inventory and based on Holland's theory. This instrument is computer scored. Mail-in scoring is available.	6th grade reading level	35–40 min.	Content, construct, and concurrent validity	Test-retest data for less than 3 month intervals
Career Key: Jones, L. K. (1987) (Originally published by Ferguson in Chicago, IL)	Not reported	This instrument assesses the six personality types hypothesized by Holland. Originally developed in a paper and pencil version and later transferred to an on-line version.	Not reported	20–30 min.	Internal consistency and retest reliability reported for paper and pencil version. None reported for on-line version.	Criterion-related validity and construct validity reported for pencil and paper version. None reported for on-line version.
Geist Picture Interest Inventory-Revised: Western Psychological Services	8th grade through adult	This interest inventory was developed for individuals who are culturally limited, educationally deprived, or have verbal disabilities. Instrument includes male and female booklets that contain illustrations of occupation. Individual or group administration.	4th grade reading level; can be read to the individual	20 to 40 min.	None reported	Test-retest data varies considerably

Kuder Form DD Occupational Interest Survey-Revised: Publisher Test Service	10th grade through college	This instrument is intended to identify occupational and college major interests. It compares interests of the individual with interests commonly found in individuals in particular occupations or college majors. Norms available for both men and women. This instrument must be machine scored.	Not reported	35 mins.	Predictive validity reported	Test-retest for vocational interest estimates (.70 to .84)
Occupational Aptitude Survey and Interest Schedule-Second Edition IS: PRO-ED	8th through 12th grade	Used with aptitude measurement to assist in career planning. 12 interest areas. This interest inventory can be group or individually administered.	Not reported	30–45 min.	Concurrent validity is reported to range from mid .70s–.80s; manual provides more validity evidence	Reliability generally fall within .80 to .90 range
Reading Free Vocational Interest Inventory-Revised: The Psychological Corporation	13 years and older	This instrument was developed to assess interests of individuals with mentally retardation, a learning disability, or other disability. It contains 55 triad of pictures that cover 11 occupational areas. Individually or group administered.	Non-reading	20 min.	Content validity, concurrent validity, occupational validity reported but questioned	None reported

Title: Publisher	Grade/ Age	Features	Reading Level	Time	Adm. Validity	Reliability
Strong Interest Inventory: National Computer Systems, Inc.	16 years and older	One of the oldest and scientifically developed instruments. It is based on Holland's theory. It is mainly applicable to those interested in professional, semiprofessional, or managerial occupations. It requires computer scoring.	6th grade reading level	25 to 35 min.	Content validity, concurrent validity, and predictive validity reported	Test-retest reliability reported
The Self-Directed Search: Psychological Assessment Resources	High school through adult	This instrument is based on Holland's theory of career development. It provides a self-interpretation guide. It can be administered individually or in a group setting.	Between 7th and 8th grade reading level	30 to 40 min.	Adequate and comparable to other vocational interest inventories.	Internal consistency, test-retest data
Wide Range Interest-Opinion Test: Guidance Associates of Delaware, Inc.	5 years and older	This instrument is a non-reading interest inventory where the individual is shown triads of pictures and is asked to indicate, through pointing, most and least preferred activities. Individually or group administration	Non-reading	40 min.	Evidence of validity is lacking	Split-half reliability estimates are high, ranging from .82 to .95. No test-retest data is reported

Figure 5.1.

Aptitude Assessment

Title: Publisher	Grade/ Age	Features	Reading Level	Time	Adm. Validity	Reliability
General Aptitude Test Battery (GATB): U.S. Employment Service	Senior high school students/ adults	Consists of 8 paper-and-pencil tests and 4 apparatus tests; nine aptitudes are measured by these 12 tests; Group administered.	High	2.5 hours	Considerable validity evidence is available	Test-retest reliability is substantial
USES Nonreading Aptitude Test Battery (NATB): U.S. Employment Service Office	High school students/ adults	Nonreading alternative to the GATB; intended for use with students who have limited reading skills.	Low	Not reported	Validity is based upon its apparent similarity to the GATB	No evidence of reliability is provided
Occupational Aptitude Survey and Interest Schedule–Second Ed. Aptitude Survey (OASIS): Pro ed	Grades 8–12	Consists of 5 subtests which yield aptitude scores in 6 areas; specific time limits are placed on each subtest; test can be individually or group administered; may be hand- or machine-scored.	Not reported	35–40 mins.	Concurrent validity is reported to range from mid .70s–.80s; manual provides more validity evidence	Reliability coefficients generally fall within .80 to .90 range

Title: Publisher	Grade/ Age	Features	Reading Level	Time	Adm. Validity	Reliability
The Differential Aptitude Test (DAT): The Psychological Corporation Grades	7–12 and adults	Two levels are available: Level 1 is designed for students in 7th–9th grade while Level 2 is used with students in 10th–12th grade. Two forms (C and D) are available at each level. Nine scores, in addition to a composite score, are provided. The test can be hand-or machine-scored. A computerized version is also available.	Not reported	3 hours	Validity is based on correlations with standardized achievement tests, other aptitude tests, and cumulative GPAs	Reliability ranges from .82–.95; Alternate form reliability ranges from .73–.90
Armed Services Vocational Aptitude Battery 18/19 Career Exploration Program (ASVAB-CEP): U.S. Dept. of Defense	16–23 years	Consists of 334 items arranged in ten subtests, each of which yields a percentile rank score; 3 composite scores also derived; test may only be administered by specially trained examiners from the DOD or Office of Personnel Management. Most recent version contains a Career Exploration Program to help provide students with occupational guidance in both military and civilian careers.	Not reported	3 hours	Criterion-related validity provided (.55 to .60 with military training school grades and .35–.47 with job performance)	High reliability (overall in .90 range; individual subtests .71–.91)

Figure 5.2.

discussed in this book. When conducting vocational and transition assessments, this comprehensive approach should underlie and guide transition plans in order to increase the success and satisfaction a student will experience in an educational program or occupation.

REFERENCES

Aiken, L. R. (1985). *Psychological testing and assessment,* 5th ed. Boston, MA: Allyn & Bacon.

Alston, R. & McCowan, C. (1994). Aptitude assessment and African American clients: The interplay between culture and psychometrics in rehabilitation. *Journal of Rehabilitation, January, February, March,* 41–46.

Anastasi, A. (1982). *Psychological testing,* 5th ed. New York: Macmillan.

Blustein, D. (1993). Applying current theory and research in career exploration to practice. *The Career Development Quarterly, 41,* 174–184.

Blustein, D. L., Walbridge, M. M., Friedlander, M. L., & Paladino (1991). Contributions of psychological separation and parental attachment to the career development process. *Journal of Counseling Psychology, 38,* 39–50.

Buchan, B., & Levinson, E.M. (2003). A comparison of the web-based and pencil and paper versions of the career key interest inventory. Paper presented at the 2003 Annual Convention of the National Association of School Psychologists, Toronto, Canada, April 2003.

Clark, G., & Kolstoe, O. (1995). *Career development and transition education for adolescents with disabilities.* Needham Heights, MA: Allyn & Bacon.

Cook, E. P. (1994). Role salience and multiple roles: A gender perspective. *The Career Development Quarterly, 43,* 85–95.

Einarsdottir, S., & Rounds, J. (2000). Application of three dimensions of vocational interests to strong interest inventory. *Journal of Vocational Behavior, 56,* 363–379.

Gati, I. (1991). The structure of vocational interests. *Psychological Bulletin, 109*(2), 309–324.

Gottfredson, G. D., Holland, J. L., & Ogawa, G. D. (1982). *Dictionary of Holland occupational codes.* Palo Alto, CA: Consulting Psychologists Press.

Gottfredson, L. (1981). Circumspection and compromise: A developmental theory of occupational aspirations. *Journal of Counseling Psychology, 28,* 545–580.

Goffredson, G., & Holland, J. (1990). A longitudinal test of the influence of congruence: Job satisfaction, competency utilization, and counterproductive behavior. *Journal of Counseling Psychology, 37*(4), 389–398.

Henderson, S. (2000). Follow your bliss: A process for career happiness. *Journal of Counseling and Development, 78*(3), 305–316.

Herr, E. L. & Cramer, S. H. (1972). *Vocational guidance and career development in the schools: Toward a systems approach.* Boston, MA: Houghton Mifflin.

Hoffman, J. J., Hofacker, C., & Goldsmith, E. B. (1992). How closeness affects parental influence on business college students' career choices. *Journal of Career Development, 19*, 65–73.

Holland, J. (1985). *The Self-Directed Search: Professional manual.* Odessa, FL: Psychological Assessment Resources.

Hood, A. B., & Johnson, R. W. (1997). *Assessment in counseling*, 2nd ed. Alexandria, VA: American Counseling Association.

Johnson, L. (1995). A multidimensional analysis of the vocational aspirations of college students. *Measurement and Evaluation in Counseling and Development, 28* (1), 25–45.

Jones, L. K. (1990). The Career Key: An investigation of the reliability and validity of its scales and its helpfulness to college students. *Measurement and Evaluation in Counseling and Development, 23*, 67–76.

Kinnier, R. T., Brigman, S. L., & Noble, F. C. (1990). Career indecision and family enmeshment. *Journal of Counseling and Development, 68*, 309–312.

Krumboltz, J. D. (1991). *Manual for the Career Beliefs Inventory.* Palo Alto, CA: Consulting Psychologists Press.

Lent, R. W., Brown, S. D. & Hackett, G. (1994). Toward a unifying social cognitive theory of career and academic interest, choice, and performance. *Journal of Vocational Behavior, 45*, 79–122.

Leong, F. T. L. (1991). Career development attributes and occupational values of Asian American and White American college students. *Career Development Quarterly, 39*, 221–230.

Levinson, E.M., Ohler, D.L., & Zeman, H. (2002). A critical evaluation of the web-based version of the career key. *Career Development Quarterly, 51*(1), 26–35.

Levinson, E., (1993) *Transdisciplinary vocational assessment: Issues in school-based programs.* Brandon, VT: Clinical Psychology Publishing Company, Inc.

Naylor, F. D., & Krumboltz, J. D. (1994). The independence of aptitudes, interests, and career beliefs. *Career Development Quarterly, 43*(2), 152–161.

Parker, R. (1991). *Occupational Aptitude Survey and Interest Schedule*, 2nd ed. Austin, TX: PRO-ED.

Power, P. W.(2000). *A guide to vocational assessment*, 3rd ed. Austin, TX: Pro-Ed.

Prediger, D. J. (1976). A world-of work map for career exploration. *Vocational Guidance Quarterly, 24*, 192–208.

Prediger, D. J. (1982). Dimensions underlying Holland's hexagon: Missing link between interests and occupations? *Journal of Vocational Behavior, 21*, 259–287.

Reardon, R., Lenz, J., Sampson, J., Peterson, G. (2000). *Career development and planning: A comprehensive approach.* Belmont, CA: Brooks/Cole, Thomson Learning.

Reisman, B. L., & Banuelo, D. (1984). Career fantasy in the barrio. *Journal of Non-White Concerns in Personnel and Guidance, 12*(3), 99–104.

Salomone, P. R. (1996). Career counseling and job placement: Theory and practice. In E.M. Szymanski & R.M. Parker (Eds.), *Work and disability* (pp. 365–415). Austin, TX: Pro-Ed.

Savage, C. T., & Fouad, N. A. (1994). Traditionality of college major and attitudes towards work-family balance: Vocational correlates. *Journal of Career Assessment, 2*, 163–178.

Seligman, L. (1980). *Assessment in developmental career counseling.* Cranston, RI: The Carroll Press.

Siegal, C. L. F. (1973). Sex differences in the occupational choices of second graders. *Journal of Vocational Behavior, 3,* 15–19.

Spitzer, D., & Levinson, E. (1988). A review of selected vocational interest inventories for use by school psychologists. *School Psychology Review, 17*(4), 673–692.

Spokane, A. R. (1991). *Career intervention.* Englewood Cliffs, NJ: Prentice-Hall.

Steele, J., & Barling, J. (1996). Influence of maternal gender-role beliefs and role satisfaction on daughter's vocational interests. *Sex Roles, 34*(9/10), 637–648.

Super, D. E. (1949). *Appraising vocational fitness.* New York, NY: Harper & Row.

Tokar, D. M., & Jome, L. M. (1998). Masculinity. Vocational interest, and career choice traditionality: Evidence for a fully mediated model. *Journal of Counseling Psychology, 45*(4), 424–435.

Tracey, T. & Rounds, J. (1993). Evaluating Holland's and Gati's vocational-interest models: A structural meta-analysis. *Psychological Bulletin, 113*(2), 229–246.

Tracey, T. J., & Rounds, J. B. (1996). The spherical representation of vocational interests. *Journal of Vocational Behavior, 48,* 1–41.

Trice, A. D., & King, R. (1991). Stability of kindergarten children's career aspirations. *Psychological Reports, 68,* 13–78.

Trice, A. D., & Knapp, L. (1992). Relationship of children's career aspirations to parents' occupations. *The Journal of Genetic Psychology, 153*(3), 355–357.

Trice, A. D., & Tillapaugh, P. (1991). Children's estimates of their parents' job satisfaction. *Psychological Reports, 69,* 63–66.

Tuck, B., Rolfe, J., & Adair, V. (1994). Adolescents' attitude toward gender roles within work and its relationship to gender, personality type, and parental occupation. *Sex Roles, 31,* 547–558.

United States Employment Service Office (1983). *General Aptitude Test Battery.* Washington, DC: Government Printing Office.

Wahl, K., & Blackhurst, A. (2000). Factors affecting the occupational and educational aspirations of children and adolescents. *Professional School Counseling, 3*(5), 367–374.

Wang, L. (1995). Differential aptitude tests. *Measurement and Evaluation in Counseling and Development, 28*(3), 168–171.

Zunker, V. (1998). *Career counseling: Applied concepts of life planning,* 5th ed. Pacific Grove, CA: Brooks/Cole Publishing Company.

Chapter 6

ASSESSMENT OF CAREER MATURITY AND SELF-ADVOCACY SKILLS

HEATHER BEAUCHAMP AND KATHLEEN R. KIEWRA

INTRODUCTION: ASSESSMENT OF CAREER MATURITY AND SELF-ADVOCACY SKILLS

For the average young person and his or her family, the transition to life after high school represents an important change in the family's life cycle. It is a time fraught with a variety of emotions and types of decisions for family members. For the average young person, it may be a time of excitement and anticipation, as he or she envisions experiencing new levels of personal choice, freedom, and independence. For parents, it may be a time of letting go emotionally, but not necessarily financially. The average young person may choose from a number options: he or she may choose to enter the work force on a full or part-time basis, to attend either a post-secondary school or college on either a full or a part-time basis, combine working and going to school, or perhaps join a branch of the armed services. For some young people who choose to attend college, they and their parents may view the college years as an opportunity to borrow time; having not yet made up their minds as to what they want to do when they "grow up", the college years are viewed as a time in which young people can engage in a new level of self-awareness and career exploration. This is probably why so many college students change their major more than once.

Transition for students with disabilities and their families is often a time of increased anxiety, confusion, and even dread. Too often students with disabilities and their parents face a discouraging and daunting future. Unfortunately, goals for independence, both financial and residential, appear to be illusive. In fact, many students with disabilities face a future of under or unemployment (Pennsylvania Departments of Education and Labor and Industry, 1986). Several U.S. states report that between 64 percent and 82 percent of individuals with disabilities report living at home with a parent or guardian (Fardig, Algozzine, Schwartz, Hengel & Westling, 1985; Edgar, 1987; Mithaug, Horiuchi, &Fanning, 1985; Schalock & Lilley, 1986).

Students who have been identified as "learning disabled" tend to possess at least average intelligence, demonstrate below-average academic skills, and may be at risk for a lower level of career maturity. For instance, they frequently demonstrate social and interpersonal skills deficits, short attention spans, and hyperactivity (Levinson, 1998).

However, it is estimated that more than 130,000 students with learning disabilities go on to attend college in this country and the numbers are on the rise (Matthew, Anderson, & Skolnick, 1987). This trend can be in part attributed to Section 504 of the Rehabilitation Act of 1973, which requires colleges receiving federal funds to provide services and programming to individuals with learning disabilities. These postsecondary institutions are required by law to make reasonable accommodations to ensure the success of students with disabilities.

The Transitional Needs of Students with Disabilities

Levinson and Ohler (1998) suggest that transition from school to life after school for the student with learning disabilities should be an outcome-oriented process which encompasses a broad array of services and experiences that leads to, among other goals, employment. Baxter (1995), Levinson, Ohler, & Baxter (1996), and Levinson & Ohler (1997), identify the following as academic predictors of success for college-bound students with learning disabilities: Average intelligence, completion of an academically-oriented curriculum, success in English classes, a grade point average of 2.5 or better, motivation and persistence, well-developed study skills and strategies, and well-developed social and interpersonal skills. Furthermore, successful students have well-developed problem-solving skills, social support, and adequate self-awareness. These students are aware of their strengths and weaknesses, they can articulate the accommodations they need, and are able to successfully advocate for themselves.

Unfortunately, research suggests that students with learning disabilities demonstrate a slower rate of career maturity than do students without learning disabilities (Bingham, 1975, 1978, 1980; Kendal, 1980, 1981). It appears that students with learning disabilities make incongruent career decisions because they fail to understand how their own characteristics are related to career choice (Jagger, Neukrug, & MCAuliffe, 1992). Levinson and Ohler (1998) propose that students with learning disabilities often need assistance in making decisions involving appropriate occupational choices, whether or not they should pursue postsecondary training, which postsecondary institutions would be appropriate for their needs, the types of accommodations they might need to be successful, and so on.

In an attempt to assist individuals who work with students with disabilities, this chapter will examine two important aspects of the transition to life after high school: career maturity and self-advocacy skills. We will provide an historical overview, as well as an examination of the theoretical and conceptual issues related to both career maturity and self-advocacy skills, discuss a best practice approach in their assessment, and review instruments used in the assessment of career maturity and self-advocacy skills.

History and Overview of Career Maturity Theory

Definition of Career Maturity

Levinson (1993) defines career maturity as "the extent to which an individual processes the knowledge and skills necessary to make realistic and informed vocational choices." Implicit in this definition is an individual's level of self-awareness about the kinds of work activities which bring personal pleasure. The definition also assumes the individual's knowledge base about vocations ultimately requires a realistic self-appraisal about abilities and skills. For example, it is probably safe to say that the high school sophomore student with Attention Deficit Hyperactivity Disorder and a specific learning disability in the area of mathematics who reports he will probably just follow in his tax accountant father's footsteps may be said to have a low level of career maturity.

Theoretical and Conceptual Issues

The concept of vocational or career maturity was first introduced by Super (1957). In examining the psychology of careers, Super theorized that there are actually several dimensions of vocational maturity, which include an orientation to vocational choice, information and planning about preferred occupations, the consistency of vocational preferences, a crystallization of traits, and wisdom of vocational preferences.

Shortly thereafter, Crites proposed a comprehensive model of career development in early adulthood which considered two dimensions to career maturity–affective and cognitive. He speculated that the cognitive dimension considers attitudes toward career decision-making skills, while the affective dimension considers attitudes toward career development (1965, 1971). Crites is also known for his development of the original *Career Maturity Inventory* (1978), the most popular instrument of its kind. A review is included in the Review of Instrumentation section of this chapter.

Factors Impacting Career Maturity

There are, quite naturally, a number of factors which can influence an individual's level of career maturity. According to Stewart (1995), the lack of specific information and the lack of knowledge of where to access such information may result in inappropriate vocational choices. Exposure to vocational choices is key in occupational exploration, which is an important component of career maturity. Occupational exploration is described as those behaviors and beliefs which facilitate the acquisition of information about careers, jobs, or business organization (Strumpf, Colarelli, & Hartman, 1983).

However, there is more to career decision making than simply obtaining information. The way in which an individual problem-solves and makes decisions further impacts the process. Amundson (1995) notes that the way in which people make decisions is heavily influenced by factors such as their culture, economic and political events, the interpersonal roles that they have assumed throughout life, and their basic self-structure.

Although there are a number of decision-making models described in the literature, Harren (1979) is most widely recognized and cited. Harren describes three different styles of decision making: rational, intuitive, and dependent. His theory allows for a blending of styles, but suggests that most people operate under a predominant style. The rational decision-making style is characterized by the ability to perceive, understand, and anticipate the consequences of previous decisions upon later decisions. Rational decision makers take responsibility for their decisions and systematically gather and evaluate information about the decision in a logical, deliberate, and objective manner. The intuitive decision-making style is characterized by a lack of anticipation of future events, little information-seeking behavior, and little or no logical weighing of decision-making factors. Present emotional factors, impulsivity, fantasy, and emotional self-awareness are the guiding principles for the intuitive decision maker. The dependent style of decision making is characterized by a denial of personal responsibility with instead a projection of responsibility onto external events of other individuals. The dependent decision maker is typically passive, compliant, has a high need for social approval, and is heavily influenced and easily directed by the others' opinions and expectations (Westcot &Tokar, 1991).

According to Larson, Busby, Wilson, Medora, and Allgood (1994), there can be various intrapersonal motivations or problems which can interfere with the career decision-making process, such as anxiety, an external locus of control, lack of self-awareness, and other "personality problems." Locus of control (Rotter, 1966) refers to the general expectations about whether the results of one's actions are under one's own control (internal) or beyond one's control (external). Perry and Penner (1990) suggest that a student who has an external locus of control is likely to experience cognitive, motivational, and affective deficits that result in a lack of effort.

Stewart (1995) suggests that a lack of realism in vocational choice is also an important factor in the career choice process. For example, an underutilization of the individual's skills and abilities can result in poor job satisfaction and less production, while the aspiration of the individual to a vocational choice which requires different skills and abilities than the individual possesses may result in frustration and/or reality shock as the person attempts to meet the demands of an occupational work choice beyond his or her capabilities.

According to Morris and Levinson (1995), intelligence has been used as a factor in personnel selection as early as 1910. Gottfredson (1986) felt that the importance of intelligence in the workplace has been underestimated, and suggests that a worker's skills and abilities influence the worker's adaptability, trainability, promotability, and problem-solving ability. Additionally, Gottfredson identified 12 factors which place individuals especially at risk for experiencing career choice difficulties: low intelligence, poor education, cultural isolation, low self-esteem, functional limitations, non-traditional interests, social isolation, low-high intelligence in comparison to family/peers, primary caretaker, and primary economic provider.

In a study investigating the factors associated with career maturity of college students with learning disabilities, few differences were actually found between students with and without learning disabilities (Ohler, Levinson, & Barker, 1996). However, results suggested that students who are able to articulate their needs for accommodations, and to advocate for themselves experience higher levels of career maturity.

Current Trends in the Assessment of Career Maturity and Self-Advocacy Skills

Limitations of Traditional Vocational Assessments

In discussing the career development system in the United States in general, Downing and D'Andrea (1994) suggest that the majority of children in this country are provided little systematic assistance in planning for their education and career, proposing that the career development system in the United States operates on a "run until you hit the wall" philosophy. In other words, from their earliest years, children are encouraged to plan to attend college, obtain a degree, and land a high-paying job. However, Downing and D'Andrea contend that the U.S. educational system does little to prepare students for their next formal learning experience–the world of work. In fact, only 20 percent of the adult population in the United States have a baccalaureate degree ("The Nation," 1990). As Stewart (1995) points out, career indecision, or the inability to specify a vocational choice, may lead to floundering between educational programs or jobs such that much capital and energy are expended with little results.

Since students with disabilities are particularly vulnerable in terms of developing an appropriate level career maturity, they are in need of specially tailored assessments and interventions in order to successfully maneuver the transition form high school to life after high school. In fact, school districts are required by law to provide services designed to assist them in this process. According to P.L. 101-476, a student's transition needs are addressed in his or her Individual Education Plan (IEP) which is to be initiated by at least age 14. Halloran (1989) proposes that an effective transition program should include three essential components: (1) parent participation in the planning and implementation of activities designed to encourage independent functioning; (2) a community-based program with opportunities to succeed in employment and community life, and (3) a partnership between schools, businesses, and community agencies to help facilitate post-high school employment. Unfortunately, many school districts fail to establish an effective transition plan, in part because there has not been a comprehensive assessment of student's needs and strengths with regards to vocational and independent living skills.

A Multifactored Approach to the Assessment of Career Maturity

There are two basic considerations that should guide a best-practice approach to any vocational assessment: (1) an understanding of vocational/career development theory, and (2) an identification of the skills needed by the individual for successful employment. Implicit in this approach is the idea that there should be an understanding of the traits which should be assessed as part of the comprehensive assessment (Levinson,1995). Facilitating a student's readiness to make career decisions is the cornerstone of effective career counseling, and can be the basis for further assessment and exploration of interests, aptitudes, work values, and personality (Levinson, Ohler, Caswell, & Kiewra, 1998).

In his book *Transdisciplinary Vocational Assessment: Issues in School-based Programs,* Levinson (1993) delineates a best-practice approach to vocational assessment which takes the following information into account: (1) psychological functioning (emotional stability, needs, temperament, values, intelligence, behavioral tendencies); (2) social functioning (adaptive behavior, social/interpersonal skills, independent living skills, hygiene); (3) educational and academic functioning (receptive/expressive language, reading and mathematics skills, range of knowledge); (4) physical/medical functioning (vision, hearing, health, strength, dexterity/motor skills, endurance); and (5) vocational functioning (vocational interests and aptitudes, work habits/attitudes, vocational/career maturity).

This approach requires a movement from a multidisciplinary approach to a transdisciplinary approach. In other words, this approach requires the thoughtful participation and cooperation of a variety of individuals who have an important role to play and contribution to make to the assessment. A transdisciplinary approach considers the assessment data and recommendations from parents and members inside as well as outside the school district (community personnel, social service agencies, vocational rehabilitation specialists, etc.).

Age Appropriateness of Evaluation and Phases of Assessment

In order to promote and eventually assess career maturity, students' interests in the world of work and in the types of careers available ideally should be encouraged from an early age. Children are in the "growth" stage of career development during the elementary years, a period of time characterized by fantasy, growing interest, and growing self-awareness of aptitudes values, and the relationship of their academic choices and post-high school alternatives. As children enter adolescence they enter the "exploration" stage in which they develop tentative career goals, identify vocational options, and begin acquiring skills needed for post-high school plans/employment. Later adolescence is marked by making a vocational choice and the transition from school to work (Levinson, 1988).

Anderson, Hohenshil, Buckland-Heer, and Levinson (1990) outline three levels of assessment for a best-practice approach to vocational assessment. Level I assessments begin during the elementary school years, focus on the student's needs, values, interests, abilities, interpersonal skills, and decision-making skills, utilize vocational and career exploration activities, and have the goal of building self-awareness. Level II assessments generally occur during the middle school/junior high school years, focusing more specifically on an assessment of vocational interests and aptitudes, work habits and career maturity, utilizes interviews, observations, and standardized norm referenced assessment instruments, and has the goal of continuing to encourage career exploration and assisting individuals in making tentative choices regarding educational and career goals. A level III assessment generally occurs during the high school years, often employs more experientially-based assessment devices like work samples and situational assessment, and focuses upon the specific training the student needs to obtain post-high school education or employment.

Appropriate Choices of Assessment Tools

In deciding upon which tools should be used in an assessment of career maturity, there must be a proper understanding of the student's cognitive, academic, emotional, and physical functioning. For example, if the student is motorically impaired, consideration must be given to how paper and pencil assessment instruments will be administered. Likewise, many instruments require a reading level of sixth grade and may not be appropriate for the student, even if the evaluator reads the questions to the student. Furthermore, whenever instruments are selected, a best-practice approach assumes that evaluators take psychometric and norming information into account.

Although there are several standardized tests which provide norms for students with disabilities, other appropriate methods of assessment include interviews, observation of the student in a variety of work settings, performance tasks which assess specific abilities, work samples which allow the student to experience work activities related to a particular job, and situational assessments designed to test a person's interests, aptitudes and work habits in a real or simulated work situation. Curriculum-based assessment can also be helpful in assessing a student's potential to acquire the skills/competencies necessary to enter or to successfully complete a vocational program (Levinson, 1995). Additionally, Miner, Osborne, and Jaeger (1997) recommend that biographical inventories could be devised to ascertain relationships among childhood or adolescent experiences and interest inventory scores.

As information about a student is obtained through ongoing assessment, students and counselors may find valuable information in a variety of reference books, such as *VGM's Career Encyclopedia* (1997) and the *Occupational Outlook Handbook* (2000). These books provide information and descriptions of jobs, descriptions of places of employment and working conditions, necessary qualifications (including education, training, and desirable personality traits), the job's potential for advancement, income, and other sources to check for additional information. Additionally, the *Dictionary of Occupational Titles* (*DOT,* 1977) provides rehabilitation professionals with information to use in critical rehabilitation activities (e.g., determining eligibility, identifying transferable skills, and job-matching). Although this resource contains more than 100 different characteristics for each of the 12,000 jobs, Geyer, Johnson, and Hunter (1998) do not consider the occupational information perfectly reliable.

Review of Instrumentation

There has been an increased interest in the development of instruments to assess a student's vocational or career maturity in the last 20 years. Along with instruments specifically designed to measure the specific construct of career maturity, this section will also provide a brief review of instruments which measure compatible or component aspects of career maturity, providing information which may be helpful in assessing a student's overall career decision-making skills and abilities.

Adult Career Concerns Inventory (ACCI)

The Adults Career Concerns Inventory (ACCI), devised by Super, Thompson, Lindeman, Jordaan, and Myers (1988), is a 61-item instrument which can be used with both high school students and adults. The *ACCI* was developed in response to Super's work and theory of career development, with Super's Career Pattern Study in mind. Super found that many individuals make a number of career choices throughout their lives, and as a result, Super and Knasel (1979) proposed the concept of career adaptability, or the exploration attitudes and necessary planfulness that are basic to coping with changing work and work conditions. This definition guided the development and validation of the *ACCI* (Levinson, Ohler, Caswell, & Kiewra, 1998).

Sixty of the 61 items on the *ACCI* are divided into five major stages, exploration, establishment, maintenance, disengagement, and career change. For each question, the individual is asked to respond to the statement on a Likert scale from *1 (no concern)* to *5 (great concern).* The 61st item simply addresses career change concerns and is left unscored.

Although it can be self-scored, it is a complicated process that requires a calculator and some basic knowledge of statistics.

As described by Super, the *ACCI* can be used in two ways: for career counseling and planning, and for needs analysis in groups of employees and adult applicants for counseling (Rounds, 1994). However the *ACCI* may be best used to identify vocational tasks with which the individual is concerned. It may be useful in individual or group counseling situations to identify career concerns which could be used as a springboard for discussion and additional exploration of problematic career/life planning issues among adults. The psychometric data presented for the *ACCI* is limited, therefore this instrument should be used with caution. While internal consistency seems sufficient (Halpin, Ralph, & Halpin, 1990), test-retest reliability is not reported. It should be noted that the data on the norm group are limited by its size, and the sample is not representative. In addition, data on construct and concurrent validity are not presented.

Assessment of Career Decision Making (ACDM)

Assessment of Career Decision Making (ACDM) is based on the Harren Model of Career Decision Making (Harren, 1979), which itself is based on the research by Tiedeman and O'Hara (1963). The *ACDM* contains 94 true/false items and can be used individually or with groups. It consists of three 10-item Decision-Making styles (Rational, Intuitive, and Dependent) and the Decision-Making Tasks scales, which included three major areas (School Adjustment, Occupation, and Major). The *ACDM* can be used in three ways: as a screening device to decide who can best benefit from career counseling, to generate hypotheses about a student prior to seeing him or her, and to facilitate client's career decision making (Sharf, 1994).The *ACDM* has been developed to be used in conjunction with the publisher's *Career Planning Program* (Sharf, 1994). It can be implemented in a high school or college class in career planning and is accompanied by a *Leader's Handbook* and a *Student's Handbook*.

Although the *ACDM* is one of the few instruments that evaluates decision-making style and progress on critical decision-making tasks, such as selection of an occupation or college major, Levinson, Ohler, Caswell, and Kiewra (1998) suggest that the instrument be used with extreme caution due to it's psychometric properties. For example, the standardization was not planned and was based on a conglomeration of studies, and the size of the norm group for high school students and minorities is small. No test-retest reliability data is available for high school students and the internal consistency reliability on the *ACDM* scales was quite variable. Furthermore, overall evidence for the validity of the *ACDM* is weak, according to the criterion-related and construct validity data presented in the manual. Another limitation to the *ACDM* is that it has not been normed on individuals outside of an educational setting (Westcot & Tokar, 1991). However, Sharf (1994) believes that there are sufficient data for counselors to use the scales, particularly with college students.

Career Beliefs Inventory (CBI)

The *Career Beliefs Inventory (CBI),* developed by Krumboltz (1994), is a 96-item instrument designed to help individuals identify certain attitudes that might be hindering the attainment of their career goals. Individuals are asked to indicate their agreement or disagreement to each item on a five-point scale. Twenty-five scales can be derived from the *CBI,* and scores are weighed and range from 10-50 for each scale. Scores of less than 39 indicate to the counselor that there may be potential blocks to career goals. Completion of the instrument takes about 30 minutes.

The psychometric properties of the *CBI* suggest that further research is warranted (Levinson, Ohler, Caswell, & Kiewra, 1998). For example, evidence for the sample's representativeness is lacking and research has not yet demonstrated that the *CBI's* scale scores are related to attainment or failure of career goals (Wall, 1994). The *CBI* was designed to assist individuals plan transition in their lives (Krumboltz, 1994). However, Wall (1994) suggests that without further research, the instrument may best be used as an interview schedule, useful as a springboard for counselors to facilitate in-depth discussions with individuals about any misconceptions that may be preventing the pursuit of a particular career. Wall (1994) further suggests that empirical verification is needed to shed light on whether or not specific types of profiles are more likely to encourage career attainment in particular occupational groups or kinds of career environments.

Career Decision Diagnostic Assessment (CDDA)

The *Career Decision Diagnostic Assessment (CDDA),* was developed by Bansberg & Sklare (1986) in order to assist career counselors in the identification of these career blocks and the degree to which they are blocking career decision making. The *CDDA* is a self-report consisting of 37 items. The first item asks the individual if they have made a specific decision about a career choice or change. The second item asks how certain the individual is in their choice. Items three through 36 consist of statements about career decision making, to which individuals indicate their degree of agreement or disagreement on a 6-point scale. The last item asks if the individual has answered each of the items honestly. The *CDDA* provides a total career decisions problems score and five subscale scores. The subscales and the number of items within each are: life/goal awareness (7 items); anxiety (9 items); secondary gain (6 items); authority orientation (5 items); and luck and fate orientation (7 items).

A study conducted by Larson, Busby, Wilson, Medora, and Allgood (1994) confirms the internal consistency reliability of the *CDDA* for a university student sample. The results were nearly identical to Bansberg and Sklare's (1986) study with high school and community college students. The reliability of the *CDDA* with other samples, young adults who are not students, for example, is yet to be determined. Larson et al. suggest that the *CDDA* potentially may be rated as one of the few valid and reliable instruments for assessing career decision-making problems. However, caution is recommended when using this instrument with high school students until further research is conducted.

Career Decision Scale (CDS)

The *Career Decision Scale (CDS);* Osipow, Carney, Winer, Yanico, & Koshier, 1976) is an inventory with 19 items, 18 of which are answered on a four-point Likert scale (*1 = not at all like me* to *4 = exactly like me*). The 18 items comprise two scales: the two-item Certainty scale and the 16 item Indecision scale. The remaining item is an open-ended question that reflects the concerns of the individual completing the inventory. The instrument typically takes 10–15 minutes to complete. The *CDS* is over 25 years old, has been revised three times, and is accompanied by a manual which was revised once in 1986.

The purposes of the *CDS* are to estimate career indecision and to assess the effects of career development interventions on high school and college students. Significant scores, as suggested by the manual, fall at or below the fifteenth percentile for the Certainty scores, and at or above the eighty-fifth percentile for the Indecision scale. A low Certainty score with a high Indecision score is considered to be indicative of a need for intervention.

The *CDS* is reported to be a reliable and valid measure of career maturity (Rogers & Westbrook, 1983; Slaney, Palko-Nonemaker, & Alexander, 1981). Furthermore, since the *CDS* seeks to clarify the antecedents of indecision and provides a total indecision score, it may be a very useful instrument when working with high school and college students who are undecided about their future educational and career direction (Levinson, Ohler, Caswell, & Kiewra et al., 1998).

Career Development Inventory (CDI)

The *Career Development Inventory (CDI)* developed by Super, Thompson, Lindeman, Jordaan, and Myers (1988), is based on over 40 years of research in the area of vocational/career maturity. It consists of two forms, the School Form, designed for students in grades eight to twelve, and the University form, for college-aged students. Each form for the *CDI* is comprised of 120 items, and has two parts. Part I includes four subtests that measure four key aspects of career maturity: Scale I–career planning, Scale II–career exploration, Scale III–decision-making, and Scale IV–the world of work. Part II may not be suitable for high school students in grade seven to ten, due to the reading level. Eight scaled scores can be obtained from the instrument and computerized scoring is available.

Although evidence for both content and construct validity is provided in the *CDI* Technical Manual (Super et al., 1992), Pinkey and Bozik (1994) note that there are areas of psychometric difficulties, such as the lack of representation in the norms for minority students, uneven reliability in its eight scales, and a potential problem with social desirability on the art of raters who choose an obviously "right" answer. However, the *CDI* may be a useful instrument for career planning, planning guidance programs, and evaluating programs and research. Additionally, the *CDI* may also be used to spark student interest in career planning and exploration (Levinson, Ohler, Caswell, & Kiewra, 1998).

Career Maturity Inventory and the Career Maturity Inventory–Revised

The *Career Maturity Inventory* (1978a; 1978b) was developed by Crites in order to assess career attitudes and competencies of children and adolescents in grade six to twelve, and was considered by Savikas (1984) to be the most popular career decision-making instrument for years. It consisted of 50 diverse statements concerning career maturity issues and used a true/false format. The scale was designed to elicit a greater number of mature responses as a child's grade level advanced (Healy, 1994).

The Competence Test consists of five subtests: Knowing Yourself (Self-Appraisal), Knowing About Jobs (Occupational Information), Choosing a Job (Goal Setting), Look Ahead (Planning), and What Should They Do (Problem-solving). Each form has 20 items and takes 20 minutes to complete. Raw scores can be converted to yield standard scores and percentiles. Several studies have supported the validity of the *CMI* (Crites, 1978a; Healy 1994; Jepsen & Prediger, 1981; Stowe, 1985; Westbrook, Sanford, & Donnelly, 1990).

The *Career Maturity Inventory–Revised* (Crites, 1995; Crites & Savickas, 1995) includes 25 items for each of the two scales (Attitude and Competence). New items were written for the competence test which would be applicable to both school and non-school populations. The revision was designed to reduce administration and testing time, extend the CMI to the adult level, eliminate the original Attitude scale and Competence subscales, construct the Career Developer (CDR) as a supplement to the CMI, to be used to facilitate improved career maturity, and prepare the CMI and CDR for a variety of scoring and data analysis purposes.

Although no reliability or validity data are reported for the CMI-R, Crites (1995) indicates that items in the revised edition were taken from the original edition and therefore have the same reliability, and that ongoing research would be conducted and reported periodically. In the interim, Levinson, Ohler, Caswell, and Kiewra (1998) caution counselors about its use with post-secondary populations with the CMI-R until additional data is generated.

Self-Advocacy and Career Maturity

Career maturity and self-advocacy skills are inseparable issues when assessing adolescents at the various junctures of transition. The development of self-advocacy skills must be part of the career development process that begins in early childhood and continues throughout adult life. Self-advocacy involves knowing about one's disability, being able to communicate effectively to others about the disability, being aware of one's rights, and being aware of accommodations that are necessary, available, and offered. Self-advocacy skills and career maturity specifically involve an individual realizing one's strengths and weaknesses and being able to make decisions about appropriate career choices based on those strengths and weaknesses. In so far as career maturity is the extent to which an individual has acquired the necessary knowledge and skills to make intelligent, realistic career choices (Levinson, 1993), so is being aware of one's disability, including strengths and weaknesses, necessary in order to make realistic career choices. For example, if a student with a reading disability wishes to pursue a job as an actor, this may not be the best career choice. This student may vaguely be aware that he or she has a disability because of attending meetings yearly with teachers and getting extra help in school. However, the student may not realize the extent of his or her disability and what he or she can and can't do. This student may not have adequate knowledge of the job requirements of an actor and may not be aware of his or her specific weaknesses in reading. This can be a bad combination when thinking about career choices because he or she has not linked his or her weaknesses with possible career choices. Realizing strengths and weaknesses is an important step in the career development process. If a student with a disability is not aware of their strengths and weaknesses, he or she may choose careers for which they are not well suited. Hence, self-advocacy skills are very important for a student with disabilities, and are essential for students to be successful in life after high school.

Because self-advocacy skills are critical to success after school, they need to be assessed and taught while the student is still in school. In so far as these skills are often not taught directly in high school (Aune & Ness, 1991; Dalke & Franzene, 1988; Ryan & Price, 1992), several college programs hold seminars in teaching self-advocacy skills.

Self-Advocacy Versus Self-Determination

Throughout the literature, the terms self-advocacy and self-determination are used almost interchangeably. Self-advocacy is generally con-

Table 6.1. Sample Instrumentation Table

Title: Publisher	Grade/ Age	Features	Reading Level	Admin Time	Validity	Reliability
The Adults Career Concerns Inventory (ACCI): Consulting Psychologists Press	HS–Adult	61 items divided into five major stages. Individuals are asked to respond to statements on a Likert scale measuring degree of a concern with a task at this point in his/her career.	N/A	15–30 min	N/A	Sufficient internal consistency
Assessment of Career Decision Making (ACDM): Western Psychological Services	HS–Adult	94 True/False items that can be individually or group administered. Contains items on Decision-Making styles and Decision-Making Tasks scales. One of the few instruments that measure decision making style and progress on critical decision-making tasks.	N/A	N/A	Weak criterion-related and construct	Variable internal consistency
Career Beliefs Inventory (CBI): Consulting Psychologists Press	MS–Adult	96 items that help individuals identify certain attitudes that might be hindering the attainment of their career goals. Individuals indicate agreement/ disagreement to each item on a five-point scale.	N/A	30 min	N/A	Variable test-retest, weak internal consistency
Career Decision Diagnostic Assessment (CDDA): McGraw-Hill	HS–Adult	37 items about career decision-making, five subscales. Individuals indicate agreement/disagreement on a six-point scale.	N/A	N/A	N/A	Sufficient internal consistency

Career Decision Scale (CDS): Marathon Consulting and Press	HS–Adult	19 items to help estimate career indecision and to assess the effects of career development interventions. Individuals respond to items on a four-point Likert scale. Two scales: Certainty scale and Indecision scale	N/A	10–15 min	Sufficient construct	Sufficient test-retest
Career Development Inventory (CDI): Consulting Psychologists Press	HS–Adult	120 items divided into two parts. Part I includes four subtests that measure four key aspects of career maturity. Part II assesses an individual's knowledge of a preferred occupational group. School form and University form.	N/A	55–65 min	Sufficient content and construct	Sufficient internal consistency variable test-retest
Career Maturity Inventory-Revised (CMI): McGraw Hill/CTB	MS–Adult	50 items True/False items concerning career maturity issues. Two scales: Attitude and Competence.	N/A	N/A	Sufficient evidence	Sufficient internal consistency test-retest
Transition Planning Inventory (TPI): Pro-Ed.	MS/HS	46 transition planning statements reflecting 9 planning areas. Individuals are asked to respond to statements on a Likert scale. Student, parent, and school forms.	N/A	30 min	Sufficient content and concurrent.	Sufficient internal consistency and stability reliability

sidered to be a subset of self-determination, in that self-advocacy refers to taking action on one's own behalf. These actions of self-advocacy then lead to greater self-determination (Wehmeyer & Berkobien, 1991). In other words, self-determination refers to the general construct, while self-advocacy refers to the actions taken by one with a disability. In this chapter both of these topics will be discussed and the terms will be used interchangeably.

History and Movements in Self-Advocacy

Ancient Views of Disabilities

Self-advocacy has a rich history and through many movements has opened doors to many opportunities today for people with disabilities. Throughout history, people with disabilities have been viewed as lower class citizens with little or no rights. This way of thinking was prevalent in biblical times. Throughout the Old and New Testament a disability was typically viewed as a sign of God's disfavor or as a result of personal sin (Shapiro, 1993). Throughout classical literature, people with disabilities have been depicted as beggars, heroes, and thieves. These images did not portray people with disabilities as being valued, able to contribute, or even being average members of society.

Towards a Modern View

Rehabilitation programs developed in the 1940s and 1950s allowed people with disabilities to live longer. With these advances, people with disabilities were living longer and consequently needed more specialized and extensive care. Consequently, movements started to take place to give more rights to disabled people. The first step was to allow more educational opportunities for children with disabilities.

Legislation for Individuals with Disabilities

Classic court cases such as *Mills vs. D.C. Board of Education* and the *Pennsylvania Association for Retarded Children vs. the Commonwealth of Pennsylvania* were forerunners of the Education of All Handicapped Children Act (P.L. 94-142). This law stated that children with disabilities were guaranteed a free, appropriate, and public education. This allowed many children with disabilities to attend public school for the first time. The second and concurrent step came from the independent living and disability rights movements. This started in the 1960s and was influenced by the social and political consciousness of other civil rights movements taking place at the time.

The first civil rights legislation for people with disabilities was Section 504 of the Rehabilitation Act of 1973 (P.L. 93-112) which stated that, "No otherwise qualified person shall be denied the benefits of Federal assistance on the basis of a handicap." This went beyond physical accommodations by requiring program accommodations. Now schools, universities, and all state and local government agencies had to accommodate all people with disabilities to the extent reasonably appropriate. These laws and movements paved the way for people with disabilities and the development of self-advocacy skills.

For the first time, people with disabilities were standing up as a group like other oppressed groups of the time. Self-advocacy started as a civil rights movement by people with developmental disabilities who were rebelling against being underestimated, deprived of choices, and believed to lead lesser lives (Shapiro, 1993). Self-advocacy began in Sweden with the ideas of Benget Nirje. Self-advocacy and self-determination grew out of his normalization principle. This principle required ". . . making available to the mentally retarded patterns and conditions of everyday life which are as close as possible to the norms and patterns of the mainstream of society" (Nirje, 1976, p. 363.) Nirje extended this principle by teaching such skills as decision making and finance control in adult education coursework. These are considered essential skills for success by self-advocacy groups.

The "People First" Movement

The "People First" movement in the United States grew out of one of the first self-advocate groups known as "People First." This group began to discuss housing, business, and equality in society as alternatives to living in institutions. Through groups like this, members learned to support one another and to help one another become active participants in decisions that affected their lives. This group caused a rapid increase in self-advocacy groups across the country. By 1974, there were 16 self-advocacy groups in the United States. By 1994, a survey identified 505 self-advocacy groups in 43 states and the District of Columbia (Longhurst, 1994). The first national organization of self-advocates was formed in 1992 and was called Self-Advocates Becoming Empowered (SABE). People with disabilities were finally getting the support they needed and at the same time were becoming empowered by these groups.

In 1988, the Office of Special Education and Rehabilitative Services (OSERS) began an initiative to help support the disability rights and self-advocacy movements. They began a self-determination initiative which focused on system-wide activities that would help people with disabilities have more input in the decisions that affected their own lives (Ward & Kohler, 1996). One of the major activities that came out of this initiative was a conference held in 1989 to recommend activities to promote self-determination at the federal level. This was just another stepping stone to empower people with disabilities, and to allow them to make decisions that would affect their lives in a profound way.

Definition of Self-Advocacy/Self-Determination

There are many definitions of self-advocacy/self-determination. However, they all have commonalties. Self-advocacy involves the student being aware of their disability (including their learning strengths and weaknesses), being effectively able to communicate his or her needs, knowing his or her rights, and knowing what accommodations he or she is entitled to. These skills are essential when a student moves from high school to the real world. Most people would argue that students with disabilities should and do know these, but it is surprising that these students often are not aware of these issues. When a student with a disability progresses through school, the school is often responsible for their needs and many of the students may not be actively involved in this process. The school assesses the student, designs an instructional program, and assists the student based on his or her individual needs.

However, the students often do not know specifics about their disabilities, how to communicate their needs effectively, or what services they are entitled to. In an informal survey that was conducted at Boston University at a college orientation program with high school graduates with learning disabilities, out of a group of 30 students, only half of the students in the group recalled having an I.E.P. in high school. Only a handful of the students knew what an I.E.P. was designed for or even knew what the letters I.E.P. stood for (Brinckerhoff, 1994). When students with disabilities come out of high school and go into the real world, the responsibility shifts and they are responsible for communicating their needs and knowing their rights.

Being able to effectively communicate one's needs is one of the most critical elements of self-advocacy. If a student is aware of their disability, but does not communicate his or her needs to the college professor or the supervisor on the job, they are not going to be successful. Being able to communicate effectively about one's disability and needs involves being able to portray strengths in spite of limitations and to present concerns in a positive light. These students must also have a thorough knowledge of the functional implications of their specific situation and how their needs may impact their success (Lynch & Gussel, 1996). Therefore, the communication skills of these students is an important area to assess when assessing self-advocacy skills.

The last two components of self-advocacy are being aware of one's rights and being aware of accommodations that are offered. These components are often not taught to students with disabilities. The laws involving students with disabilities guide school personnel when working with these students, but these laws often are not conveyed to the students themselves. These laws require that the student be involved in the process, be made aware of the rights they have, and be made aware of the accommodations that are offered. For example, the Individuals with Disabilities Education Act of 1990 (IDEA) emphasizes self-advocacy and requires that the student be an active participant in their transition planning. This law requires that students preferences and interests be taken into account when transition services are being planned. School districts are also required to include students in transition planning meetings. There is increasing evidence that students who are involved in the planning and implementation of their educational programs perform better than peers who are not involved (Field, 1996).

The 1992 Rehabilitation Act Amendments also emphasize self-advocacy and student involvement in transition planning, stating that a "Disability is a natural part of the human experience and in no way diminishes the right of individuals to: Live independently, enjoy self-determination, make choices, contribute to society, pursue meaningful careers, and enjoy full inclusion and integration in the economic, political, social, cultural, and educational mainstream of American society. . ." (Section 2. Findings; Purpose; Policy). This requires that individuals with disabilities have the opportunity to be active participants in their rehabilitation programs. This participation includes the encouragement to make meaningful and informed choices about vocational goals and objectives and vocational rehabilitation services. Students need to be aware of their rights and need to realize that they must be active participants in the plans that will impact the rest of their lives.

Because students with disabilities often lack self-advocacy skills, it is imperative to teach these skills before they enter postsecondary education or the work force. These skills are essential for success in life after school. In order to maximize their success in life after school, students with disabilities need awareness of their academic and social strengths and weaknesses. They need the ability to express awareness to faculty or supervisors, and they need awareness of service needs and appropriate accommodations. They also need the ability to request information, assistance, and accommodations when appropriate and necessary (Durlak, Rose, & Bursuck, 1994). These skills are essential in self-advocacy and for making complex decisions. It has been shown that self-advocacy in employees is related to more effective employee performance and is positively associated with employer satisfaction, quality of work life, and organizational effectiveness (Field, 1996). Self-advocacy skills are also important when entering postsecondary education. A smooth transition from high school to postsecondary education is dependent on the student's ability to state their needs for supports and accommodations.

Models of Self-Determination/Self-Advocacy

The following models have been developed through the OSERS' self-determination initiatives. These models represent some of the first attempts to operationally define and describe the concept of self-determination.

Model Focused on Individual Beliefs, Knowledge, and Skills

The Model focused on Individual Beliefs, Knowledge, and Skills involves internal factors and skill components that promote self-determination. Field and Hoffman (1994) describe self-determination as either promoted or discouraged by factors within the individual's control and variables that are environmental in nature. Factors within the individual's control may include values, knowledge, and skills. Variables that are environmental in nature may include opportunities for choice making and attitudes of others. There are five components involved in this model: (1) Know Yourself, (2) Value Yourself, (3) Plan, (4) Act, and (5) Experience Outcomes and Learn. The first two components describe internal processes that provide a foundation for acting in a self-determined manner. The next two components identify the skills that are needed to act on this foundation. The individual must have internal awareness, and strengths and ability to act on the internal foundation in order to be self-determined. If an individual only has the self-awareness and self-esteem but not the skills, he or she is not fully self-determined. Conversely, if the individual has the skills but no self-awareness or self-esteem, he or she is not fully self-determined. In order to be fully self-determined, the individual must know and value what he or she wants and possess the necessary skills to seek what is desired.

The final component celebrates the success and reviews efforts to become self-determined, so that skills and knowledge are enhanced. The environmental variables that affect self-determination according to Field and Hoffman (1994) are availability of role models, curriculum variables, opportunities for choice, types of responses to student behavior, and availability of student supports. These factors will ultimately help or hinder an individual in their process of becoming self-determined.

Model Based on Self-Determination as an Adult Outcome

The model based on Self-Determination as an Adult Outcome focuses more on the outcome rather than the process. Wehmeyer (1992) proposes that for the purposes of education, self-determination is best conceptualized as an outcome, a set of attitudes and abilities that are learned across the life span and that are associated primarily with achieving adulthood and fulfilling adult roles. Wehmeyer proposes that in order for an individual to be self-determined, they must have four essential characteristics: (1) the person acted autonomously; (2) the behaviors were self-regulated; (3) the person initiated and responded to events in a "psychologically empowered" manner; and (4) the person acted in a self-realizing manner.

Individuals who consistently demonstrate these four characteristics are viewed as being self-determined. These characteristics are also the product of a set of related components including choice making, decision making, problem solving, goal setting and attainment, self-observation skills, self-evaluation skills, self-reinforcement skills, internal locus of control, positive attribution of efficacy and outcome expectancy, self-awareness, and self-knowledge. In order to increase self-determination, these components must be targeted in instruction.

Model Based on Self-Regulation Theory

The model based on Self-Regulation Theory is, as its name implies, rooted in self-regulation theory. This model developed by Mithaug, Campeau, and Wolman (1994) proposes that individuals who are self-determined self-regulate their choices and actions more successfully than others. They are less influenced by others and their environments in setting their goals and deciding how well they will accomplish them. This model focuses on internal factors. According to the authors of this model, self-determination is a special form of self-regulation that is effective and free of external influences. This model includes six major steps: (1) the individual identifies and expresses their own needs, interests, and abilities; (2) the individual sets expectations and goals to meet his or her needs and interests; (3) the individual makes choices and plans to meet goals and expectations; (4) the individual takes action to complete plans; (5) the individual evaluates the results of actions; and (6) the individual adjusts plans and actions until the goal is achieved. This model emphasizes the self-regulation theory by focusing on an individual's ability to self-regulate their choices and actions.

Model Developed from an Ecosystems Perspective

The final model that will be discussed is the Model Developed from an Ecosystems Perspective. This model developed by Abery (1994) proposes that self-determination has a skills base, a knowledge base, and a motivational base. This model also proposes that self-determination is influenced by environmental elements. This model is developed from an ecosystems perspective in that self-determination is viewed as a by-product of interactions between an individual and the numerous environments in which they function. The skills base involves personal choice/decision making, self-regulation, personal advocacy, and problem solving. The knowledge base includes declarative knowledge, procedural knowledge, and self-knowledge. Declarative knowledge involves factual knowledge the individual possesses about their environment. Procedural knowledge involves knowing how to engage one's environment. Self-knowledge involves an individual's awareness of and ability to accurately assess their competencies and skills. The last component, the motivational base, involves a sense of self-efficacy (which is the degree to which an individual expects to successfully behave in the way necessary to achieve desired outcomes), locus of control, and attributions for success and failure. This model, unlike other models, places a stronger emphasis on relationships and interrelationships between an individual and the different environments in which he or she functions.

Barriers to Becoming Self-Determined

Students will inevitably encounter barriers along the way to becoming self-determined. These barriers may include a failure to acknowledge or a limited understanding of their disability, a lack of self-awareness and low self-esteem, lack of skills, and a failure to disclose important information about the disability to key individuals. If these issues are not addressed before the student graduates from high school, the student may not achieve full self-determination, which will in turn limit success in the world beyond school.

The first barrier, a failure to acknowledge or having limited understanding of one's disability is crucial to overcome. Many students may not acknowledge that they have a disability once they get out of school, especially students with learning disabilities. Many students want to see if they can manage without acknowledging that they have a disability. A learning disability is often "hidden," and many successful adults with learning disabilities have learned to compensate. Not acknowledging the disability, however, may hinder those students who have not learned to compensate. If students who have more difficulties do not acknowledge their disability, they may flounder in the workplace or in college and will not come forward to request accommodations that they may need. This will ultimately negatively impact their performance in school or on the job. A proper understanding of their disability is also important. Students need to understand their learning strengths and weaknesses in order to be able to ask for accommodations. The understanding of a disability is the foundation of self-determination.

A lack of self-awareness and low self-esteem are also barriers that many students with disabilities encounter. Many students with disabilities have low self-esteem and a poor level of self-awareness, which may hinder their ability to communicate their disability to others. Because they cannot or will not communicate their needs, they may not succeed in life after school. If they do not have the courage to let others know that they have a disability, they may not receive accommodations which they may desperately need.

A lack of skills is yet another barrier to becoming self-determined. Many skills that are necessary for becoming self-determined are often absent in students with disabilities, especially students with learning disabilities (Field, 1996). The abilities to plan, initiate behavior, and respond flexibly to situations are often linked to self-determination. These skills are related closely to executive functioning skills such as organizational and planning ability, mental flexibility, and task initiation. These skills are often difficult for students with learning disabilities to learn. A failure to develop these skills puts the student at risk for not becoming self-determined.

Disclosure of one's disability is another barrier that many individuals with disabilities face. While it is important to be aware of one's disability, it is even more important to be able to disclose information concerning the disability. While in high school, the student does not have the responsibility of telling teachers that they have a disability or self-advocating, because the school takes on this responsibility. However, when the student enters postsecondary education or the work force, the responsibility shifts and it is the responsibility of the student to disclose their disability to their professors or supervisors and to self-advocate. Accommodations are offered at the post-secondary level, but a student has to come forward in order to receive those accommodations. Similarly, arrangements can be made at the workplace, but again the individual with a disability has to come forward and disclose information about his or her disability.

Issues Related to Disability Disclosure

There are many issues that need to be taken into consideration when disclosing information. According to Lynch and Gussell (1996), timing is one of the most crucial issues when dealing with disclosure. The timing of disclosure can impact its success. Individuals need to disclose information early on in the class at the university or at the job site. If disclosure of a disability is not done early enough, the individual may end up seeking help only after a problem has occurred. Take for example, a student in a college classroom who discloses a disability only after the student has failed a test due to lack of appropriate accommodations. Obviously, after a failure has occurred is not the correct time to disclose important information regarding needed accommodations because this creates an awkward situation for both the student and the professor. The same example can be applied to the workplace. Picture an individual who is working on a project and fails to meet a deadline. Only after the individual has failed to meet the deadline does he or she disclose that he or she has a disability. Waiting until the last minute places undo stress on the employee with a disability and places the project and the relationship between the employee and employer in jeopardy. Other concerns in disclosing information involve when to disclose, how to disclose, how much to disclose, and to whom to disclose (Nutter & Ringgenberg, 1993).

There are benefits and concerns of disclosing information about a disability. Simply relieving the stress from keeping the disability hidden will allow the individual to better concentrate in the classroom or at the workplace. In the classroom, a student may need an accommodation which may provide help to other students in the classroom (Lynch & Gussell, 1996). Another benefit is that disclosing information about the disability may allow the individual to participate in and be successful at activities which the individual may have previously avoided.

Assessing Self-Advocacy Skills

A Best Practice Approach

Assessing for self-advocacy skills is very important. Because these skills are essential in succeeding in life after school, school professionals need to address these before these students with disabilities leave high school. Assessing these skills can help in determining what these students need to be taught. According to Wehmeyer (2000), this assessment information is important because it will ultimately be used to make decisions about educational programs, track student progress, and make predictions about student needs.

Because there are so many facets to self-advocacy skills, there are a number of different areas to assess, such as communication skills, decision-making skills, self-awareness, and self-esteem. Using information from other sources such as intelligence tests is also important. Cognitive measures, adaptive functioning, and other areas provide useful information when assessing self-advocacy. Communications skills are key because a student has to be able to effectively communicate the extent of their disability and strengths and needs to professors or supervisors in the workplace. Decision-making skills are also important to assess, especially in making career choices. Self-awareness is also important to assess, because students with disabilities need to be aware of their interests, strengths, and limitations. Self-esteem is important because these students need to be able to stand up for themselves, disclose private information when needed, and let people know their needs.

There are few standardized instruments that focus on self-advocacy skills. This may be due to the fact that this is a difficult construct to measure. Self-advocacy skills cannot be summarized by a number, like many other measures that we use to assess the skills and abilities of individuals with disabilities. For the assessment of these skills, more subjective measures are often used. Interviews and observations are especially valuable in assessing self-advocacy skills. With these tools, a school professional can investigate what skills the individual has that are necessary for self-determination. With any assessment, a multimethod approach should be used. This is especially important in assessing self-advocacy skills. Some facets are better assessed by one method, and other facets are better assessed by another. Observations, interviews, subjective and objective measures, and standardized measurements can all be used in assessing self-advocacy skills.

Observations

Much information can be gathered about a student by simply watching and listening to them. This can be especially useful in assessing self-advocacy skills. The assessor can observe the student asking for accommodations from teachers in the classroom, communicating their limitations in the vocational education workplace, etc. Observations should take place in a variety of settings, at different times, and by different team members (Levinson, 1993).

Salvia and Ysseldyke (1991) describe six steps that should be followed when preparing for and conducting a systematic observation. The first step is defining a target behavior. This behavior must be described in measurable and observable terms and must be clearly defined. In assessing self-advocacy skills, this may be difficult. However, behaviors like the number of times a student asks for an accommodation in the classroom can be observed. The second step to conducting a systematic observation is to select a setting. Observations should occur in at least three different settings in order to ensure validity and to determine if the behavior is situationally specific. The third step is selecting an observation schedule. Choosing the session length, determining whether to observe continuously or non-continuously, and observing at different times of the day are important facets of this. The fourth step is developing a recording procedure or the type of recording schedule. The fifth step is selecting a means of observation, whether the observer uses an electronic device or simply tallies the number of times a student demonstrates a certain behavior. The sixth and final step is carrying out the observation. This should be done in an unobtrusive manner, so that the behavior of the student will not change because he or she knows they are being observed. These steps should be followed in order to obtain observational data that is valid and reliable.

Interviews

Interviews provide excellent opportunities to assess self-advocacy skills. Interviews can be used to assess the many facets of self-advocacy, including the understanding the student has of their disability, their communication skills, the awareness of their rights, and the awareness of accommodations that are offered. Interviews should have a clear focus, be structured, planned, and organized ahead of time. Interviews can be standardized with highly structured topics or they can be unstructured with few constraints. Again, they are useful because they can assess all facets of self-advocacy.

In conducting an effective interview, there are a number of principles that should be used as guidelines for best practice according to Lentz and Wehmann (1995). The first principle is that the interview should always be ecological in nature and directed toward the examination of variables in natural situations, observable behaviors, and the beliefs and perceptions of the interviewee. The second principle is that desired outcomes should be set up prior to the interview (in this case, what specific self-advocacy skills the student possesses) and these outcomes should be used in making further decisions about the student's program. Third, interviews should be focused and economical, in that the interviewer should use questions and statements to direct the course of the interview. Fourth, structured questions and responses should be related to objectives of the interview. Fifth, the interviewer must be an active listener using verbal and non-verbal communication. This is especially important when assessing self-advocacy skills, because the interviewer must convey to the student that they have their full attention, because this may be a difficult subject for the student to talk about. Sixth, interview information should be connected to a decision about the next plan of action.

Some other issues to take into consideration when conducting an interview are establishing rapport and achieving the ability to process and evaluate information. Establishing rapport involves building a sense of trust and confidence, and developing an open means of communication. Levinson (1993) suggests that this can be accomplished through eye contact, maintaining a relaxed posture, speaking slowly and calmly, using a warm and expressive tone of voice, being nonjudgmental, accepting what is said, demonstrating interest, and being sensitive. A sense of trust is very important in assessing self-advocacy because discussion of one's disability can often be an emotional issue for the student. Another element in conducting an effective interview is to be able to process and evaluate the information collected within the interview. Effective interviewing involves being able to judge when sufficient information on a topic has been obtained, being able to determine when the topic has become uncomfortable, and responding to a topic that has been brought up by the interviewee.

Subjective and Objective Measures

Subjective and objective measures are also a good way of assessing self-advocacy. These can be especially useful when assessing such constructs as self-esteem and self-awareness. There are many informal methods of assessing these two areas. Informal checklists, teacher reports, and even some projective methods may be useful in assessing these areas. These methods can add to the information obtained through other measures.

Standardized Measurements

While standardized measurements are a good method for assessing various other areas, they may not be the best method for assessing self-advocacy. There has been research done on standardized instruments that assess self-advocacy, however, there are few instruments in the literature. Baker, Horner, Sappington, and Ard (2000) suggest that critical features need to be present in a self-determination assessment instrument. First, the instrument must be based on a conceptual model of self-determination. Secondly, the instrument must be psychometrically sound. Third, it must generate a quantifiable index of self-determination. Fourth, it must be based on observable measures, considering both important choices such as where to live and less important choices such as where to go on vacation. Fifth, it must have results that are useful for making policy and clinical decisions. Sixth, it must be usable with the full range of individuals with disabilities. Seventh, the instrument must use efficient data collection procedures. Eighth, it must be sensitive to changes in the lives of persons with disabilities. Finally, the instrument must weigh specific factors based on individual preferences. These features are important in developing a sound way to measure self-determination. One standardized instrument which measures the construct of self-determination/self-advocacy and embodies many of these principles is the Transition Planning Inventory.

Transition Planning Inventory

While the *Transitional Planning Inventory (TPI)* is a measure that addresses all transition needs of students with disabilities, there is a section devoted to self-determination/self-advocacy. The following information concerning this measurement is from the 1997 edition.

The purpose of the *TPI* is to identify and plan for the comprehensive transition needs for students (Clark & Patton, 1997). This scale measures nine areas including Employment, Further Education-Training, Daily Living, Leisure Activities, Community Participation, Health, Self-

Determination, Communication, and Interpersonal Relationships. Ratings and written comments are obtained from the student, parents or guardians, and one or more school professional using one of four forms. Ratings are obtained using a six-point Likert scale from *Strongly Disagree (0) to Strongly Agree (5),* along with Not Appropriate (NA) and Don't Know (DK) options. The 1997 edition of the test only has five questions in the self-determination category. An expanded version of a self-determination scale was developed and included in the 1998 edition. This scale consists of 26 statements in which the rater checks yes, no, or don't know. The rater checks the appropriate box for behavior in school and at home or in the community. Administration can be independent self-administration, guided self-administration, or oral administration. Administration time is approximately 15-20 minutes, but may take up to 20-30 minutes if orally administered.

Evidence is offered in support of the instrument's content validity. Limited correlational evidence is presented to support concurrent validity. There is also no confirmation of construct validity. In terms of reliability, impressive internal consistency and stability reliabilities are reported. Internal consistency reliability coefficients ranged from .70 to .94 across the nine planning areas. Stability coefficients ranged from .70 to .98 across the three survey forms.

The TPI addresses critical transition areas required by IDEA including information from the nine domains across three raters: student, parent, and school personnel. It also provides a framework to assist the IEP team in linking assessment data to IEP goals and activities. The manual is very detailed and contains many supplemental materials including case studies, suggested transition goal statements, and additional forms

Summary

Career maturity and self-advocacy skills are ultimately about self-awareness. Career maturity involves a realistic self-appraisal about abilities and skills and the kinds of work activities which bring personal pleasure, and requires an adequate knowledge base about vocations, generally and specifically. Self-advocacy requires an understanding of one's disability and rights, the ability to effectively communicate one's needs, and the skills to appropriately request accommodations for those needs in order to achieve one's goals in life.

Transition from school to life after school for students with disabilities should be an outcome-oriented process which encompasses a broad array of services and experiences that leads to, among other goals, employment. Since students with disabilities are particularly vulnerable in terms of developing an appropriate level career maturity and self-advocacy skills, they are in need of specially tailored assessments and interventions in order to successfully maneuver the transition from high school to life after high school.

For optimum results, thoughtful and cooperative transition teams need to move from a multidisciplinary to a transdisciplinary approach. In other words, they consider the assessment data and recommendations from parents and members inside, as well as outside, the school district (community personnel, social service agencies, vocational rehabilitation specialists, etc.). Additionally, these transdisciplinary teams need to take the psychological, social, educational and academic functioning. physical/medical, and vocational functioning, all into consideration.

A best-practice approach to vocational assessment begins during the elementary school years, focusing on the student's needs, values, interests, abilities, interpersonal skills, and decision-making skills, utilizing vocational and career exploration activities, and having the goal of building self-awareness. During the middle school/junior high school years, the focus is specifically on an assessment of vocational interests and aptitudes, work habits and career maturity, utilizing interviews, observations, and standardized norm referenced assessment instruments, and having the goal of continuing to encourage career exploration and assisting individuals in making tentative choices regarding educational and career goals. The high school years is marked with a more experimentally-based assessment devices, such as using work samples and situational assessment, and focuses upon the specific training the student needs to obtain post-high school education or employment.

REFERENCES

Abery, B. (1994). A conceptual framework for enhancing self-determination. In M.F. Hayden & B.H. Abery (Eds.), *Challenges for a service system in transition.* Baltimore: Brookes.

Amundson, N. E. (1995). An interactive model of career decision-making. *Journal of Employment Counseling, 32*(1), 11–22.

Anderson, W. T., Hohenshil, T. H., Buckland-Heer, K. & Levinson, E.M. (1990). Best practices in vocational assessment of students with disabilities. In A. Thomas & J. Grimes (eds.) *Best practices in school psychology - II.* Washington, DC: National Association of School Psychologists.

Aune, E., & Ness, J. (1991). *Tools for transition: Preparing students with learning disabilities for post-secondary education.* Circle Pines, MN: American Guidance Service.

Baker, D.J., Horner, R.H., Sappington, G., & Ard, Jr., W.R. (2000). A response to Wehmeyer (1999) and a challenge to the field regarding self-determination. *Focus on Autism & Other Developmental Disabilities, 15*(3), 154–156.

Bansberg, B. & Sklare, J. (1986). *The career decision diagnostic assessment.* Monterey, CA: CTB/McGraw-Hill.

Baxter, J. (1995). Transition needs of learning disabled students for success at post-secondary institutions. Unpublished manuscript.

Bingham, G. (1975). Career attitudes and self-esteem among boys with and with out specific learning disabilities. (Doctoral Dissertation). *Dissertation Abstracts International 36,* 02A-75347. (University Microfilms No. 75-17, 340).

Bingham, G. (1978). Career attitudes among boys with and without specific learning disabilities. *Exceptional Children, 44,* 341–342.

Bingham, G. (1980). Career maturity of learning disabilities adolescents. *Psychology in the Schools, 17,* 135–139.

Brinckerhoff, L.C. (1994). Developing effective self-advocacy skills in college-bound students with learning disabilities. *Intervention in School & Clinic, 29*(4), 229–232.

Clark, G.M. & Patton, J.R. (1997). *Transition Planning Inventory.* Austin, TX: Pro-Ed.

Crites, J. O.(1965). Measurement of vocational maturity in adolescence. Attitude Scale of the Vocational Developments Inventory. Psychological Monographs, 79(2), Whole No. 595.

Crites, J. O. (1971). *The maturity of vocational attitudes in adolescence.* Washington, DC: American Personnel and Guidance Association.

Crites, J. O. (1978a). *Administration and use for the Career Maturity Inventory,* 2nd. ed. Monterey, CA: McGraw-Hill/CTB.

Crites, J. O. (1995). *Career Maturity Inventory Sourcebook.* Monterey, CA: McGraw Hill/CTB.

Crites, J. O. & Savickas, M. L. (1995). *Career Maturity Inventory.* Monterey, CA: McGraw Hill/CTB.

Dalke, C.L. & Franzene, J. (1988). Secondary-postsecondary collaboration: A model of shared responsibility. *Learning Disability Focus, 4,* 38–45.

Downing, J. & D'Andrea, L. (1994). Parental involvement in children's career decision-making. *Journal of Employment Counseling, 31,* 115–126.

Durlak, C.M., Rose, E., & Bursuck, W.D. (1994). Preparing high school students with learning disabilities for the transition to postsecondary education: Teaching the skills of self-determination. *Journal of Learning Disabilities, 27,* 51–59.

Edgar, E. (1987). Secondary programs in special education: Are they justifiable? *Exceptional Children, 53*(6), 555–561.

Fardig, D. B., Algozzine, R. F., Schwartz, S. E., Hensel, J. E., & Westling, D. L.. (1985). Postsecondary vocational adjustment of rural, mildly handicapped students. *Exceptional Children, 52*(2), 115–121.

Field, S. (1996). Self-determination instructional strategies for youth with learning disabilities. In J.R. Patton & G. Blalock (Eds.), *Transition and students with learning disabilities: Facilitating the movement from school to adult life.* Austin, TX: Pro-Ed.

Field, S. & Hoffman, A. (1994). Development of a model for self-determination. *Career Development for Exceptional Individuals, 17*(2), 159–169.

Geyer, P. D., Johnson, V.A., & Hunter, J. E. (1998). Empowering career decision-making: a practical strategy for using occupational information. *Journal of Rehabilitation, 64*(4), 423–434.

Gottfredson, L. S. (1984). Special groups and the beneficial use of vocational interest inventories. In W.B Walsh & S. H. Osipow (Eds.) *Advances in vocational psychology* (pp. 127–188).

Halloran, W. (1989). Foreward. In D. E. Berkell & J. M. Brown (eds.) *Transition from school to work for persons with disabilities* (pp. xiii–xvi). New York: Longman.

Halpin, G., Ralph, J., & Halpin, G. (1990). The adult career concerns inventory: Validity and reliability. *Measurement and Evaluation in Counseling and Development, 22*(4), 196–202.

Harren, V. A. (1979). A model of career decision-making for college students. *Journal of Vocational Behavior, 14,* 119–133.

Healy, C. C. (1994). Review of the Career Maturity Inventory. In J. T. Kapes, M. M. Mastie, & E. A. Whitfield (Eds.), *A counselor's guide to career assessment instruments,* 3rd ed. Alexandria, VA: National Career Development Association.

Jagger, L., Neukrug, E., & McAuliffe, G. (1992). Congruence between personality traits and chosen occupation as a predictor of job satisfaction for people with disabilities. *Rehabilitation Counseling Bulletin, 36,* 53–60.

Jepsen, D. A. & Prediger, D. J. (1981). Dimensions of adolescent career development. A multi-instrument analysis. *Journal of Vocational Behavior, 19,* 350–368.

Kendal, W. S. (1980). *Affective and career education for the learning disabled student.* Prairie View, Texas: Prairie View A & M University (ERIC Document Reproduction Service No. Ed. 188772).

Kendal, W. S. (1981). Affective and career education for the learning disabled student. *Learning Disability Quarterly, 4,* 69–75.

Krumboltz, J. D. (1994). The Career Beliefs Inventory. *Journal of Counseling & Development, 72,* 424–428.

Larson, J. H., Busby, D. M., Wilson, S., Medora, N., & Allgood, S. (1994). The multidimensional assessment of career decision problems: The career decision diagnostic assessment. *Journal of Counseling & Development, 72*(3), 323–338.

Lentz, Jr., F.E. & Wehmann, B.A. (1995). Interviewing. In A. Thomas & J. Grimes (Eds.) *Best practices in school psychology.* Washington, DC: The National Association of School Psychologists.

Levinson, E.M. (1988). Correlates of vocational practice among school psychologists. *Psychology in the Schools, 25*(3), 297-305.

Levinson, E.M. (1993). *Transdisciplinary vocational assessment: Issues in school-based problems.* Brandon, VT: Clinical Psychology Publishing Co.

Levinson, E. M.(1995). Best practices in vocational assessment in the schools. In A. Thomas & J. Grimes (eds.), *Best practices in school psychology - III.* Washington, DC: National Association of School Psychologists, pp.741–751.

Levinson, E. M. (1998). *Transition: Facilitating the post-school adjustment of students with disabilities.* Boulder, CO: Westview Press.

Levinson and Ohler (1998). Transition from high school to college for students with learning disabilities: Needs, assessment, and services. *High School Journal, 82*(1), 62--73.

Levinson, E. M., Ohler, D. L., & Baxter, J. (1996). *Transition from high school to college for students with learning disabilities.* Paper presented at the 1996 Meeting of the National Association of School Psychologist, Atlanta, GA.

Levinson, E. M., Ohler, D. L., Caswell, S. & Kiewra, K. R. (1998). Six approaches to the assessment of career maturity. *Journal of Counseling & Development, 76*(4), 475–488.

Longhurst, N.A. (1994). *The self-advocacy movement by people with developmental disabilities: A demographic study and directory of self-advocacy groups in the United States.* Washington, DC: American Association on Mental Retardation.

Lynch, R.T. & Gussel, L. (1996). Disclosure and self-advocacy regarding disability-related needs: Strategies to maximize integration in postsecondary education. *Journal of Counseling and Development, 74*(4), 352–358.

Miner, C. U., Osborne, W. L., & Jaeger, R. M. (1997). The ability of career maturity to predict interest score differentiation, consistency, and elevation. *Measurement & Evaluation in Counseling & Development. 29*(4), 187–207.

Mithaug, D., Campeau, P., & Wolman, J. (1994). *Self-determination assessment.* Unpublished manuscript.

Mithaug, D.E., Horiuchi, C. N., & Fanning, P. N. (1985). A report on the Colorado statewide follow-up survey of special education students. *Exceptional Children, 51*(5), 397–404.

Morris, T. W. & Levinson, E. M. (1995). Relationship between intelligence and occupational adjustment and functioning: A literature review. *Journal of Counseling and Development, 73*(5), 503–526.

Nirje, B. (1976). The normalization principle and its human management implications. In M. Rosen, C.R. Clark, & M.S. Kivitz (Eds.), *The history of mental retardation: Collected papers.* (Vol. 2). Baltimore: University Park Press.

Nutter, K.J. & Ringgenberg, L.J. (1993). Creating positive outcomes for students with disabilities. *New Directions for Student Services, 64,* 45–58.

Occupational Outlook Handbook 2000-2001. (2000). U. S. Labor Bureau of Labor Statistics, Bulletin 2520.

Ohler, D. L., Levinson, E. M., & Barker, W. F. (1996). Career maturity in college students with learning disabilities. *Career Development Quarterly, 44*(3), 278–288.

Osipow, S. H., Carney, C. G., Winer, J., Yanico, B. J., & Koshier, M. (1976). *The Career Decision Scale,* 3rd rev. Columbus, OH: Marathon Consulting and Press.

Pennsylvania Departments of Education and Labor and Industry (1986). *Pennsylvania transition from school to workplace,* pp. 3, 7, 83.

Perry, R. P. & Penner, K. S. (1990). Enhancing academic achievement in college students through attributional retraining and instruction. *Journal of Educational Psychology, 82,* 262–271.

Pinkney, J. W. & Bozik, C. M. (1994). Review of the Career Development Inventory. In J. T. Kapes, M. M. Mastie, & E. A. Whitfield (Eds.), *A counselor's guide to career assessment instruments,* 3rd ed. Alexandria, VA: National Career Development Association.

Rehabilitation Act Amendments of 1992, 2, 29, U.S.C. 701.

Rogers, W. B. & Westbrook, B. W. (1983). Measuring career indecision among college students. Toward a valid approach for counseling practitioners and researchers. *Measurement and Evaluation in guidance, 16,* 78–85.

Rotter, J. B. (1966). Generalized expectancies for internal versus external control of reinforcement. *Psychological Monographs, 80* (Whole no. 609, 1–28).

Rounds, J. (1994). Review of the Adult Career Concerns Inventory. In J. T. Kapes, M. M. Mastie, & E. A. Whitfield (Eds.), *A counselor's guide to career assessment instruments,* 3rd ed. Alexandria, VA: National Career Development Association.

Ryan, A. & Price, L. (1992). Landmarks in the '90's: Addressing the needs of students with learning disabilities. *Intervention in School and Clinic, 28,* 6–20.

Salvia, J. & Ysseldyke, J.E. (1991). *Assessment,* 5th ed. Boston: Houghton-Mifflin.

Savikas, M. L. (1984). Career maturity: The construct and its measurement. *The Vocational Guidance Quarterly, 32,* 222–231.

Schalock, R. L. & Lilley, M.A. (1986). Placement from community-based mental retardation programs: How well do clients do after 8 to 10 years? *American Journal of Mental Deficiency, 90*(6), 669–676.

Shapiro, J.P. (1993). *No pity: People with disabilities forging a new civil rights movement.* New York: Times Books.

Sharf, R. S. (1994). Review of the assessment of career decision making. In J. T. Kapes, M. M. Mastie, & E. A. Whitfield (Eds.), *A counselor's guide to career assessment instruments,* 3rd ed. Alexandria, VA: National Career Development Association.

Slaney, R. B., Palko-Nonemaker, D. & Alexander, R. (1981). An investigation of two measures of career indecision. *Journal of Vocational Behavior, 18,* 92–103.

Stewart, J. (1995). Counselling individuals who experience career decision-making difficulties. *Guidance & Counseling, 10*(4), 52–61.

Stowe, R. W. (1985). Convergent and discriminant validity of Crites Career Maturity Inventory Attitude Scale, Counseling Form B-1. *Educational and Psychological Measurement, 45,* 763–770.

Strumpf, S., Colarelli, S., & Hartman, K. (1983). Development of the career exploratory survey (CES). *Journal of Vocational Behavior, 22,* 191–226.

Super, D.E. (1957). *The psychology of careers.* New York: Harper.

Super, D. E. & Knasel, E. (1979). *Development of a model, specifications, and sample items for measuring career adaptability (vocational maturity) in young blue-collar workers.*

Cambridge, Untied Kingdom: National Institute for Careers Education and Counseling.

Super, D. E., Thompson, A. S., & Lindeman, R. H., Jordaan, J. P., & Myers, R. A., (1988). *Manual for the Adult Career Concerns Inventory and the Career Development Inventory.* Palo Alto, CA: Consulting Psychologists Press.

The nation. (1990). *Chronicle of Higher Education, 9,* 14–15.

Tiedeman, D. V. & O'Hara, R. P. (1963). *Career development: choice and adjustment.* New York: College Entrance Examination Board.

U.S. Department of Labor (1977). *Dictionary of Occupational Titles,* 4th ed. Washington, DC: U.S., Government Printing Office.

VGM's Career Encyclopedia (1997). The editors of VGM Career Horizons. Lincoln Wood, Ill: VGM Career Horizons.

Wall, J. E. (1994). Review of the Career Beliefs Inventory. In J. T. Kapes, M. M. Mastie, & E. A. Whitfield (Eds.), *A counselor's guide to career assessment instruments,* 3rd ed. Alexandria, VA: National Career Development Association.

Ward, M.J. & Kohler, P.D. (1996). Promoting self-determination for individuals with disabilities: Content and process. In L.E. Powers, G.H.S. Singer, & J. Sowers (Eds.), *Making our way: Building self-competence among children with disabilities.* Baltimore, MD: Brookes.

Wehmeyer, M.L. (1992). Self-directed learning and self-determination. In M. Agran (Ed.), *Student-directed learning: A handbook of self-management.* Pacific Grove, CA: Brooks/Cole.

Wehmeyer, M. L. (2000). Assessment of self-determination-Negotiating the mindfield: A response to Baker et al. *Focus on Autism & Other Developmental Disabilities, 15*(3), 157–158.

Wehmeyer, M.L. & Berkobien, R. (1991). Self-determination and self-advocacy: A case of mistaken identity. *The Association for Persons with Severe Handicaps Newsletter, 17*(7), 4.

Westbrook, B. W., Sanford, E. E., & Donnelly, M. H. (1990). The relationship between career maturity test scores and appropriateness of career choices: A replication. *Journal of Vocational Behavior, 36,* 20–32.

Westcot, A. M. & Tokar, D.M., (1991). The assessment of career decision-making. *Guidance & Counseling, 6*(4), 28–35.

Chapter 7

TRANSITION ASSESSMENT: FOCUS ON LIFE SKILLS

M. ALICIA JENKINS AND LESLIE A. LATOCHE

INTRODUCTION: TRANSITION ASSESSMENT: FOCUS ON LIFE SKILLS

The ultimate goal of the transition planning process is to maximize the likelihood that an individual will be able to effectively deal with the multifaceted demands of adulthood, which may lead to a higher level of personal fulfillment. To function successfully in an adult role, individuals must have the knowledge and skills needed to handle the various situations that may arise. Likewise, one must be able to access these supports and services when needed. Comprehensive transition planning, if conducted appropriately, makes an effort to even the playing field by providing a process for identifying, planning for, and acting on the needs students have in dealing with the complexities of life (Patton, & Cronin, 1997).

Among the many accepted and validated models for developing the competencies needed to function independently as an adult, there is a great deal of agreement with regards to the major skills needed in adult life. These skills are maintaining a home, becoming appropriately involved in the community, and experiencing satisfaction in personal and social relationships (Sitlington, 1996).

Overview

Life skills are those skills which are needed to function independently in day-to-day living situations. Life skills is a broad spectrum of many subcategories that focus on the goal of being able to take care of oneself in an adult role. Levinson (1998) further indicated that many experts propose that life skills are critical to functioning independently in the community and indicate that they are a critical component in transition planning. Skills associated with life skills include maintaining a home, cooking, shopping, and organizing of a personal living environment.

The Division on Career Development and Transition of the Council for Exceptional Children published a statement in 1994, which included "Transition refers to a change in status from behaving primarily as a student to assuming emergent adult roles in the community. These roles include employment, participating in postsecondary education, maintaining a home, becoming appropriately involved in the community, and experiencing satisfactory personal and social relationships. . . ." In looking at this definition, there is an obvious link between transition and life skills, and research has continuously demonstrated that many positive effects have resulted from transition planning. Therefore, it is unfortunate that the general high school curriculum, into which many special education students are being integrated, places a very low priority on Life Skills.

Four Major Domains of Life Skills

Maintaining a Home

Home living skills are those skills that are used in the place where the individual lives. Typically, such skills include safety skills, housekeeping skills, clothing care, bathroom activities, bedroom activities, kitchen activities, living room activities, and yard care. Safety skills include basic first aid, use of the telephone for emergencies, and knowledge of the handling of hazardous materials. Housekeeping includes basic cleaning and maintenance skills such as sweeping, mopping, etc. Bathroom skills may include showering, brushing one's teeth, using the toilet, and so on. Bedroom skills include making the bed, dressing, and undressing. Kitchen skills consist of appropriate handling of food, food preparation, using appliances, storing food, and skills associated with eating. Living room skills may include skills such as using electrical equipment such as a stereo or television, socialization, and cleaning. Yard care skills include basic skills such as mowing the lawn, planting flowers, shoveling, and watering. Also, skills of managing finances, budgeting, and paying living expenses are included in home management (Levinson, 1998).

A number of studies have been conducted addressing living status. One study by Sitlington (1996) examined the living status of disabled students one year after graduation from high school. It was found that after one year of leaving school, between 54 percent and 70 percent of the individuals studied were living with parents or relatives. The study went on to report that 22 percent to 39 percent were living independently, while eight percent to 10 percent were married. An earlier study found that after three years, 49 percent were living independently. We can probably conclude from the presented studies that students may not be ready to function on their own due to lack of appropriate transition planning and life skills training in the high school years.

Community Involvement

Being able to use the many services available in a community along with being able to negotiate within a community setting are important skills that are needed to function independently. Mobility skills that may be taught to promote community involvement include walking up and down stairs, climbing in and out of vehicles, knowing how to enter and exit buildings, crossing the street, and using public restrooms. Individuals may also need to be taught how to use the various forms of public transportation including bicycles, cars, buses, taxis, trains, and wheelchairs. These skills are especially important because individuals need to use them in order to get around within the community for work, grocery shopping, going to the bank, and for leisure activities (Levinson, 1998).

Social/Interpersonal Skills

Social and interpersonal skills are needed to function in a variety of roles. In order to communicate effectively with others, one must be able to incorporate interpersonal skills that are accepted by those with whom one interacts. Social and interpersonal skills include being able to appropriately greet someone, praise, tone of voice, loudness of voice, eye contact, facial expressions, knowing personal space, and appropriate physical contact. Levinson (1998) explains that social skills can be viewed from two perspectives: a vocational perspective, and a leisure perspective. The vocational perspective expresses a need for social skills in that they greatly influence the degree to which one is capable of maintaining a job. Similarly, the leisure perspective notes that the skills are important in that they influence social acceptance and friendships with others.

Individuals with learning disabilities have more difficulty in the area of social and interpersonal skills compared to their non-disabled peers. According to Sitlington (1996), the Learning Disabilities Association sponsored an adult adjustment study that included a report on the areas of life with which individuals with Learning Disabilities had the most difficulty. Number one on the list was social relationships and social skills. One study reported by Sitlington (1996) indicated that students with learning disabilities had difficulty making friends and relating to parents and relatives. Students with learning disabilities also expressed more social dissatisfaction with their employment and reported lower aspirations for further education or training.

Leisure Skills

One must not neglect the importance of leisure skills. The development of leisure skills is essential life fulfillment. Also, the development of leisure skills has been shown to reduce inappropriate social behaviors and may also enhance other areas of development, such as cognitive, domestic, language, and motor skills. Leisure activities may include but are not limited to games, hobbies, and sports (Levinson, 1998).

Career Education and Life Skills Training Models

There is a great deal of agreement across career education and life skills education models that maintaining a home, becoming appropriately involved in the community, and experiencing satisfaction in personal and social relationships are major skills needed in adult life. Each of these models provides a framework for preparing individuals to function effectively in these life roles. Readers are referred to the appendix for examples of existing career education and life skills models.

Historical Perspectives

Life skills have been, and are still closely related to adaptive behavior. Adaptive behavior is often associated with professional practice and legal issues relative to addressing needs of individuals with mental retardation. Federal law requires assessment of adaptive skills in determining classification for mental retardation. In particular, life skills are a component of adaptive behavior, and although closely related, should not be confused with adaptive behavior. Living skills is a more general and basic concept and looks at what an individual can or cannot do. On the other hand, adaptive behavior is a more comprehensive area that often assesses what individuals can or cannot do and also incorporates maladaptive behaviors that may have a negative effect on performance. Nolan et al. (2000) expanded on this idea, and presented information from numerous authors. They reported that much of the literature that deals with assessment of youth self-sufficiency and life skills has been divided into two categories: tangible and intangible skills. Tangible skills are considered those skills needed for daily living, self-maintenance, and obtaining and sustaining employment. They can be described as skills we know or do. Intangible skills are those skills that are needed for successful interpersonal relationships and for skills necessary to maintain employment. These skills are socially based and include decision making, problem solving, planning, communication, self-esteem, anger and grief management, and overall social skills.

Initially, special educators saw the state rehabilitation agency as an appropriate link to employment and successful community living for graduates with disabilities. In the 1960s, schools took notice of state rehabilitation agencies giving a considerable amount of attention to special education populations, with a focus on students classified as mildly mentally retarded. Between 1960 and 1975, the increase in the number of cases closed by vocational rehabilitation agencies raised the expectations of special educators in regards to having someone assume responsibility for students after they left school. This "closed employment status" of special education graduates was welcomed by school personnel and assumed to be a personal policy commitment (Clark & Kolstoe, 1995).

As cited in Clark and Kolstoe (1995) the term transition was used in the late 1960s to describe an orderly passage from school or institutional programming to adult services and full community participation. In the late 1970s, during the beginning stages of the implementation of public law 94-142, the momentum decreased as state vocational rehabilitation agencies began to change their focus to meet the needs of individuals who were more severely disabled.

The literature identifies two movements that opened the door for a return to the concept of transition and the context of ending school programming and beginning adult living. These movements include the career education movement and independent living movement. For the purposes of this chapter, the focus will be the independent living movement. The concept of independent living rehabilitation began as a disability rights movement due to legislation and policies that neglected to address vocational rehabilitation for students with severe disabilities. Historically, federal policy restricted vocational rehabilitation services to individuals from whom there was a "reasonable expectation" that the services would result in profitable employment. The goal of many vocational rehabilitation professionals was to develop independent living services for those individuals who would not be entering the field of work. The vocational rehabilitation professionals did not believe it was possible for these individuals to function independently in a work environment.

Current Trends in Transition Assessment: Focus on Life Skills

In recent years, there has been a shift in the perspective of the importance of life skills and its link to vocational development. Updated literature has pointed out that there is an overlap between daily living skills and job skills. This obvious overlap makes it clear that it is possible for disabled students to use living skills and apply them to a vocational setting. Clark and Kolstoe (1995) support this notion by giving examples of this in the work force. The basic skills needed for reading a recipe in order to cook a meal at home parallels the skills needed for fulfilling the cooking requirements in a restaurant. Similarly, skills required for operating a car or truck for personal reasons parallels skills required to do so in a work environment. In addition, skills that are necessary to select and purchase personal items are the same skills required for working in a retail-oriented job setting.

In contrast to the historical perspective, where the focus of life skills was geared towards those student with disabilities and those not expected to enter the work force, current trends address life skill as a much needed component of both transition to independent living and transition to work. Life skills are relevant for all children, and although most children acquire life skills on their own, reinforcement of such skill is needed. Children with disabilities do not spontaneously acquire these skills on their own, and therefore must be taught directly. Non-disabled students often learn these skills vicariously and can generalize and apply these skills in multiple settings. This is not the case for disabled students who need to be taught directly and in the natural environment in which the skill is needed. For example, it would not be productive to simply offer a written step-by-step explanation of the process of doing laundry. The most effective way of teaching this skill would be to teach the lesson in a Laundromat with hands-on experience.

Another focus has been on implementing transition planning earlier in the curriculum. Most educational institutions focus on transition planning in high school, and research now suggests that this is almost too late. Life skills should be included in the curriculum long before transition from school to community. Patton and Blalock (1996) reported that some research suggests that life skills should be taught throughout the curriculum rather than being presented as isolated tasks that are in a separate category from the core content covered in school. In addition, life skills instruction should be formally included in each of the academic areas as a way of communicating its importance and linking academics to everyday activity. Social skills is one particular area of life skills that is critical to transitioning from high school to independent living and work environments which can be incorporated into the curriculum.

Implications of Life Skills Assessment

The ability to live independently brings quality to the life of most individuals. Having appropriate life skills has been known to reduce inappropriate social behaviors along with dropout, underemployment, and unemployment rates. When individuals stay in school and find employment, they are likely to have a higher quality of life. Essentially this is one of the goals for most, if not all individuals and is therefore a vital area of assessment for transition planning.

Another factor that contributes to having a quality of life is obtaining and maintaining employment. Although we might not think about it often, basic life skills are needed to get and keep a job. Often students with disabilities have difficulty maintaining positions once they obtain them. This could be due to poor social skills, lack of knowledge of community resources, and lack of skills related to functioning independently in a work setting. These issues are important to address since students with learning disabilities or with low cognitive functioning are often faced with more challenges compared to their non-disabled peers.

Future Directions in Transition Assessment: Focus on Life Skills

Why Assess Life Skills?

As professionals who are constantly faced with the challenge of assessment, we are expected to begin nearly all evaluations by determining the student's current level of functioning. This applies to life skills assessment as well. Although we talk about the need for life skills to be included in the curriculum for all students, presently we deal with this primarily in the special education classroom. After assessment of life skills, focus can be placed on skill deficits and educators may individualize their teaching based on the student's needs.

During the assessment process it is important to identify the strengths of the student. This will facilitate the process in determining vocational options in which the student is likely to be most successful. These strengths can also be used to promote the learning of skills in which improvement is needed. For example, a student who possesses strong interpersonal and social skills may be steered towards vocational options involving interaction with people. On the other hand, someone who has limitations in motor skills may not be suited for jobs requiring high levels of physical mobility.

Keeping in mind that we want students to obtain and maintain jobs, identifying areas in which improvement is needed is equally important as the identification of strengths. When assessing areas in which skill is lacking, we want to be certain that we consider the types of skills that will inevitably be needed for job success.

As professionals well trained in data-based decision making, it is vital that we use the information gathered during assessment to effectively plan for transition to adult life. It is important that professionals give special consideration to choosing appropriate assessment measures. Later in the chapter, appropriate assessment techniques addressing the data-based decision process will be discussed.

How Do We Assess Life Skills?

Observations

Observations involve gathering information by studying or examining carefully. Specific information about an individual's skill level can be gathered through the process of thorough observation. This method of collecting data is a critical part of life skills assessment and should be conducted in a natural setting. In comparison to non-disabled students, students with disabilities are less likely to generalize what they learned to different settings or to be able to apply their skill in different situations. Moreover, observations in the students' natural environment can provide a true measure of his or her ability and skill level. It also allows for verification of the accuracy of parent and teacher reports regarding student behavior (Levinson, 1996).

To assure the most accurate measure of a student's behavior or skill in a particular environment, observations should be carried out by more than one person. As Levinson stated in 1993, the use of multiple observers and different settings can contribute to the reliability and validity of the information gathered and it also increases the representativeness of the behaviors observed. Keeping in mind that we would like to provide the most complete assessment of all students, it is important that we involve several different team members in this data-collection process.

The observation process falls into two categories. They can be either informal or formal. Informal observations can assist in answering a number of meaningful questions about a person's life skills and may help to guide additional, more structured assessment. According to Harrison (1991), informal observations of individuals provides opportunities for assessment in a variety of settings and also allows for additional analysis of behavior.

On the other hand, structured observations focus on direct and systemic explanations of individuals in natural settings, such as the classroom, home, lunchroom, and workplace (Harrison & Robinson, 1995). In the measurement of life skills, two types of observational methods that can be used are the descriptive method and the quantitative method. For the most part, the descriptive method can generate an overall picture of life skills including consistency and frequency of behavior, or more detailed information about events that occur prior to and immediately following the life skill that was demonstrated.

The quantitative method provides more concrete information that is measurable and deals with specific skills. For example, this method is likely to yield information about the exact number of occurrences of a life skill within a specific time frame, the precise length of the demonstration of the skill from beginning to end, and the measurement of the number of times a skill is demonstrated during a specified amount of time. The latter might involve recording the presence or absence of a skill every 20 seconds.

Rating Scales/ Adaptive Measures

The use of rating scales can assist professionals with obtaining specific information about a student's level of skill. For example, while checklists often allow for concrete "yes" or "no" answers, rating scales in a Likert-type format allows the respondent to rank the level of particular skills. Similarly, adaptive measures provide specific information due to their comprehensive nature. Evaluators can benefit from using an entire Adaptive Behavior Scale, or just the life skills domain in a life skills assessment.

Clark and Kolstoe (1995) describe rating devices as an attempt to assess a person by way of a report from a second person who reacts to the individual personally. With this in mind, responses should be elicited from a variety of individuals who work closely with the student. As with any assessment, multiple sources allow for a more thorough evaluation process. Unfortunately, functional living skills programs and classrooms vary with regards to the exposure of students to real-life environments and situations. In the case of such limited exposure, parents can offer information about a student's life skills at home and in other settings that might not be evident to the teacher.

Teachers, who work with students primarily in school and community settings, can provide information about life skills that require social interaction and other skills that are likely to be more frequently used outside of the home environment. For example, a teacher might be more frequently exposed to students as they socialize with their peers as well as people in the community, and can offer information about the student's skill level in those particular areas.

In addition to collecting information from those who work closely with a student on a regular basis, it is just as beneficial to get the student's perception of their own skill level and ability. Getting a self-report from the student might provide information that neither teachers nor parents can contribute. For instance, students' interpretation of their experiences will affect their behavior with regards to how they view their skills in particular areas. In turn, this affects their ability to perform or demonstrate adequate life skills. It also gives students the opportunity to think about what it is they are able to do and what skills need to be improved.

Semi-structured Interviews/Consultation

In general, interviews are interpersonal encounters in which there is an exchange of information (Sattler, 1988). This process should be two-way, with the goal of the interviewer being to facilitate the flow of information. Interviews allow for the resolution of ambiguous responses, clarification of misunderstandings, obtaining of information about the consistency and history of skills, learning about the beliefs, values, and expectations of the parents, teachers, and students, and assess receptivity of the parent, teacher, and student to various interventions.

When specifically dealing with the semi-structured interview format, general and flexible guidelines for conducting the interview and recording the information are provided. This format allows for freedom in phrasing questions, follow-up questions about information provided by the interviewee, and interpretation of responses (Sattler, 1988). Semi-structured interviews and consultative methods are particularly effective in the assessment of life skills due to the conversational nature and given opportunity for interviewees to expand and give examples of the types of skills the student is capable of demonstrating.

Best Practices in Assessing Life Skills

Life skills assessment should be incorporated into assessment for all children experiencing learning and behavioral difficulties. However, this is not often the case in many school systems. Unfortunately, it seems to be more common for life skills assessment to take place with students who have been diagnosed or classified with mental retardation. As life skills are important for all students, school professionals are encouraged to move away from the common practice of neglecting to include life skills assessment in evaluations.

Many times, students who are referred for demonstrating learning and behavioral difficulties are "labeled" both formally and informally (amongst school faculty). Once students obtain such a reputation, progressing through the school system successfully presents a challenge. Although the reputation is oftentimes generated and maintained in the school environment, it has a tendency to carry over into and affect the students in their work settings. For example, these students may not have gained the life skills necessary to survive at work due to attention being placed on their negative attributes throughout school. This is another reason that life skills assessment should be incorporated in the evaluation of such students.

When planning an assessment, vital questions about a student's functioning should be addressed. In other words, the methods or tools chosen, specifically for life skills assessment, should be directly related to the *reason* for the assessment. For example, if there is concern about a student lacking skill in a particular domain area, then the assessment should be focused on that area. Neglecting to take this into consideration may result in the feeling of conducting a meaningless evaluation.

After establishing a focus for assessment, it is important that different methods are incorporated so that all of the data gathered is not coming from one assessment technique. Both formal and informal assessment tools should be utilized. Norm-referenced instruments (which would be considered formal) are useful because it allows a comparison of the student to a population of students outside of the immediate school and community. Also, this type of method looks more closely at general competencies of the student.

In contrast, criterion referenced instruments (which are also formal methods of assessment) focuses on more specific skills. This type of tool may be used to determine how many competencies were acquired in a particular training program. Both of these informal methods can facilitate assessment, however there are some limitations that should be considered prior to their use.

Of course, validity and reliability of instruments should be strongly considered before including them in an assessment. Particularly, when using standardized rating scales, inter-rater reliability should be taken into account. Another limitation that should be given attention is applicability to questions you want answered in the assessment. For example, an instrument that focuses primarily on maintaining a home is probably not the best to use if the purpose of your assessment is to evaluate a student's community involvement.

The time factor is also often an issue with anyone involved in the assessment process. With teachers and parents who are asked to complete rating scales, they are less likely to do so if they feel that the scale is time-consuming. Moreover, when administering a scale to a student for a self-report, the likelihood of a short attention span must be considered. Many times students with learning and behavioral difficulties are easily distracted and will not provide valid answers when filling out a lengthy scale.

Comprehensiveness of the instrument that is chosen is another essential component to consider when looking at the limitations of assessment tools. Often, evaluators may find that it is still beneficial to use instruments that are limited with regards to specific skill areas, as long as such instruments are supplemented. For example, a norm-referenced scale might be considered vague and general. However, if the evaluator is able to recognize this limitation, using the strength of the scale (national norms for example) and then supplementing the assessment with additional methods that focus on specific skill areas can only result in a more thorough interpretation of the information gathered.

In addition to previous examples of structured observations provided earlier in the chapter, quantifying the amount of prompts needed before a student can successfully perform a task independently is a form of structured observation. Data gathered from this approach can give specific information leading to measurable goals for the student. The use of interviews, again, is important because it yields qualitative information that can offer a clear picture of students' skills. Self-report measures can give information about the student's perception of his or her own skills. This report might be far from accurate when assessing students of very low cognitive ability. However, the information provided can still be useful.

Similar to general assessment practices, *life skills assessment tools should be based on the individual's current needs.* For example, many times when a reevaluation is conducted, specifics about a student's skill are not necessary if they have been previously and consistently demonstrated over time. In this case, less comprehensive measures such as checklists might be sufficient as opposed to an entire adaptive behavior scale.

Review of Instrumentation

When assessing skills associated with independent living, it is necessary to consider two areas: adaptive behavior and living skills. As stated earlier, life skills is a component of adaptive behavior, and although closely related, should not be confused with adaptive behavior. Living skills is a more general and basic concept and looks at what an individual can or cannot do, whereas adaptive behavior is a more comprehensive area that often assesses what one can or cannot do and also incorporates maladaptive behaviors that may have a negative affect on performance. When choosing instruments to assess life skills, it is important to research the various psychometric properties to ensure that the instrument being chosen is appropriate for the child being evaluated. This section of the chapter will provide a brief review of popular instruments being used in the field today.

Adaptive Behavior

The Vineland Adaptive Behavior Scales

The Vineland Adaptive Behavior Scales are a revision of the Vineland Social Maturity Scale from 1935 and assesses personal and social sufficiency of individuals from birth until 18 years, 11 months of age. The later version was developed in 1984 and is appropriate for both handicapped as well as non-handicapped individuals. The Vineland Adaptive Behavior Scales requires that someone familiar with the behavior of the individual being evaluated answer questions raised by a trained examiner. The instrument has three forms: the Survey Form, the Expanded form, and the Classroom Edition. Each version examines behavior in four domains: Communication, Daily Living Skills, Socialization, and Motor Skills. The four domains are combined to generate an Adaptive Behavior Composite. Included in the Survey and Expanded forms is a Maladaptive Behavior Composite (Sattler, 1993).

Each domain has been designed to assess various aspects of adaptive behavior. The Communication domain measures receptive, expressive, and written skills associated with communication. The Daily Living Skills domain addresses questions associated with independent living such as personal hygiene, behavior in community settings, along with domestic skills. The Socialization domain examines the individuals interactions with others, more specifically, friendships, play, sensitivity towards others, etc. The final component is the Motor Skills domain, which focuses on fine and gross motor skills. This domain is used only for those children under the age of six years old. The Maladaptive Behavior component addresses unwanted behaviors that may interfere with the child's adaptive functioning (Sattler, 1993).

The survey and expanded forms are presented in an interview format and are typically orally administered to the individual. The survey form contains 297 items and can be administered in about 20 to 60 minutes. The expanded form contains 577 items and takes approximately 60 to 90 minutes to administer. The third form, Classroom Edition, was designed for children ages three years, 0 months to 12 years, 11 months and contains 244 items. This form is given to the teacher to complete about the child's classroom behavior. It takes approximately 20 minutes to complete (Sparrow, Balla, and Cicchetti, 1984).

Levinson (1993) explains that domain and composite scores can be transformed to standard scores, percentile ranks, age equivalents, and adaptive levels. The survey and expanded forms had a population sample of 3,000 individuals with ages ranging from newborn to 18 years, 11 months. The sample was stratified based on sex, race or ethnic group, geographical region, community size, and parents' educational level. The Classroom Edition had a representative sample of 2,984 individuals from ages 3 years, 0 months to 12 years, 11 months. This sample was stratified based on the same variables as the interview editions.

Reliability and validity of the Vineland Adaptive Behavior Scales are at least adequate. Split-half reliabilities range from .83 to .94. Test retest reliability coefficients fell between .80 and .90. Interrater reliability was measured to be between .96 and .99. Levinson (1993) cited Salvia and

Ysseldyke and noted that the test was adequately normed and appears to have adequate validity. This instrument appears to be a useful tool for the assessment of adaptive behavior (Sattler, 1993).

AAMD Adaptive Behavior Scale for Children and Adults

The AAMD Adaptive Behavior Scale for Children and Adults is an individually administered instrument used to assess "personal independence in daily living." The scale is administered to an informant who is familiar with the individual being evaluated. The scale has two parts. Part 1 evaluates behavior in 10 domains: independent functioning, physical development, economic activity, language development, numbers and time, domestic activity, vocational activity, self-direction, responsibility, and socialization. Part 2 addresses 14 domains including violent and destructive behavior, antisocial behavior, rebellious behavior, untrustworthy behavior, withdrawal, stereotyped behavior and odd mannerisms, inappropriate interpersonal manners, unacceptable vocal habits, unacceptable or eccentric habits, self-abusive behavior, hyperactive tendencies, sexually aberrant behavior, psychological disturbance, and use of medication.

The AAMD Adaptive Behavior Scale for Children and Adults converts raw scores into deciles. High deciles in Part 1 indicate the presence of more adaptive behavior, unlike Part 2, where a high decile score indicates less adaptive behavior. This instrument is reportedly designed for use with persons with a variety of disabilities, however, normative data for the instrument is based only on a sample of an institutionalized population of mentally retarded individuals. Interrater reliability was reported as ranging from .71 to .93 for Part 1 and .37 to .77 for Part 2. Questions have been raised about this instrument's content validity and standardization procedures. Also, this test now possesses outdated norms, and has no evidence of internal consistency or stability. Therefore, this test should probably not be used as a norm-referenced device (Levinson, 1993).

Scales of Independent Behavior-Revised (SIB-R)

The Scales of Independent Behavior Revised is a comprehensive measure of adaptive and problem behaviors, and was primarily designed to "measure functional independence and adaptive functioning in school, home, employment, and community settings (Bruininks, Woodcock, Weatherman, & Hill, 1996). The SIB-R is similar to its predecessor, the Scales of Independent Behavior (SIB). The SIB-R is an individually administered instrument that gathers information from an examinee's parents or caregivers. The SIB-R is used to plan education and training activities and to monitor support programs to enhance an individual's adaptive functioning. The instrument was designed for use in individual evaluation, program planning, selection and placement, and to assess students needs. However, it can be used in a variety of other roles including guidance, research, appraising skill gains, program evaluation and management, and psychometric training.

The SIB-R is appropriate for individuals between three months and 80+ years of age. The scales can be administered either by the structured interview format, which was used by the previous SIB, or by using the checklist procedure that is new to the SIB-R. The checklist procedure is recommended for when respondents assess several individuals, when the respondent is knowledgeable, or when the interview is not convenient or too time-consuming. There are no special qualifications needed to administer or score this instrument, however, a higher level of competency is needed to interpret and use the results.

The scale measures two broad constructs: the Adaptive Full Scale and the Problem Behavior Scale. The Adaptive Behavior items assess the extent to which an individual can perform a task. The Problem Behavior categories address the frequency and severity of problem behavior.

The SIB-R has three forms: The Full Scale, the Short Form Screening, and the Early Development Scale. The Full Scale assesses a comprehensive list of behaviors including gross-motor skills, fine-motor skills, social interaction, language comprehension, language expression, eating and meal preparation, toileting, dressing, personal self-care, domestic skills, time and punctuality, money and value, work skills, and home-community orientation (from the adaptive composite). The Problem Behavior Scale measures hurtful to self, unusual or repetitive habits, withdrawal or inattentive behavior, socially offensive behavior, uncooperative behavior, hurtful to others, destructive to property, and disruptive behavior. The Short Form is appropriate for individuals at any developmental level and requires 15 to 20 minutes to complete. On the other hand, the Early Development Form is used for young children and for individuals with developmental functioning levels below eight years of age. It also takes approximately 15 to 20 minutes to complete.

Those who have used the Woodcock-Johnson Psychoeducational Battery will be familiar with the scoring system of the SIB-R. Raw scores are used in calculating Relative Mastery Indexes, standard scores, percentile ranks, and adaptive behavior skills levels. The SIB-R requires the calculation of difference scores, which are used to compute standard scores. Scoring the instrument by hand may lead to computational errors, therefore, a computer-scoring program is available. The SIB-R can also be used in conjunction with the Woodcock-Johnson Psychoeducational Battery, as they include some of the same standardization sample. This provides for a comprehensive profile of an individual's current functioning in a variety of areas.

The SIB-R was standardized on 2,182 individuals in 15 states and more than 60 communities throughout the United States. The sample ranged in age from three months to 90 years and stratification variables were used to ensure a representative sample of the United States population. For adaptive behavior, split-half reliability coefficients ranged from .88 to .98 for the four cluster and full scale scores. Individual subscales ranged from .70 to .88. When examining children with mental retardation, split-half reliabilities were in the .90s. Test-retest reliabilities for children without disabilities ranged from .83 to .97 for the 14 subscales and .97 to .97 for the clusters. The problem behavior indexes were in the low .80s. In looking at interrater reliabilities, studies indicated that similarities were reported between independent examiners (Maccow, & Zlomke, 1999).

The San Francisco Vocational Competency Scale

The San Francisco Vocational Competency Scale is an individually administered instrument that is completed by an informant that is familiar with the person being assessed. The scale was developed to measure vocational competency in mentally retarded individuals in sheltered workshop settings. The scale measures four areas: motor skills, cognition, responsibility, and social-emotional behavior. The scale has 30 items, and yields a vocational competency score. The total score can then be converted into percentiles.

The standardization sample consisted of 562 mentally retarded individuals from various workshops around the country. Internal consistency reliability coefficients were reported to be .95, while test-retest coefficients were reported as being .85. Unfortunately, no validity information is reported in the manual. One researcher suggested that the San Francisco Competency Scale has value in working with mentally retarded individuals who may be entering placement in a work setting. The scale may also be beneficial for assisting in program evaluations and in instructional planning (Levinson, 1993).

Vocational Adaptation Rating Scale (VARS)

The Vocational Adaptation Rating Scale measures maladaptive behavior in severely, moderately, and mildly retarded workers in vocational settings. Specifically, the scale addresses maladaptive behaviors that may interfere with employment. The scale was designed for employment supervisors or vocational education teachers. The VARS is 133-item scale that focuses on six domains: verbal manners, communication skills, attendance and punctuality, interpersonal behavior, respect for property, rules and regulation, and grooming and personal hygiene. The VARS yields two scores, a frequency score and a severity score. Internal consistency reliabilities fell between .86 and .93. Interrater reliability coefficients ranged from .40 to .72. Concurrent validity has been assessed by comparing the Adaptive Behavior Scale and the San Francisco Competency Scale (Levinson, 1993).

Living Skills

Developmental Assessment of Life Experiences (D.A.L.E.)

The Developmental Assessment of Life Experiences is a criterion-referenced instrument designed to assess home living and community skills in individuals with disabilities, including severely disabled persons. The D.A.L.E. can be used in a variety of settings including public schools, small community residences, and larger residential facilities. The system was designed for use in prioritizing goals and objectives and for developing individualized programs. The system is appropriate for school-aged to adult individuals, but is most applicable for older school-aged students and adults. Minimal training is required to administer the D.A.L.E., however, it is suggested that examiners go through some formal training prior to administering the test.

The D.A.L.E. system includes two separate inventories that address a wide range of self-care and community living skills. Level I was designed for individuals with severe disabilities. This inventory included the following areas: sensory motor, language, self-help, cognition skills, and socialization. The Level II system was designed for higher functioning individuals and includes subscales in personal hygiene, personal management, communication, residence-home maintenance, and community access. One criticism of the system is that it is too general and does not apply to specific settings and specific skills that are necessary to complete daily living tasks (Block, Bunker, & Jones, 1990).

The D.A.L.E. system utilized formal observations and reports from care providers to measure functional living skills. D.A.L.E. does not use standardization procedures, but presents a systematic approach to observation, assessment, and program planning through the use of qualitative and quantitative components. Since qualitative data is collected, reliability may be affected. There was no evidence of reliability in the manual. For looking at quantitative data, a graphing system can be used to chart progress. Despite the lack of psychometric information, it was reported that the D.A.L.E. System can be a useful instrument for special education teachers working with students being transitioned into the community as well as direct care workers working with young adults (Block, Bunker, & Jones, 1990).

The Checklist of Adaptive Living Skills (CALS)

The Checklist of Adaptive Living Skills is a criterion-referenced instrument that measures approximately 800 specific adaptive behaviors. Areas that are addressed include behaviors related to self-care, personal independence, and adaptive functioning in leisure, work, community, and residential environments. The CALS is independently administered and was designed for use with a wide range of individuals with or without disabilities. The CALS is appropriate for infants to adults in a variety of settings, such as educational, residential, day care, rehabilitation, work activity, employment training, and other human service settings (Morreau & Bruininks, 1991).

The CALS is organized in four broad domains: Personal living skills, home living skills, community living skills, and employment skills. These broad domains are comprised of subcategories that focus on 24 specific skill modules: Socialization, eating, grooming, toileting, dressing, health care, sexuality, clothing care, meal planning and preparation, home cleaning and organization, home leisure, social interaction, mobility and travel, time management, money management and shopping, community safety, community leisure, community participation, job search, job performance and attitudes, employee relations, and job safety.

An appropriate instrument for program planning, the CALS may be used to determine the specific skills an individual has mastered or needs to master in various environments. The CALS also may be used to determine instructional needs, develop individualized training objectives, and monitor the progress of individuals toward achieving instructional goals.

Since the CALS does not yield normative scores, formal training is not required for completion. Administration involves collecting responses to individual items from a respondent who knows the assessee well. The respondent is asked to mark the items that the individual can perform independently. For an item to be scored, the individual must be able to perform the task independently with good quality, at least 75 percent of the time, when needed, and without being asked or reminded. Respondents who are familiar with the instrument can complete the entire CALS in about 60 minutes. Those who are qualified to complete the CALS are parents, caregivers, rehabilitation counselors, teachers, instructional assistants, and other direct-service personnel who have had the opportunity to observe the learner in natural environments for a period of three or more months.

The CALS was field tested on 627 individuals nationally. The instrument was given to individuals ranging in age from infancy to over 40 years of age. The sample was comprised of approximately 50 percent of persons with disabilities. The remaining population was made up of individuals without disabilities. Internal consistency reliability appears to be high with coefficients ranging from .74 to .99 for persons without disabilities, and .79 to .97 for students with disabilities. Spit-half reliability coefficients ranged from .67 to .96. for individuals without disabilities and .65 to .95 for individuals with disabilities. Bachelor and Van Haneghan (1991) reported that test authors relied heavily on prior research to establish an accepted conceptualization of adaptive living skills from which test items were constructed, revised, and refined. Researchers in the field judged the skills assessed by the CALS to be important for successful living in the home, community, and employment settings and supported claims of content validity. Based on the information available on the CALS, it appears to be a sound psychometric instrument and is appropriate as a descriptive measure of adaptive living skills.

Informal Measures

Clark, Patton, and Moulton (1994) note that the intent of transition assessment is to gather information in an organized fashion that will aid in the development of appropriate transition plans. In order to serve students with disabilities well, transition assessment should be comprehensive and responsive to students' interests and preferences. Life skills functioning may also be assessed through the use of informal instruments. Although these instruments are not based on norms, they can be used to assess more specific behaviors in depth. When looking at life skills, there are many sub-domains to assess. Informal measures may aid in pinpointing specific strengths and weaknesses in particular domains. One publication, *Informal Assessments for Transition Planning* is a compilation of many short checklists and interviews focusing on specific areas important to transition assessment. When assessing life skills, the following informal instruments may be useful in transition planning and may be reprinted with permission from the authors: (Daily Living)–Independent Living Assessment Instrument, Parents of Teenagers Survival Checklist, Assessment of Financial Skills and Abilities, Transportation Needs, Leisure Activities–Survey of Indoor and Outdoor Recreational Activities, Recreation and Leisure Survey, (Community Participation)–Community Assessment, (Interpersonal Relationships)- School and Community Social Skills Rating Checklist, and Let's Look At Interpersonal Relationships.

SUMMARY

This chapter discussed the various aspects of life skills assessment. Specifically, the various domains of life skills, historical as well as current

Table 7.1. Career Education and Life Skills Education Models.

Source	Major Components
Life-Centered Career Education (Brolin, 1991)	Three Major Areas: *Daily Living *Personal/Social *Occupational guidance and preparation
School-Based Career Development and Transition Education Model (Clark & Kristoe, 1990)	Four Major Areas: *Values, attitudes, and habits *Human Relationships *Occupational information *Acquisition of job and daily living skills
Hawaii Transition Project (1997)	Four Major Areas: *Vocation/education *Home and family *Recreation/leisure *Community/citizenship
Community-Referenced Curriculum (Smith & Schloss, 1988)	Five Major Areas: *Work *Leisure *Consumer *Education and Rehabilitation *Transportation
Community Living Skills Taxonomy (Denver, 1988)	Five Major Areas: *Personal Maintenance and development *Homemaking and community life *Leisure *Vocational *Travel

Sitlington, P. L. (1996)

perspectives of life skills assessment, and best practices in assessment were addressed. The chapter concluded with a brief review of popular instruments used in transition planning today. Four domains of life skills include maintaining a home, community involvement, social/interpersonal skills, and leisure skill. Life skills assessment has evolved considerably over time. It has moved from a perspective that centered on those individuals who had no opportunity to further their education or enter the work force to being a focal point to preparing disabled as well as non-disabled students for success in postsecondary education or a vocational setting. Key points identified in best practices of assessing life skills include: giving consideration to why we assess life skills, how we assess life skills, and the goals included in the evaluation process. Although life

Table 7.2. Table of Test Summaries

Title: Publisher	Age	Features	Reading Level	Admin. Time	Validity	Reliability
Vineland Adaptive Behavior Scales (Survey Form): American Guidance Service (AGS)	Birth to 18–11	Assesses personal and social adaptability of individuals; 4 Domains: communication, daily living skills, socialization, motor skills	Interview format	20 to 60 minutes	Adequate	Adequate
Vineland Adaptive Behavior Scales (Expanded Form): American Guidance Service(AGS)	Birth to 18–11	Assesses personal and social adaptability of individuals; 4 Domains: communication, daily living skills, socialization, motor skills	Interview format	60 to 90 minutes	Adequate	Adequate
Vineland Adaptive Behavior Scales (Classroom Edition): American Guidance Service (AGS)	3-0 to 12-11	Assesses personal and social adaptability of individuals; 4 Domains: communication, daily living skills, socialization, motor skills	Completed by classroom teacher	20 minutes	Adequate	Adequate
AAMD Adaptive Behavior Scale	N/A	Assesses "personal independence in daily living"; 2 domains: measures adaptive and maladaptive behavior	N/A	N/A	Questionable	Questionable
Scales of Independent Behavior-Revised (SIB-R) Comprehensive Form: Riverside Publishing	3 months to 80+	Designed to measure functional independence in school, home, employment, and community settings; uses 2 broad constructs: Adaptive Behavior Full Scale and Problem Behavior Scale; May be used in conjunction with the WJ Psychoeducational Battery	Interview format	60 minutes	Adequate	Adequate

Scales of Independent Behavior-Revised (SIB-R) Short Form: Riverside Publishing	3-0 to 80+	Designed to measure functional independence in school, home, employment, and community settings; uses 2 broad constructs: Adaptive Behavior Full Scale and Problem Behavior Scale; May be used in conjunction with the WJ Psychoeducational Battery	Interview format	15 to 20 minutes	Adequate	Adequate
Scales of Independent Behavior-Revised (SIB-R) Early Development Form: Riverside Publishing	Dev. Level up to 8 years of age	Designed to measure functional independence in school, home, employment, and community settings; uses 2 broad constructs: Adaptive Behavior Full Scale and Problem Behavior Scale; May be used in conjunction with the WJ Psychoeducational Battery	Interview format	15 to 20 minutes	Adequate	Adequate
San Francisco Vocational Competency Scale	Adults	Developed for mentally retarded adults in sheltered workshop settings; 4 areas assessed: motor skills, cognition, responsibility, social-emotional behavior	N/A	N/A	Adequate	No evidence in manual
Vocational Adaptation Rating Scale	N/A	Looks at maladaptive behavior that may jeopardize the employment status of mentally retarded individuals in a vocational setting	N/A	N/A	Adequate	Adequate

Table 7.2. (Continued)

Title: Publisher	Age	Features	Reading Level	Admin. Time	Validity	Reliability
Developmental Assessment of Life Experiences (DALE): The Barber Center Press Inc.	School-aged to adult-hood	Designed to assess motor, intellectual, and adaptive skills of disabled persons; 2 levels: level 1 scales are for those with severe disabilities, Level 2 scales are for higher functioning individuals	N/A	N/A	Not reported	Not reported
Checklist of Adaptive Living Skills (CALS): Riverside Publishing Company	Infants to Adults	Measures adaptive living skills in personal independence, self-care, adaptive functioning in work, leisure, community, residential environments; appropriate for individuals with or without disabilities	N/A	N/A	Adequate	Adequate

skills assessment has evolved considerably over the years, educators are encouraged to begin transition planning early and ensure that the process of identifying strengths and weakness is ongoing.

REFERENCES

Bachelor, P. & Van Haneghan, J. (1991). Checklist of adaptive living skills. *12 Mental measurements yearbook.* Burrows Institute of Mental Measurements, University of Nebraska.

Block, M., Bunker, L. & Jones, E. (1990). *Developmental test of life experiences. 12 Mental measurements yearbook.* Burrows Institute of Mental Measurements, University of Nebraska.

Bruininks, R., Woodcock, R., Weatherman, R. R. & Hill, B. (1996). *Scales of independent behavior revised: Comprehensive manual.* Itasca, Il: Riverside Publishing Company.

Clark, G. M. & Kolstoe, O. P. (1995). *Career development and transition education of adolescents with disabilities,* 2nd ed. Needham Heights, MA: Allyn and Bacon.

Clark, G. M., Patton, J. R., & Moulton, R. L. (2000). *Informal assessment for transition planning.* Austin, TX: Pro-ed.

Harrison, P. L. (1991). Assessment of adaptive behavior. In B. A. Bracken (Ed.), *The psychoeducational assessment of preschool children,* 2nd ed. (pp. 168–186). Boston: Allyn and Bacon.

Levinson, E. M. (1993). *Transdisciplinary vocational assessment: Issues in school-based programs.* Brandon, VT: Clinical Psychology Publishing.

Levinson, E. M. (1998). *Transition: Facilitating the postschool adjustment of students with disabilities.* Boulder, Colorado: Westview Press.

Maccow, G. & Zlomke, L. (1999). Scales of independent behavior-revised. *14 Mental measurements yearbook.* Burrows Institute of Mental Measurements, University of Nebraska.

Morreau, L. & Bruininks, R. (1991). *Checklist of adaptive living skills manual.* Itasca, Il: Riverside Publishing Company.

Nolan, K. A., Wolf, M., Ansell, D., Burns, J., Barr, L., Copeland, W., and Paddock, G. (2000). Ready or not: Assessing youths' preparedness for independent living. *Child Welfare, 79* (2), 156–176.

Patton, J. R., & Blalock, G. (Eds.). (1994). *Transition and students with learning disabilities: Facilitating the movement from school to an adult life.* Austin, TX: Pro-ed.

Sattler, J. (1993). Vineland adaptive behavior scales. *10 Mental measurements yearbook.* Lincoln, Ne: Burrows Institute of Mental Measurements, University of Nebraska.

Sattler, J. M. (1988). *Assessment of children,* 3rd ed. San Diego: Author

Sitlington, P. L. (1996). Transition to living: The neglected component of transition programming for individuals with learning disabilities. *Journal of Learning Disabilities, 29*(1), 31–41.

Sparrow, S. Balla, D. & Cicchetti, D. (1984). *Interview edition survey form manual: Vineland adaptive behavior scales.* Circle Pines, MN: American Guidance Service.

Chapter 8

ISSUES IN TRANSITION FROM SCHOOL TO POSTSECONDARY EDUCATION: FOCUS ON STUDENTS WITH LEARNING DISABILITIES

JENNIFER J. SMITH AND KRISTEN YOUNG

INTRODUCTION: ISSUES IN TRANSITION FROM SCHOOL TO POSTSECONDARY EDUCATION

The transition from high school to postsecondary education settings can be an exciting time for young adults. But along with that excitement can be a fear of the unknown and frustration with the challenges related to new and greater responsibilities. Imagine then the mix of emotions that a student with a learning disability may feel, along with the greater challenges he/she might face when approaching graduation and considering postsecondary education options after high school. A student with a learning disability may not have many of the prerequisite academic skills or personal care skills that typical students without disabilities have mastered upon graduation. This puts them at a greater disadvantage than their non-disabled peers when considering postsecondary education options.

In this chapter we will discuss the need for transition services for students with learning disabilities considering attending postsecondary education programs. The reader will find that there are many misconceptions about students with learning disabilities and oftentimes broader need areas for these students. In addition, we will review assessment factors and issues related to preparation for transition planning. Finally, we will present some guidelines for transition planning with students with learning disabilities that are considering postsecondary education options, beginning before high school and continuing on throughout high school until graduation.

The Need for Transition Services for Students Attending Postsecondary Education

Relevant Legislation

There are two primary pieces of federal legislation that affect the rights of students with disabilities and their ability to access and participate in educational programs. The Individuals with Disabilities Education Act (IDEA) and the Vocational Rehabilitation Act of 1973, Section 504 offer guarantees of protection from discrimination on the basis of a disability and confirm equal access participation rights. Both laws also utilize criteria to determine who is eligible for protection. While there are a number of similarities between IDEA and Section 504, it is the critical and practical differences in scope and goals that must be fully understood in order to effectively prepare students with disabilities for their transition from high school to postsecondary education (Scott, 1991; Vess, 2000).

IDEA is special education legislation applicable to students with disabilities while in elementary and secondary school programs. To receive protection under IDEA, students must meet eligibility requirements according to the IDEA's categorical restrictions. In addition to guaranteeing students with disabilities access to a free and appropriate education, IDEA is an affirmative action law that mandates special education and related services regardless of the cost or inconvenience to the school district. IDEA also makes provisions that ensure the effectiveness of educational efforts (Scott, 1991; Vess, 2000).

In contrast, Section 504 is civil rights legislation that applies to persons with disabilities in postsecondary education programs. In order for a person to be considered eligible under Section 504, the student must meet the admission criteria of the institution and also have a documented disability that substantially limits a major life functioning such as learning. If at any time the student is unable to maintain the institution's academic requirements, then that student is no longer eligible under Section 504. Postsecondary institutions are not legally obligated to accept or maintain students with disabilities simply because they are disabled. Students with disabilities seeking to attend postsecondary education programs must meet all of the same academic and technical standards required to perform the essential functions within a given program as are their non-disabled peers. Under Section 504, postsecondary institutions are afforded the right to protect their programs from inferior or substantially modified standards. While section 504 guarantees non-discriminatory access to postsecondary education programs to those qualified individuals, it does not provide for the types of services and programs that a student with a disability may have received in their elementary and/or secondary programs. The function of accommodations and services at the postsecondary level is to simply level the academic playing field for students with disabilities. Some common accommodations and services for students with disabilities include extended time on tests, note-takers, sign-language interpreters, and enlarged print. Programs and accommodations that are designed to enhance personal study or competency such as tutoring, personal counseling, academic progress monitoring, etc., are only offered to students with learning disabilities as they are offered to non-disabled students. Essentially, the education of a student with a disability is equivalent to the education received by a non-disabled student. There is no separate programming or standards. Finally, in order to receive services and accommodations, students with disabilities must self-disclose their disability to the institution and supply all of the necessary documentation required by the institution. The student's parents are legally no longer permitted to seek disability services for their child or receive information about their child's progress and use of accommodations. The student must access accommodations on their own (Vess, 2000).

In reviewing the fundamental differences between IDEA and Section 504, practical implications for postsecondary education transition planning emerge. Students with disabilities must be prepared to face the challenges of increased academic and technical requirements and decreased services. They must also learn to be assertive and to utilize self-advocacy skills in order to obtain the services and accommodations that they are entitled to and may critically need to be successful in the higher educational setting. To properly prepare students with disabilities for postsecondary education, public schools must provide transition programs that consider the implications of the student's change in legal status after graduating and the subsequent academic and personal skills that they will need to be successful in higher education.

Statistics in Postsecondary Education

Numerous studies have been completed on students with disabilities enrolled in postsecondary education programs. These studies have revealed some differences in the enrollment status of students with disabilities when compared with students without disabilities and in the accommodations or support services provided by public versus private institutions. These studies will be discussed in the following section.

A 1993 study found very few students with disabilities go on to postsecondary education within five years of leaving high school. When broken down into postsecondary education options, it was found that 12 percent of students with disabilities went on to attend two-year colleges, 4 percent went to four-year colleges, and 16 percent went to vocational schools (Wagner, M., Blackorby, J., Cameto, R., Hebbeler, K. & Newman, L., 1993). The reason for these very low statistics is unknown. While postsecondary education may not be a realistic option for many students with disabilities, it seems it certainly could be for students with learning disabilities.

According to the 1995-96 National Postsecondary Student Aid Study, 6 percent of undergraduate students had disabilities, with the majority (29%) of those being students with learning disabilities. Other categories of disability represented by undergraduate students included: orthopedic (23%), other health-related disabilities or impairments (21%), hearing impairments (16%), visual impairments (16%), and speech impairments (3%), (U.S. Department of Education, National Center for Education Statistics, 1999).

There appears to be some differences in the postsecondary education programs attended by students with disabilities compared to those attended by students without disabilities. According to the 1995-96 National Postsecondary Student Aid Study, students with disabilities and students without disabilities were equally likely to attend private, not-for-profit four-year institutions (14% with disabilities and 15% without). However, students with disabilities were less likely than students without disabilities to attend public four-year colleges and universities (25% for students with disabilities, compared to 32% for students without disabilities). Additionally, students with disabilities were more likely to attend public two-year institutions or vocational programs than students without disabilities (U.S. Department of Education, National Center for Education Statistics, 1999).

There were also differences found in the attendance rates of students with disabilities when compared to students without disabilities at public versus private institutions. While almost all (98%) public two-year and four-year institutions enrolled students with disabilities, only 63 percent of private four-year institutions and 47 percent of private two-year institutions enrolled students with disabilities (U.S. Department of Education, National Center for Education Statistics, 1999).

Some may argue that the differences in enrollment rates of students with disabilities at two-year versus four-year programs or public versus private institutions could be a reflection of the enrollment policies provided at these institutions. However, according to the Postsecondary Education Quick Information System (PEQUIS) survey conducted in the spring of 1998, the majority of schools (72%), public or private, two-year or four-year, accepted and enrolled students with disabilities into their programs (U.S. Department of Education, National Center for Education Statistics, 1999).

Others may argue that differences in enrollment rates of students with disabilities at postsecondary education programs is a reflection of the support services or accommodations provided at those schools. While almost all (98%) two-year and four-year postsecondary education institutions provided at least one accommodation or support service to students with disabilities, differences were found in the quantity of support services or accommodations in public versus private institutions. Public two-year and four-year institutions were more likely than private two-year and four-year institutions to provide accommodations or support services. Additionally, large and medium institutions were more likely to provide accommodations or support services than small institutions, with large institutions providing the most accommodations or support services (U.S. Department of Education, National Center for Education Statistics, 1999). This may be in large part due to the federal funding provided to public institutions for providing accommodations or special services to students with disabilities and the greater availability of funds at larger institutions.

Given these statistics, it seems highly probably that the accommodations and support services provided affects the enrollment rates of students with disabilities, as public institutions enrolled more students with disabilities than private institutions and they were also found to provide more accommodations/support services.

The types of accommodations/support services most commonly provided at the surveyed institutions and the percentage that provided them were as follows: alternative exam formats or additional time (88%), tutors to assist with ongoing coursework (77%), readers, classroom notetakers, or scribes (69%), registration assistance or priority class registration (62%), adaptive equipment (58%), textbooks on tape (55%), and course substitutions or waivers (42%) (U.S. Department of Education, National Center for Education Statistics, 1999).

The Beginning Postsecondary Students Longitudinal Study (1990-1994) was completed to determine the percentage of students with disabilities that completed their postsecondary education programs. They found that students with disabilities were equally likely as students without disabilities to earn a postsecondary credential from a two-year public institution. However, students with disabilities were more likely to receive their associate's degree (18%) than students without disabilities (7%). Also, both students with disabilities and students without disabilities that started their postsecondary education in public two-year institutions were equally likely (6%) to go on to receive their bachelor's degree (U.S. Department of Education, National Center for Education Statistics, 1999).

Of those enrolled in public four-year institutions, students without disabilities were more likely to receive their bachelor's degree (48%) than students with disabilities (33%). However, it was noted that this study only lasted five years, thus not accounting for all students who may still have been working on their degrees. This factor is important since students with disabilities often take longer than four to five years to finish their degree. Given this finding, it was found that about half of the students with disabilities beginning a postsecondary education program (53%) go on to obtain their degree or certificate. These percentages were comparable to students without disabilities, as 64 percent were found to obtain their degree or certificate (U.S. Department of Education, National Center for Education Statistics, 1999). This certainly implies then, that students with disabilities are equally capable of completing a postsecondary education program as students without disabilities.

Misconceptions About Students With Learning Disabilities

Increasingly, the focus of education for all students has been placed on long-term outcomes. Whether it is entering the work force or moving on to additional training in a postsecondary setting, the success of all students in their chosen paths is largely a reflection of the quality of their elementary and secondary school educations (Reiff & deFur, 1992). While transitioning to work or school can be a difficult period for all students, students with learning disabilities by definition have additional obstacles to overcome. Specialized planning and preparation is needed if they are to be successful after graduation. However, despite the clear link between preparation and success, many in the field of education are reluctant to consider the importance of transition planning as it pertains to students with learning disabilities (Dunn, 1996). One possible explanation as to why educators are reluctant to seriously consider and plan appropriately for the transition needs of students with learning disabilities may be due to some commonly held misconceptions. In their 1992 study, Reiff and deFur identified several pervasive myths that surround students with learning disabilities and may in part explain why appropriate transition planning for these students is often not taken seriously and has also lagged behind that of other disability groups (Dunn, 1996).

The first misconception is that students with learning disabilities often do not encounter employment difficulties. In fact, there has been much research to show that students with learning disabilities experience much higher rates of unemployment, underemployment, and part-time employment than their non-disabled peers (Reiff & deFur, 1992). A second misconception is the belief that students with learning disabilities can and do achieve basic academic competencies consistent with their non-disabled peers because both receive high school diplomas. In actuality, an estimated 27–29 percent of students with learning disabilities drop out of school with minimal academic skills and vocational training (Reiff & deFur, 1992). A third commonly held misconception is that students with learning disabilities have average to above average levels of intellectual ability and will be able to pursue higher education. Again, in their study, Reiff and deFur reported that students with disabilities have a wide range of intellectual ability. In 1993, a study by Wagner and others, 52.8 percent of learning disabled students had an IQ between 75 and 90; 13.1 percent of learning disabled students had an IQ below 75, and the mean IQ of students with learning disabilities was 87.1 (Wagner, Blackorby, Cameto, Hebbeler, & Newman, 1993). A fourth and final misconception involved the hidden nature of learning disabilities. Often because learning is not a readily observable disability there is a tendency to invalidate the seriousness of its nature. Consequently, many educators view a learning disability as only a school-related problem. This misconception often leads to the belief that comprehensive services are not necessary for students with disabilities and that these students will not need special supports to make a successful transition to adulthood. Unfortunately, the research shows that students with disabilities experience difficulties in multiple aspects of life including social and interpersonal relationships, independent functioning, and as stated earlier, employment (Reiff & deFur 1992).

Differences Between High School and College

When a student with a learning disability considers the possibility of attending college or a university, it is important to realize the differences between high school and college. First and foremost, public high school programs are mandated to provide a variety of special education services, including specially designed instruction and replacement curriculums, to students with disabilities. However, colleges or universities may provide only a handful of accommodations or special services. It is also important to note given the statistics mentioned previously that different colleges or universities may provide different accommodations or support services.

In addition to special services available, there are differences in the teaching styles, learning environments, and classroom expectations that may have a huge impact on a student's functioning in the classroom. The following information, drawn from Shaw, Brinckerhoff, and McGuire (1991) detail some of these differences. For example, the amount of time spent in classes at the high school level is typically six hours a day for 180 days of the year. In college, a student typically attends classes 12 hours per week for 28 weeks. One class in high school might last about 40 minutes, but in college it could last from one to three hours. The length of time spent in class could be an important factor for a student with a learning disability who also has difficulty attending for long periods of time.

The number of students attending one class will vary at the college level. In high school, 20–30 students may attend one class. While in college, up to 300 students could attend one class. A student with a learning disability may want to plan to sit near the front of the room, if attending a class with 300 other students. The amount of time spent studying is considered to increase greatly at the college level. Typically a high school student might study one to two hours per day, while a college student is expected to study three to four hours per day. Additionally, the college student is expected to study for classes on their own, while a high school student with a learning disability may have scheduled study times during their school day in the learning support room.

Other factors to regard when considering college are testing and grading. A high school student may have weekly tests, end of chapter tests, or frequent quizzes. This frequency of testing allows the student to monitor their progress and plan/study better the next time, if needed to improve their grade. It also requires the memorization and understanding of smaller bits of information at a time. Whereas, in college, a student may have two to four tests per semester, often encompassing four or more chapters of a textbook at a time. In addition, tests in college may be given very early in the morning (8:00 a.m. classes) and after Homecoming weekends or Spring Break. This requires the student to study and be ready very early in the morning or after a holiday weekend or long break full of socializing. Grading is also different at the college level. In high school, a student with a learning disability may be graded based on subjective information, such as improvement over the course of the year or level of effort given. In college, grades are typically dependent on performance-based mastery of course content material and most institutions require grades of a C or better. For a student with a learning disability in general education courses in high school that has typically been graded on more subjective measures, they may have difficulty maintaining C or better grades at the college level.

Teaching styles at the college level are very different from typical teaching styles in high school. In high school teachers often take attendance, they may regularly check a student's homework assignments, they usually lecture from the textbook and use the blackboard or worksheets to supplement instruction, and their goal is to transmit knowledge or facts. However, in college professors typically do not take attendance, they generally do not check homework, they may often lecture from their own notes and not the textbook, they usually require additional library research, and their goal is to challenge students to integrate information from a variety of sources. These differences in teaching styles could pose additional challenges for a student with a learning disability.

Finally, the level of freedom provided and independence required at the college level differs from what is typical at the high school level. In high school, limits are set by teachers, parents, and other adults, the school day is structured providing for free periods and extracurricular activities, school buildings are usually monitored, and the student is generally not responsible for daily living needs (shopping, laundry, money management, etc.). In college, an individual student is responsible for scheduling their day, managing their time and personal freedom, and taking care of their daily living (shopping, laundry, money management, etc.) and social needs (social activities, intramurals, sports, clubs, etc.).

All of these factors are important to take into account when considering postsecondary education options and preparing a student with a learning disability for the transition after high school. Not only are there educational factors to consider, but also social and daily living factors to consider when deciding if a student has the skills to succeed in a postsecondary educational program after high school.

Areas of Need For Students With Learning Disabilities In Postsecondary Education

While transitioning to postsecondary education can be a difficult time for all students, it can be a particularly trying time for students with learning disabilities. Many students with learning disabilities face the challenge of higher education with additional educational, personal, and emotional obstacles to overcome (Dalke & Schmitt, 1986; Gartin, Rumrill, Serebreni, 1996). Subsequently, students with learning disabilities may be less inclined to be successful in higher education and demonstrate a more significant need for transition services than their non-disabled peers.

In their "Higher Education Transition Model," Gartin, Rumrill and Serebreni (1996) identified three key domains that educators need to consider when preparing students with disabilities for their transition to postsecondary education. According to their theory, educational activities designed to remediate, build skills, and increase information in the areas of psychosocial-adjustment, academic development, and college/community orientation are necessary to make a successful postsecondary transition for the student with disabilities. The importance of these need areas in the transition process, as described by Gartin, Rumrill and Serebreni (1996), and discussed below.

As described as part of the transition model, psychosocial adjustment is the process of moving from the dependence of adolescence to the more independent life of adulthood. As a natural part of the route to independence, students must be able to make friends, establish and maintain social networks, and build adult relationships. The process of developing psychosocial adjustment in students with learning disabilities should be started early in the student's school career. To help teachers facilitate psychosocial adjustment as part of the transition plan, several guidelines have been offered. First, students with disabilities need to be able to be self-advocates. They need to be able to express personal needs, suggest options for meeting those needs, and defend their choice of coping methods. Students with disabilities also need to be able to manage frustration and learn to be assertive rather than aggressive. Direct instruction of frustration management and/or assertiveness training through role playing, may be helpful in developing alternative, more appealing behavioral choices. Another recommendation is to directly teach social skills and provide opportunities for students to discuss social situations and problem solve with peers on topics of problems of a particular concern. As students get older, they will need guidance to be able to problem solve in more adult-like scenarios and community situations. Creating mock adult situations will help students with learning disabilities to better transfer and generalize communication and social skills (Gartin, et al., 1996).

Students with disabilities need special academic preparation to be successful in postsecondary settings. Specialized academic development is needed for students with disabilities to adjust to the academic rigors of higher education. For example, students with disabilities should be provided with information on standardized college entrance exams such as the Scholastic Achievement Test (SAT), including information about test preparatory courses and how to appropriately request accommodations (if needed) for these tests. Students with disabilities need to be connected with the disability services personnel at their postsecondary institution. Disabilities service personnel are often able to provide the student with information regarding how they should request in-class accommodations in their postsecondary setting and what those accommodations might include. Students with learning disabilities will need the opportunity to routinely practice using the types of accommodations in the secondary setting that they will likely have in higher education. Also, careful assessments should be done of the student's transcripts to ensure that they are enrolled in the proper coursework necessary for admission into postsecondary institutions. Opportunities and occupational experiences should be provided to assist students with disabilities to develop appropriate career goals. As the student takes preparatory classes in line with their career choices, progress monitoring should occur to assess the appropriateness and viability of the long range career plans in relation to their demonstrated levels of proficiency (Gartin et al., 1996).

Finally, students with disabilities need to become oriented to the upcoming postsecondary setting and its surrounding community and resources. They will need to develop strategies for accessing services within the community such as how to obtain medical assistance, banking, shopping, etc. Students with disabilities should be encouraged to link with their future postsecondary settings early. They should review catalogs and brochures, visit the institution, attend orientation programs and become aware of on-site activities in which they might be interested in participating. Becoming involved in the institutions activities will provide the transitioning student the opportunity to develop a campus support network and a circle of friends that will be needed for a successful transition (Gartin et al., 1996).

Current Trends in Transition from School to Postsecondary Education

Assessment Areas

Current practice in transition assessment varies from professional to professional. Most state guidelines suggest that transition assessment utilize a variety of methods, including tests, interviews, rating scales, curriculum-based assessments, and observations. Given the broad areas of need for students with learning disabilities considering postsecondary education options, it seems evident that transition assessments must cover a variety of areas not just intellectual or academic functioning, depending on the specific needs of each student.

Clark (1996) suggests that transition assessments include evaluations in the following areas, based on the individual needs of each student: learning styles, academic achievement, intellectual functioning, adaptive behavior, aptitude, personality, social skills, prevocational/vocational skills, transition knowledge, and physical fitness and health. Previous chapters in this book have discussed in great detail the issues surrounding many of these assessment areas, including academic achievement, intellectual functioning, adaptive behavior, aptitude, personality, social skills, prevocational/vocational skills, and transition knowledge. However, in this chapter we will discuss some of the current instruments available to assess learning styles and transition knowledge.

Learning styles are important to evaluate when considering appropriate accommodations for a student with a learning disability. Several informal instruments are available to evaluate learning styles. These include: Learning Styles Inventory and Learning Styles and Strategies. In addition, an individual's learning styles could be evaluated using situational/observational methods geared at answering questions such as: Does the student prefer to learn alone or in groups? Does the student prefer visual or auditory input?

Transition knowledge is important to measure, because students anticipating postsecondary education options need to be aware of their disability, community resources, and how to advocate for themselves. The following instruments measure aspects of these areas and may help in the transition planning process: Enderlee-Severson Transition Scale, Transition Behavior Scale, Transition Planning Inventory, Quality of Life Questionnaire, and Quality of Student Life Questionnaire. Unfortunately, the psychometric properties of these instruments are not particularly good, but they can be used informally to gather information for the transition planning process. For example, the Transition Planning Inventory (TPI) has adequate reliability, but low concurrent validity and criterion-related validity. The Quality of Life Questionnaire has good internal or test-retest reliability, but questionable validity.

Reassessment Considerations for Students Facing Postsecondary Planning

According to federal law (IDEA 1997), reassessment of identified students with learning disabilities should occur every three years. In addition, transition planning needs to begin by age 14 for students with disabilities. As such, the reassessment process is an excellent way of gathering the needed information for transition planning for students with learning disabilities. In Pennsylvania, for example, the state Confidential Evaluation Report (CER) form provides headings for the inclusion of transition planning information. In addition, several school districts in the Pennsylvania area have been cited for not including transition assessments in their multidisciplinary evaluation reports. Given this information it seems not only a failure to follow state guidelines but a grand disservice to students with disabilities if transition assessment information is not included in the multidisciplinary evaluation.

Current assessment practices typically have limited involvement of the student and family. However, for students planning for postsecondary education, student and parental involvement in the reassessment process is crucial. As a result, a change in roles for most multidisciplinary team members is necessary. Beginning at age 14, the role of the student in the reassessment and transition planning process should broaden, so that they are able to take a leadership role. IDEA 1997 mandates that students must be invited to transition planning meetings or efforts must be made to include their vocational interests and preferences, if they cannot attend the meeting. In addition, it is most beneficial if the student collaborates with team members to identify needs and individualized education plan (IEP) goals and objectives. This process assists the student in developing self-advocacy skills, as well as giving the student ownership of their IEP and transition plan (Hurley, 2000).

In addition to changing student roles, the transition planning for students with learning disabilities to postsecondary educational options, will also require changes in family involvement and school personnel roles. The family's involvement is a key component to transition planning. First, because the transition process can be difficult for many families to envision, let alone plan for, they need the support of others and assistance from the school to plan for the transition. Secondly, family involvement is important because questions like "Where will the student live?", "How will the student get to school?", and "What daily living skill needs are required for the student to succeed on his/her own in a postsecondary education program?" need to be discussed and parents will most likely have the greatest input into these areas of planning.

School personnel roles will also change when planning for students with learning disabilities transitioning from high school to postsecondary education options. Previously, school personnel have typically led the meetings and provided the student and family with a plan for the student's coming school year. However, with transition planning, school personnel need to support the student's vocational exploration and the family's impending needs. Their roles shift from active directors to facilitators, supporters, and resource linkers. These role changes are important to effectively assist and empower the student and family in planning for life after high school in a postsecondary educational setting where support may bc somewhat limited.

The following suggestions have been offered to help school personnel review their reassessment procedures so that they might better plan for students transitioning from high school to postsecondary education options (Hurley, 2000). The first suggestion is to incorporate information about the reassessment procedure and IEP development into existing curriculum, to help the student understand their disability, the laws guiding special education procedures, and the purposes of reassessment and IEP planning. This information needs to be understood by students so that they may then self-advocate for themselves in a postsecondary education program.

Utilization of a *trans*disciplinary reassessment team is recommended, as opposed to a *multi*disciplinary reassessment team. The differences here being that a transdisciplinary team incorporates professionals from several different disciplines, not just from the school. Whereas a multidisciplinary team consists of team members with different areas of expertise but from the same discipline (i.e., school), a transdisciplinary team might include community agencies, college coordinators, and/or professionals from the Department of Rehabilitation Services (DRS). Utilizing all of these resources will help the team better plan for postsecondary life, because the contact persons for various linkages are present and able to determine what information is needed for planning and report on what services they will be able to provide to the student and family (i.e., what accommodations are provided at the local community college).

Oftentimes a reassessment team may determine that additional information is needed about a student to effectively plan for their transition from high school to postsecondary education options. Hurley (2000) recommends minimally including additional information needed through student and family interviews, observations, and information provided by teachers and community-based instructors, in transition planning scales that cover a broad range of transition areas. For example, interviews such as the Transition Information Planning System (TIPS) covers information on Employment, Postsecondary Education and Training, Community Participation, Recreation/Leisure, and Home Living/Daily Living. This and other structured interview formats include information from all transition areas and solicits input from the student as well as other knowledgeable team members (community-based instructors, parents, etc.).

In many cases, students do not want to attend IEP or transition planning meetings because they feel ashamed or embarrassed because the focus of the meeting is often on their weaknesses. Hurley recommends (2000) addressing the relevance of the reassessment for the student and family through a strengths-based focus and a problem-solving model to help the student and family get where they want to be.

Finally, it is recommended that school professionals meet with students separately to review reassessment results. This individual meeting will provide the student with an opportunity to ask questions that they may not feel comfortable asking in a large group. This also gives the student time to think about the information presented to them and to prepare for the IEP planning meeting, which will improve their self-advocacy skills. In addition, individual meetings communicate to students that they are mature enough to process the information on their own and that they are important members of the team. This type of individual conference may also help students feel empowered and invested in their transition planning (Hurley, 2000).

Reporting Psychological Assessments

Reevaluating students with disabilities at the end of their secondary educational careers has become a very important aspect of the transition process. Not only does it fulfill legal obligations under IDEA and assist in planning appropriate transition services, but a comprehensive reevaluation can fulfill the documentation requirements of the postsecondary institution and assist in securing needed accommodations (Vess, 2000).

When completing comprehensive reports that will be used for postsecondary program planning, it is important to consider what types of assessment information will be most useful and are required for a student to be considered eligible under Section 504. As postsecondary institutions are generally not familiar with individual student's educational histories and services, it is often helpful to provide detailed information regarding the student's background. Interpretations of test findings and classroom observations should also be included and elaborated upon (Vess, 2000).

At the postsecondary level, institutions generally only provide accommodations that are designed to alter the environment rather than change the student. Many of the services such as tutoring that are offered to students with disabilities at the secondary level are no longer specially afforded to students with disabilities at the postsecondary level. The goal of accommodations in postsecondary settings is to level the academic playing field for students with disabilities and not to provide a competitive advantage through special services and assistance. As students with disabilities must demonstrate that they are otherwise qualified to participate in every stage of their postsecondary education and must meet the standards of the institution, it is highly unlikely that accommodations such as waivers of math or foreign language requirements would be accepted. In general, there are significantly fewer accommodations provided in higher education than in high school (Vess, 2000).

It is very important to clarify the functional impact of the student's disability on the immediate educational environment as well as its predicted impact as it relates to the demands of the postsecondary setting. Additionally, the functional relationship between the student's disability and the recommended accommodation must be clearly, precisely, and specifically stated and substantiated by assessment information. At the postsecondary level, inferential statements are not acceptable (Vess, 2000).

Just as there are specific documentation requirements in elementary and secondary level reports, there are also specific requirements in documentation at the postsecondary level. In general, most postsecondary institutions require a psychological report that is current at the time of student's enrollment (e.g., less than three years old). Specific diagnostic statements should be used and based upon the criteria found in the DSM-IV. Diagnostic statements should avoid inferential words such as "appears to," "seem to," or "suggests." Alternative explanations such as poor motivation, attendance, lack of academic exposure, etc. should be ruled out as factors that might account for the student's apparent disability. Finally, reasonable recommendations directly tied to the functional limitations of the disability should be included for the postsecondary institution to consider (Vess, 2000).

Components of Effective Transitions Plans:

Transitioning students smoothly from high school to their post-graduation plans is not an easy task. Generally speaking, all of the student's three to four years of high school is needed to accumulate all of the necessary skills and requirements for matriculation into a postsecondary setting. Effective transition planning begins by determining the student's postsecondary education goals. Once the student's general goals have been established, the transition planning team should work backward to develop a transition plan that will ensure that the student's high school experiences, including instruction, practical experiences, and skill building activities are geared to properly prepare them to reach their goals. Susan Vess, Director of Disabilities Services at the University of Iowa suggests three important components of effective transition plans for students with disabilities transitioning to postsecondary settings. These components, which include catalog reviews, program exploration, and the acquisition of basic skills, are important in developing comprehensive transition plans that facilitate smooth transitions (Vess, 2000).

When developing an effective transition plan, there needs to be a direct link to the student's desired goal and the path they will be on to achieve that goal. One way to clearly link the student's goals with their preparatory transition activities is to utilize a catalog review strategy. Catalogs can be easily obtained from colleges, vocational-technical schools, and so forth. They can be used in the special education classroom to help the student identify what the basic requirements are for entrance into specific postsecondary programs. Subsequently, the catalog information can be used to guide the student's development of required skills. When reviewing catalogs, students should identify required high school courses necessary for admission. As some institutions require math and foreign language credits, it is important to discover what the requirements are so that these courses can be distributed appropriately over the student's high school years. Students with disabilities should also consider other admission requirements that they will need to meet, such as GPA, placement test scores, admission deadlines, and fees. Finally, early reviewing of the institution's catalog will give the student the opportunity to practice completing admission application forms, develop personal statements and portfolios, and practice interviewing (Vess, 2000).

Another important strategy is program exploration. Students with disabilities should work together with their transition planning team to explore various postsecondary institutions and the differences among settings. Factors such as class size, faculty to student ratios, teaching formats, campus size, etc., should be considered in relation to students needs and preferences. The students should be encouraged to think realistically about their choices. Program choices should always be based upon the student's skills, interests, and aptitudes. The benefits of each program and school should be discussed with the student to hone in on the student's preferences and self-understanding. Lastly, the students should obtain information from the institution's disability services office regarding campus services, accommodations and documentation requirements (Vess 2000).

Finally, one of the most important components of an effective transition plan is the student's acquisition of basic skills and competencies. Students with disabilities must understand that when they graduate from high school they graduate into a new legal status. While in high school they were entitled to mandated special services under IDEA, in the postsecondary setting under Section 504, they are eligible for reasonable accommodations only. For students with disabilities to be successful in postsecondary education they must have the basic skills and competencies necessary to keep up with their non-disabled peers. There are many basic skills and competencies that students with learning disabilities will need in order to be successful. For example, basic computer skills such as word processing, using a keyboard and/or voice activated software and screen readers may be a very important factor in the student's success or failure. The student should practice taking different types of exams such as short answer, essay, and multiple choice and learn effective test-taking strategies for each type of test. College level texts should be acquired so that the student with learning disabilities can learn and develop strategies for understanding ideas and concepts and learning from the way information is presented through text, charts, graphs, and so forth. Math knowledge and application skills including how to use formulas as well as different types of calculators will be needed. Written language and mechanical skills should be developed, including writing for a particular audience, organizing the paper, explaining and supporting conclusions, summary writing, and utilizing correct spelling, punctuation, and grammar. The student with disabilities should also learn to develop in and out-of-class study skills. Study skills such as taking and organizing notes, prioritizing information, relating class discussion to reading material, paying attention and attending class regularly will impact the student's ability to be successful in higher education. Well-developed study skills also assist the student in moving beyond the basic memorization of facts to understanding and applying information. Finally, students with disabilities must learn to be self-advocates. To assist them in this process of skill development, it may be helpful to have the student learn to identify their disability, practice describing its impact on learning, and requesting reasonable accommodations in an assertive but non-demeaning manner (Vess, 2000).

Transition Planning: Postsecondary Education Options

Once the student's strengths, needs, vocational interests, and vocational aptitudes are assessed, transition planning can begin. When considering postsecondary educational options it is important to know what is available. The following paragraphs detail several postsecondary educational options available after high school, as was discussed in Levinson's text, *Transition: Facilitating the Postschool Adjustment of Students with Disabilities* (1998).

Apprenticeship programs typically involve manual, technical, or mechanical skills and knowledge. For example, one might complete an apprenticeship program before becoming a carpenter, electrician's lineman, or plumber. Apprenticeships typically last from one to six years and may include a pre-job program of six to eight weeks. Typically, an apprentice works under the supervision of a worker who has experience, has learned the trade, and is usually at the next highest level of certification. This supervisor is sometimes called a journeyman. The apprentice works and earns money while learning on the job. However, at least 144 hours of related classroom instruction is usually required in addition to on-the-job training. The apprentice is usually able to earn a higher wage as they complete each level within the apprenticeship program.

The requirements for apprenticeship programs vary. Some require individuals to be at least 16 years old and others at least 18 years of age. Most require a high school diploma or general education degree (GED). Additionally, some apprenticeship programs may require individuals to pass a competency test. Given the additional classroom instruction required, most programs also require apprentices to have some reading, writing, and mathematics skills.

An apprenticeship program might be good for a student with a learning disability who has high scores in Holland's Realistic personality type or someone who learns better with hands-on activities. Also, because individuals earn money while learning, this could be a good option for a student who does not have the money to go to a trade or technical school or who needs to make a living quickly after high school.

Military training is another good way for individuals to earn money while receiving vocational training. After basic training, individuals are usually given jobs based on their performance on the Armed Services Vocational Aptitude Battery (ASVAB). While serving for the military, individuals learn the skills needed for their military job, which often provide them with the training and entry-level credentials necessary for many occupations once they leave the military. In fact, all branches of the military guarantee job training for qualified individuals.

Enrollment in the military requires a high school diploma or equivalent (GED). Individuals then must go through basic training for six to ten weeks. After basic training, vocational and military training begins. Students take classes to gain needed military and vocational experience. In most military programs, individuals sign up for the number of years they would like to serve. The minimum is usually two years, but most have the option of serving in the military for their entire careers. In addition, most military programs offer tuition assistance packages for individuals who wish to attend college after they have completed their military training.

Military training programs can be good options for students with learning disabilities who need structure in their lives or those who may need some assistance providing for personal care skills. The military is very structured and they also offer health care services, housing, and meals. However, this may not be a good program for a student with a learning disability who has difficulty with many rules and people in authority, as the military is very hierarchical and individuals must learn to take orders from various supervisors who are higher in rank. The military also has high physical demands, so an individual with a learning disability that also has health concerns may not be best suited for military training.

Trade and technical schools are another postsecondary option. They are offered in a variety of occupational areas. Most trade and technical schools are privately run and cost the individual money to attend. However, many guarantee job placements after the individual completes the training. There are over 10, 000 trade and technical schools in the United States. Students can expect to attend a trade or technical school anywhere from six months to two years. In addition, some trade and technical schools offer their training as part of degree programs that are approved by state departments of education. These training programs are usually similar to other programs offered by community colleges.

Trade and technical schools would be a good option for a student with a learning disability that does not want to be in school for a long time, learns best with a hands-on approach, and has a specific vocational interest. For example, a student could attend a program in computer repair, graphic design, cosmetology, nurses assistant, or electronics repair. This would probably not be a very good option for a student without a specific vocational interest. They would need further career exploration and vocational experiences to narrow their interests before deciding upon a trade or technical school.

Community colleges or junior colleges are two-year institutions that provide vocational training, associate's degrees, or two years of college education that can be applied toward a bachelor's degree at a four-year institution. The admissions requirements of community colleges are typically not as stringent as most four-year programs. At the very least, they require a high school diploma or GED. In addition, most two-year programs offer support services for students with disabilities or other students in need.

A two-year college might be a good option for a student with a learning disability who might not have the qualifications for a four-year college or university, but wants to eventually go on to get their bachelor's degree, or for someone who wants the vocational training or associate's degrees offered. Additional benefits of community colleges are that the student can take classes while living at home so they have the support of their family and do not have the burden of taking care of their personal care needs. In addition, community colleges typically have smaller class sizes than four-year colleges or universities.

Four-year colleges or universities provide extended education to allow students to achieve bachelor's degrees and prepare a student for professional occupations (teacher, nurse, or engineer). Admissions requirements for four-year colleges or universities vary, but most require a high school transcript and standardized college admissions test scores (SAT's or ACT's). Some may require extensive written essays as part of the application procedure and others may require a personal interview. Application to a four-year college or university takes time and usually needs to be submitted well in advance. In addition, most four-year colleges and universities provide accommodations and support services for students with disabilities.

Students with learning disabilities who have received satisfactory grades in general education core courses (Algebra/Geometry or English) might want to consider applying to a four-year college or university. Because of the aforementioned differences between high school and college, a student with a learning disability should consider all of the previously discussed factors when contemplating application to a four-year program. If a student is hesitant, they may also want to consider attending a two-year program before transferring to a four-year program.

Special Considerations in Transition Planning

When preparing transition plans for students with disabilities, many factors should be considered. In the 1996 book, *Transition and Students with Learning Disabilities: Facilitating the Movement from School to Adult Life,* Caroline Dunn identified some of these important and helpful aspects and provided recommendations for transition teams to consider. A brief description of some of the special considerations identified by Dunn (1996) have been adapted and are reported below, including recommendations to transition teams.

When developing a transition plan for a student with a disability, it important to ensure that the plan is individualized to that particular student. Transition plans should always be focused on the individual's needs, interests, preferences, and aptitudes, not their disability label. Comprehensive data should be collected about the individual student and supported from a variety of sources to serve as a coordination tool in the student's transition plan.

Provisions for vocational preparation activities should be included as part of the transition plan. Vocational preparation includes comprehensive career and vocational assessments, counseling and training. Career and vocational assessment can be used to identify academic, interpersonal and vocational skills and employment interests. Vocational counseling can be helpful to help students with disabilities choose careers for which they are well suited. Vocational training can help students with disabilities develop appropriate work habits.

Job seeking and/or placement programs can be instrumental in facilitating a smooth transition for students with disabilities. Such programs typically include practical tasks and activities. For example, some job seeking/placement program curriculums teach resume writing, how to locate jobs through local resources, filling out applications, practicing job interviews, and strategies for contacting personnel/potential employers.

Academic remediation and support is another important aspect to consider when developing the transition plan. Students with disabilities are often tracked into lower level mainstream classes or take classes in a resource room where they fail to receive training and experiences that would prepare them for postsecondary level work. Students with disabilities who plan to enroll in higher education programs must have adequate skills, competencies, and exposure to academic material in order to be successful at the postsecondary level. Students with disabilities must have the opportunity to experience the nature of college demands and have access to content and critical concepts for college success.

Students with disabilities should learn to understand their disability. Developing an understanding of their disability empowers the student in social, familial, academic, and vocational situations. Understanding their disability places them in a better position to assist in selecting appropriate goals and advocating for themselves. Students who fail to develop an understanding of their disability often lack self-acceptance and/or are unable to communicate needs and abilities to others.

Self-determination activities are another important aspect to consider. Students with learning disabilities need to learn to make choices, set goals regarding their lives, and initiate actions to achieve goals. Students also need to participate in decision-making activities.

Transition teams should also consider the psychosocial issues associated with the student's disability. Students with disabilities often need help to develop self-esteem, feelings of competence, adequacy, motivation, and persistence as well as self-advocacy, communication, and group working skills. Psychosocial development can be accomplished through counseling and/or self-help groups.

Finally, students with disabilities need to develop general problem-solving skills/strategies. Weak skills can affect personal, social, and vocational aspects of life. Even the best curriculum cannot prepare students for every possible situation. Helping students with disabilities developing problem-solving strategies to handle new and challenging situations can empower them to face adult life (Dunn, 1996).

Future Directions in Transition from School to Postsecondary Education

Suggested Activities for Transition Planning Beginning Before High School and Continuing On Throughout High School

The National Joint Committee on Learning Disabilities (NJCLD; 1994) reported that many students with learning disabilities may not be considering postsecondary education options because they are not adequately prepared in high school and because of low self-esteem and feelings of failure toward school. However, the NJCLD feels that many students with learning disabilities are very capable of being successful in postsecondary education programs. They just need adequate transition planning to be successful. As such, Brinkerhoff (1996) recommends transition teams and students plan for postsecondary education by following plan, beginning prior to high school and continuing on during each year of high school until graduation. His recommendations are detailed below.

Beginning before a student with a learning disability begins High School, transition planning should begin. This allows the student with the learning disability to transition better from the middle school/junior high school level to the senior high school level and prepares the student early, so that transition planning will be more successful. At this point, students considering postsecondary education options need to focus on taking as many general education courses as possible. This will better prepare them for postsecondary settings after high school. In addition, if they haven't already received this type of instruction, the student should be taught study skills, time management skills, and test preparation and test-taking skills. Aune (1991) found only 15 percent of students with learning disabilities were taught any type of study strategy in the last year. These skills are what the student needs to be successful in general education courses and in postsecondary education settings. At this point, Brinkerhoff (1996) also recommends that students with learning disabilities begin to actively participate in their IEP meetings. This is important so that they begin to understand the process and can become invested in their transition plans. Lastly, the middle school student or eighth grader should be provided with career exploration activities to broaden their knowledge of the world of work and to help them further define their vocational interests. This could occur through visits to work sites, volunteer experiences, or "shadowing" where the student follows a worker around for part of their work day.

Once the student is a freshman, the focus of transition planning should be on: (1) developing an understanding of what learning disabilities, in general are; (2) develop an understanding of the specifics of their own learning disability as well as an understanding of their strengths; (3) develop an understanding of their rights under the law; (4) choose classes that will best prepare them for their postsecondary education choices; (5) develop greater career awareness through an understanding of how to make decisions, knowledge of how and where to get information needed for career planning, and knowledge of specific information about a variety of occupations; and (6) develop greater dependence by taking a summer job and playing a leadership role in the transition planning meetings (Cowen, 1993). These activities are geared toward helping the student to develop greater career maturity and self-determination skills which are crucial to success in postsecondary education settings and the world of work.

As the student begins their sophomore year they should understand their disability, their limitations, and their strengths. This will help them in identifying realistic vocational interests centered around their strengths, while taking into account their weaknesses. With a better understanding of their disability, the student should begin to develop their own transition planning goals and "try out" possible accommodations or technological aids, as appropriate. School officials need to encourage greater participation from students in the transition-planning process to develop their self-determination skills and empower the student. In addition, any study skills or learning strategies that the student still has difficulty with should be included in their transition plans. Finally, the sophomore student needs to continue with career exploration. At this point the student may want to take the Self-Directed Search (SDS) to categorize their interests and aptitudes and match their 3-letter personality code to possible vocational interests. Holland's Dictionary of Occupational Titles provides a list of occupations that match the 3-letter code generated from the SDS. Using this resource, students can determine what type of postsecondary education is required for occupations consistent with their vocational interests (Brinckerhoff, 1996).

For sophomores considering college, Brinkerhoff (1996) suggests that they begin to take college preparatory courses. If capable of doing this on their own they should, otherwise they are encouraged to take college preparatory courses with accommodations or support from their learning support teacher. The sophomore learning disabled student considering college should also prepare to take the PSAT's ,a preparation for the Scholastic Assessment Test I (SAT), or the Admissions College Test (ACT) in that these exams are usually required for college acceptance. They should talk to their guidance counselor or teacher about this and consider taking the exam with accommodations, if necessary. Lastly, the sophomore preparing for college should explore postsecondary education options and begin to prepare for the differences between college and high school. To accomplish this, students should review college catalogs, review sample college textbooks, review college course syllabi, and interview college students with learning disabilities. To assist students, school professionals should provide direct instruction in accessing student support services and build transition skill training into the curriculum (DuChossis & Michaels, 1994).

The junior year is considered the most important year for transition planning (Brinkerhoff, 1996). Juniors should evaluate the postsecondary education programs available and consider which option is best suited for them, taking into consideration their vocational interests, their academic strengths and weaknesses, and their transition planning needs. Students may need to be instructed on how to research postsecondary programs through catalogs and computer searches. Two possible resources for postsecondary searches include *Postsecondary Decision-making for Students with Learning Disabilities* (Vogel, 1993) and *Choosing the Right College* (DuChossis & Stein, 1993). In addition, students and parents may wish to call the HEATH Resource Center in Washington, DC (1-800-54-HEATH) to obtain up-to-date information and publications on disability issues in higher education.

Next, the student should evaluate the support services/accommodations provided at postsecondary educational programs they are considering. For students planning to attend college, *Peterson's Colleges with Programs for Students with Learning Disabilities* (Mangrum & Strichart, 1995) may be helpful. After considering these options, the student should narrow their search to just a few programs/institutions. In addition, they should schedule visits to the desired schools or plan to meet with their local union, apprenticeship program, or military recruiting office to inquire about their programs.

Juniors will next want to begin to develop a portfolio of their work or a "personal transition file" (Vogel, 1993). This portfolio should include medical records, a high school transcript, IEP's, resumes, samples of academic work, the student's most recent psychological report detailing their disability and necessary accommodations, PSAT or SAT scores, letters of recommendation, and other significant pieces of written work (autobiographies, reports, short stories, etc.).

The junior with a learning disability that is planning on attending college will also need to prepare for the SAT or ACT exam. Guidance counselors can assist students with learning disabilities in registering for the exam and determining what accommodations might be appropriate for the student. In addition, the student should review their PSAT for areas of strength and weakness, so they can better prepare for the SAT or ACT. Students who take the exam with accommodations should be advised that the schools they have their test scores sent to will be informed that the exam was taken with accommodations. In addition, the student planning to attend college may want to prepare for a college interview, if required for their prospective schools. School personnel should assist the student with their preparation for the interview by providing a demonstration, giving suggestions, and setting up a "mock interview" (Brinkerhoff, 1996).

The senior student will want to register with the Department of Rehabilitation Services (DRS) to determine if they are eligible for services. Through the DRS, the student may be eligible to enroll in internships or job shadowing experiences that provide hands-on training in their desired vocational area. If appropriate, the senior-level student should also contact their local union, apprenticeship program, or military recruiting office or begin the application to a trade or technical school. Most apprenticeship programs and the military will require that the student pass a test before entering the program. Hence, the student should inquire about the content of the test, register to take the test, and study for the test, if appropriate. Once the student obtains their test results, they should begin planning accordingly (Brinkerhoff, 1996).

Finally, activities for the senior planning to attend college will include a final narrowed search of possible programs or institutions to attend. It is recommended that students apply to a few "safe bets," several realistic options, and a few "long shots." Students would be wise to set up a timeline to assure that they get their information in on time and then turn in their applications three weeks in advance to their guidance counselor so that they can check their information. Several time-saving options are available for filling out college applications. The student may use The Common Application Form that is accepted by more than 120 colleges, apply online, or use the College Link program for a fee. Next the student will want to choose individuals to write letters of recommendation, apply for financial aid, and retake the SAT or ACT–if needed. Some students may wish to write a cover letter to their school detailing their disability, but this is not required. Other students may discuss their disability in their college essays. Either way this could be a good way for the student to self-advocate for themselves and demonstrate their writing skills (Brinkerhoff, 1996).

Once the student receives information from the schools they applied to, they will need to decide where to attend. If they did not get in to the school of their choice, they may want to appeal the decision, especially if information related to their disability was not considered. Otherwise, the student may consider less competitive colleges, attend a Learning Disabilities preparatory school, or enroll in a community college or two-year school. The student may also benefit from taking a college course for credit over the summer at a community college to add to their transition portfolio or attend a Summer Transition Program, offered for new students at some colleges (Brinkerhoff, 1996).

SUMMARY

In this chapter, we discussed various issues surrounding students with learning disabilities and their transition from high school to postsecondary education options. Our focus has been primarily on students with learning disabilities because it is the most commonly diagnosed disability in high school, the most common disability in postsecondary education programs, and is the disability category that has been the subject of much of the transition research.

In the first section of this chapter, we focused primarily on the need for transition services for students who are planning to attend postsecondary education programs. Laws that require transition planning for students with disabilities were summarized, statistics of students in postsecondary education programs and the services provided in those facilities was reviewed, the myths surrounding students with learning disabilities were presented, the differences between high school and college were addressed, and the areas of need for students with learning disabilities considering postsecondary education options were identified.

In the second section, we focused on assessment factors for students transitioning to postsecondary education programs. Here we reviewed the assessment areas to be evaluated in a multidisciplinary evaluation, reassessment considerations for students considering postsecondary education, and critical issues to address when reporting psychological assessments for postsecondary education programs.

Finally, in our third section, we discussed the various postsecondary education options available, special considerations in transition planning for students with learning disabilities, and we then recommended activities for transition planning beginning before high school and continuing on through high school.

Our main focus in this chapter has been to encourage better planning for students transitioning from high school to postsecondary education settings by encouraging greater student participation in transition planning, encouraging school professionals to teach students the necessary skills for success in postsecondary education settings, and encouraging school personnel to empower students and encourage them to attend postsecondary education programs to better provide for themselves in the future. Through these efforts we hope professionals will be able to develop better transition plans for students with learning disabilities and encourage more students with learning disabilities to attend postsecondary education programs. It is our hope that improved efforts in these areas will result in lower rates of unemployment and underemployment and a better quality of life for student with learning disabilities.

REFERENCES

Aune, E. 91991). A transition model for postsecondary bound students with learning disabilities. *Learning Disabilities Research and Practice, 6,* 177–187.

Brinkerhoff, L.C. (1996). Making the transition to higher education: Opportunities for student empowerment. *Journal of Learning Disabilities, 29,* 118–136.

Clark, G.M. (1996). Transition planning assessment for secondary-level students with learning disabilities. *Journal of Learning Disabilities, 29,* 79–92.

Cowen, S. (1993). Transition planning for LD college-bound students. In S.A. Vogel and P.B. Adelman (Eds.), *Success for college students with learning disabilities* (pp. 39–56). New York: Springer-Verlag.

Dalke, C. & Schmitt, S. (1987). Meeting the transition needs of college-bound students with learning disabilities. *Journal of Learning Disabilities, 20* (3), 176–180.

DuChossis, G. & Michaels, C. (1994). Postsecondary education. In C.A. Michaels (Ed.), *Transition strategies for persons with learning disabilities* (pp. 79–118). San Diego: Singular.

DuChossis, G. & Stein, E. (1993). *Choosing the Right College: A step-by-step system to aid the student with learning disabilities in selecting the suitable college setting for them.* New York: New York University.

Dunn, C. (1996) A status report on transition planning for individuals with learning disabilities. In Patton, J. R. & Blalock, G. (Eds.), *Transition and Students with Learning Disabilities: Facilitating the Movement from School to Adult Life.* Austin, TX: Pro-Ed.

Fairweather, J.S. & Shaver, D.M. (1991). Making the transition to postsecondary education and training. *Exceptional Children, 57,* 264–270.

Gartin, B. C., Rumrill, P. & Serebreni, R. (1996). The higher education transition model: Guidelines for facilitating college transition among college-bound students with disabilities. *Teaching Exceptional Children, 23,* 30–33.

HEATH Resource Center. (1993). *How to choose a college: A guide for the student with a disability.* Washington, DC: American Council on Education.

Hurley, C.M. (2000). Reassessment considerations for students facing postsecondary planning. *Communique, 28* (5), 22–24.

Levine, P. & Nourse, S.W. (1998). What follow-up studies say about postschool life for young men and women with learning disabilities: A critical look at the literature. *Journal of Learning Disabilities, 31* (3), 212–233.

Levinson, E.M. (1998). *Transition: Facilitating the Postschool Adjustment of Students with Disabilities.* Boulder, CO: Westview Press.

Levinson, E.M. & Brandt, J. (1999). Career development. In *Children's Needs II* (Chapter 47). National Association of School Psychologists.

Mangrum, C.T. & Strichart, S.S. (Eds.). (1995). *Peterson's Colleges with Programs for Students with Learning Disabilities,* 4th ed. Princeton, NJ: Perterson's Guides.

National Joint Committee on Learning Disabilities. (1994). *Secondary to postsecondary education transition planning for students with learning disabilities. Collective perspectives on issues affecting learning disabilities.* Austin, TX: Pro-Ed.

Ohler, D. (1993). *Intervention Strategies for High School Students with Learning Disabilities in Transition to College.* Paper written for EP 765.

Patton, J. R. & Blalock, G. (Eds.) (1996). *Transition and Students with Learning Disabilities: Facilitating the Movement from School to Adult Life.* Austin, TX: Pro-Ed.

Reiff. H.B. & deFur, S. (1992). Transition for youths with learning disabilities: A focus on developing independence. *Learning Disability Quarterly, 15,* 237–248.

Scott, S.S. (1991). A change in legal status: An overlooked dimension in the transition to higher education. *Journal of Learning Disabilities, 24* (8), 459–466.

Shaw, S., Brinkerhoff, L., McGuire, J. (1991). Differences between high school and college requirements. *LDA Multidisciplinary Journal, 2,* 22.

Terenzini, P.T., Rendon, L.I., Upcraft, M.L., Millar, S.B., Allison, K.W., Gregg, P.L. & Jalomo, R. (1993). The transition to college: Diverse students, diverse stories. *Research in Higher Education, 35* (1), 57–73.

U.S. Department of Education, National Center for Education Statistics. (1999). *Students with Disabilities in Postsecondary Education: A Profile of Preparation, Participation, and Outcomes,* NCES 1999-187. Washington, DC.

Vess, S. (2000). Reporting psychological assessments for postsecondary education. *Communique, 28* (6), 10.

Vess, S. (2000). Transition planning for postsecondary education. *Communique, 28* (7), 25–26.

Vess, S. (2000). Transition to postsecondary education: New opportunities and lost protections. *Communique, 28* (5), 18–19.

Vogel, S.A. (1993). *Postsecondary Decision-making for Students with Learning Disabilities.* Pittsburgh, PA: Learning Disabilities Association of America.

Wagner, M., Blackorby, J., Cameto, R., Hebbeler, K., & Newman, L. (1993). *The transition experiences of young people with disabilities: A summary of findings from the*

National Longitudinal Transition Study of special education students. Menlo Park, CA: SRI International.

White, W.J. (1992). The postschool adjustment of persons with learning disabilities: Current status and future projections. *Journal of Learning Disabilities, 25* (7), 448–456.

Chapter 9

ASSESSMENT FOR TRANSITION FROM SCHOOL TO WORK

Larry Fultz and Chad Kinsey

INTRODUCTION: TRANSITION ASSESSMENT FOR TRANSITION FROM SCHOOL TO WORK

The importance of transition assessment for transition from school to work cannot be underscored and emphasized enough in terms of increasing the likelihood of obtaining gainful employment and achieving positive transition outcomes for students with disabilities as they prepare for transition into the workplace. In this chapter, support is provided for completing transition assessment through discussion of statistical outcomes of students with disabilities and transition planning laws. Relevant models will be briefly presented including: career development theory, social cognitive career theory, and decision-making theory which provide solid foundations for transition assessment and planning. A more extensive discussion of transition assessment tools will be highlighted including both informal and formal assessment techniques as well as a comprehensive, multitrait/multimethod assessment model. Last, the role of local employment agencies and transdisciplinary transition teams in the transition assessment process will be discussed.

Transition Philosophy

Transition can be defined in a variety of contexts, but for our purposes transition is viewed as the process in which a student is preparing for graduation from high school and transitioning into the workplace or adult world of gainful employment. Although this transition may appear to be a natural process, it cannot be assumed to be smooth or without problems especially if left unaddressed by the student, family, and school. The *American Heritage Dictionary* defines transition as "the process . . . of changing from one form, state, activity, or place to another." Transitions occur in many aspects of life from birth to death. Some transitions are painless and hardly noticeable, while others are arduous or memorable experiences. For young people, one of the most significant transitions occurs when they leave school. The education system provides a structured, defined experience that allows individuals to not only learn content, but also to learn about themselves and to explore opportunities. The transition from school to work can cause students stress, uncertainty, and lack of direction. It is hoped that the education that they have received has prepared them to succeed in this new stage of their lives. Generally, life choices at this point fall into one of two categories: further education or employment. As mentioned already, this transition can be difficult for students. It can be particularly trying for students with disabilities. This chapter is primarily concerned with why and how the educational system prepares these students to transition from school to work through a transition assessment and planning process.

Statistics Supporting Transition Assessment and Planning

There is abundant statistical support available providing logic and reason to support the transition assessment and planning process for students with disabilities. Many of these statistics are striking and, in fact, very disconcerting. Obviously, caution should be used in interpreting some of these statistics, but the prevailing theme is that successful transition planning must receive increased focus and effort on the part of transdisciplinary transition teams.

Disabled Students' Outcome Statistics

In *Best Practices in School Psychology,* Levinson (1997) cites several studies which reveal alarming statistics for individuals with disabilities. The

President's Committee on the Employment of the Handicapped reports that following the completion of high school, only 21 percent of persons with disabilities will be employed, 40 percent will be underemployed or at the poverty level, and 26 percent will be on welfare. Other cited studies suggest that 67 percent of persons with disabilities in the United States, between the ages of 16 and 64, are not working. Of those that are working, 75 percent are employed on a part-time basis, and of those who are not working, 67 percent indicate that they would like to be employed.

Furthermore, in surveys of five states, the employment rate for persons with disabilities ranges between 45 percent and 70 percent depending on the disability and geographic location. Between 64 percent and 82 percent of the aforementioned population report living at home with a parent or guardian. Additionally, 42 percent of learning disabled and behaviorally disturbed students, and 18 percent of mentally challenged students leave school before graduation or simply drop out. Research has demonstrated consistently that "handicapped students leave school at a greater rate than their non-disabled peers" (Levinson, 1997). These statistics provide unrefutable support that schools must become better not only at keeping students with disabilities in school, but also in preparing them for employment after school.

Statistical Profile of Special Education Students

Further research has been conducted related to special education students regarding their school completion and employment outcomes. Knight and Rieck (1997) completed research in these areas that revealed that in 1992, 5.3 million students were enrolled in special education services in the United States. Their statistical profile and analysis further revealed that approximately 70 percent of these students exiting the educational system received a diploma or certificate of achievement, approximately 30 percent dropped out of school, students that failed one or more courses dropped out of school at a rate of 17 percent, and over 10 percent of students absent for 21 to 30 days of school and students absent for more than 30 days of school did not complete their course of study. Additionally, further analysis revealed three to five years after graduation 57 percent of youths with disabilities were competitively employed, as compared to 69 percent of the general population. The median hourly wage for youths with disabilities as they enter the work force was $5.72, or less than $12,000 per year for full-time employment. Lastly, five years after graduation vocational services were needed by 60 percent of youths with disabilities, and only approximately one-third were receiving these much needed services. Although these statistics paint a grim picture, there is light at the end of the tunnel for those receiving job specific career education. Students with disabilities that were receiving job specific career education were less likely to drop out of school. Also, they were more likely to have better school attendance, acquire positive social boundary skills, and have parents that were actively involved in their educational process.

Current Trends in Transition Assessment for Transition from School to Work

Transition Planning Law

As a result of some of the statistical information presented and the realization by schools, families, and legislators that outcomes of students with disabilities have been dismal at best, transition planning legislation began to be more formally developed and implemented particularly in the early 1980s. Several key additions to previously developed transition planning laws were made in the 1997 IDEA document.

Office of Special Education and Rehabilitation Services (OSERS)

The need for school to work transition planning for students with disabilities has been a focus of study and legislation for the federal government since the early 1980s. In 1984, transition was identified as major priority by the Office of Special Education and Rehabilitation (OSERS) as well. M. Will of the OSERS office stated, "Qualifications for employment is an implied promise of American education . . . yet 50 percent to 80 percent of working age adults who report a disability are jobless" (Michaels, 1994). Within this framework, transition was defined as an outcome-oriented process encompassing a broad array of services and experiences that lead to employment.

Individuals with Disabilities Education Act (IDEA)

The scope of transition outcomes was further expanded with the reauthorization of the Individuals with Disabilities Education Act (IDEA) in 1997. The IDEA of 1997 mandated the nature of the transition services to be available to students with disabilities. As described by Warger (2000), IDEA of 1997 requires that transition services "be designed within an outcome-oriented process that support movement from school to post-school activities which would include: postsecondary education, vocational training, integrated employment such as supported employment, continuing and adult education, adult services, independent living, and community participation." Additionally, Warger stated that transition services should be individualized for each person taking into account the student's needs, preferences, and interests and should include instruction, related services, community experiences, and the development of employment and other adult living objectives. When appropriate, attainment of daily living skills and a functional vocational evaluation should occur. According to IDEA, transition planning must be part of the student's Individualized Education Program (IEP) by the time the student is 14 years of age. By the time the student is 16 years of age, a well-developed transition plan must be included in the IEP. This plan must indicate what transition services are needed including which agency will be responsible for providing the identified services. Also, in accordance with IDEA, students must be invited to attend their IEP meetings if transition services are being discussed or considered. According to Best Practices, transition planning minimally including informal assessment and discussion should be initiated prior to the student being 14, and students should be invited to all IEP meetings particularly at the secondary level. Further relevant additions to the IDEA of 1997 include: the focus should be placed on self-determination for students and families in transition planning, the focus should be on both short and long-range goals rather than objectives within the IEP, and a focus should be placed on education planning and programming related to post-school outcomes.

Determination of Services

Transition planning and vocational assessment are intimately related in that successful transition planning cannot occur without the information that is gathered from a comprehensive functional vocational assessment as required by special education law. Vocational assessment data, however, is of little value if not used to recommend appropriate services designed to facilitate successful transition from school to work and community living. Skills that are needed to maintain employment and to adjust to community living are comprised of three critical evaluation areas: daily living skills, personal/social skills, and occupational/vocational skills.

At this point, brief consideration is given to the low cognitive functioning disabled student for whom transition assessment and planning must occur. Research suggests that characteristics of a transition curriculum for the one percent to three percent with the lowest cognitive functioning should focus on development of skills necessary for independence. This is most commonly referred to as community-based instruction in which individuals in this grouping are prepared to function in four basic domains in preparation for transition. These domains are identified as: independent living, community functioning, recreation and leisure, and vocational development. The chronological age of the student will determine when instruction is offered in the community or the classroom setting. Typically, as the student increases in age and development, the amount of non-school instruction should increase. In order to facilitate a smooth transition to adult life, the last two years of schooling should be primarily in a community-based setting. These students will often be most challenging for the transdisciplinary transition team to assess and the overall assessment must be directed both towards meeting their individual needs and the acquisition of realistic outcomes as reflected in their Individualized Education Program.

In theory and practice, what should be strongly considered in assessing the four previously mentioned domains in transition to the employment and work setting is what employers have stated that they value most in their employees. Research in this area has demonstrated that employers place the highest value on attitude, communication skills, and work experience. Also valuable to employers who have been surveyed is ability to comply with work hours, overall reading and communication skills, and ability to accept direction. In considering vocational assessment information, these valued areas should be assessed in order to delineate areas of need for students with disabilities prior to entering the work setting. Related services and opportunities in the areas of personal social skills and occupational/vocational skills can be provided within the school setting through appropriate use of IEP goals. Further research studies have supported this premise in that students who graduate from high school are more likely to be employed, especially if they have paid jobs while in school and/or have participated in mainstream education courses or work experiences. In summary, vocational education and assessment are vital since skill levels and expectations for new jobs are increasing and changing at a rapid pace.

Career Development Theories

Several career development theories have assisted in helping educators to realize the importance of the transition planning process and vocational assessment. Students with disabilities must be considered from the context of career development theory, social cognitive career theory, and decision-making theory in order to best understand individual student progression and development, and in order to successfully plan for the transition from school to work with students and their families.

Career Development Theory

Career development theory provides a comprehensive model for conceptualizing the school to work transition process. Savickas (1999) reviewed studies which concluded that "youth cope better with the school to work transition if as high school students they have developed an awareness of the choices to be made and of the information and planning that bear on these choices." In other words, career awareness and career planning activities have assisted students transitioning to work in coping with the emotional, psychological, and other changes that the transition process causes.

Super proposed that individuals differ in abilities, interests, and personality and are qualified by definition of these characteristics for a number of occupations. Each of these occupations requires a characteristic pattern of abilities, interests, and personality traits that are diverse enough to allow for some variance in occupations for each individual. Vocational preferences and competencies as well as self-concepts change over time with accumulated experiences which in turn make choices and adjustment an ongoing process. Career patterns also develop which are further determined by socioeconomic level, mental ability, personality characteristics, and opportunities that individuals are exposed to. Ultimately, Super's theory has provided the underpinnings of career development theory by focusing on abilities, interests, and personality characteristics and how they interact with one another.

Holland's theory is described as a "trait factor" theory in that it focuses on factors that influence the choice of a career at any given point in time in an individual's life. Holland suggests that vocational choice is the expression of one's personality, and that individuals select occupations that are consistent with their personalities. Individuals with similar personalities tend to choose occupations consistent with their personalities. Furthermore, job satisfaction is determined by how well personalities and related attributes such as interests, abilities, and work habits match requirements and demands of the selected occupation. Job satisfaction is highly correlated with congruence between work and personality. According to Holland, most persons can be categorized as possessing one of six major personality orientations: realistic, investigative, artistic, social, enterprising, or conventional.

In summary, career development theory, personality traits, characteristics, and attitudes must be continually assessed as an ongoing, explorative process. From this perspective, career development theory provides a foundation for design and implementation of assessment and transition programs. Career development theory offers guidelines for career objectives and tasks that confront students at certain points in their educational careers. Assessment programs must be developmental in nature in considering age-appropriate tasks, personality traits, and preferences in relation to individual career objectives.

Social Cognitive Career Theory

Social cognitive career theory should be utilized as a guiding principle in the vocational assessment and transition planning process. Social cognitive career theory emphasizes the interplay between three variables: self-efficacy, outcome expectations, and goals. Self-efficacy, or confidence in one's ability to successfully perform a given task, helps to determine whether an individual will initiate, persevere, and succeed at identified endeavors. Successful performance further enhances or improves self-efficacy and increases the probability of future successful performances. Failure experiences tend to diminish self-efficacy and have adverse effects upon perseverance and motivation variables. Outcome expectations refer to beliefs about what will happen contingent upon performance of certain tasks. Success or failure in attaining goals tends to strengthen or weaken respectively, self-efficacy, and outcome expectations (Lent et al., 1999).

Social cognitive career theory imposes a perspective on school to work transition that highlights six interrelated processes that are meaningful at various developmental stages and points. These interrelated processes involve: acquisition of positive, yet realistic outcome expectations; development of academic and career interests; formation of linkages between interests and career-related goals; translation of goals into progressive actions; development of academic and work skills as well as remediation of performance-related problems; and negotiations of social supports and barriers that affect the development of self and occupational beliefs and pursuit of options.

Decision-Making Theory

Decision-making theory emphasizes step-by-step procedures to be utilized in making vocational decisions and choices. Hohenshil, Levinson, and Buckland-Heer (Levinson, 1993) proposed a career-planning model based on decision-making theory which was influenced by previous research conducted by H. B. Gelatt. Gelatt advocated a chronological step-by-step process to making career decisions based on the concepts of value and probability. Value is considered as the desirability of an outcome; probability is considered to be the likelihood that an event will occur. Four basic categories of information are required in making an informed decision according to decision-making theory including: knowledge of possible alternative actions, possible outcomes of the identified actions, knowledge of the probability that each action will result in the expected outcome, and preference such as how desirable the outcome is to the individual.

Decision-making theory is relevant to the transition assessment and planning process in that components of this theory can be utilized once transition assessment data has been collected and as the transdisciplinary transition assessment team works with the student and family to further identify desired outcomes and the likelihood or probability of these outcomes. In other words, are the expected outcomes realistic with gathered data? This model has particular relevance in terms of students that have vocational interests far below or above what transition assessment data has depicted and by assisting students and other team members to identify realistic and achievable goals and potential outcomes. Decision-making theory assists in operationalizing value and probability in a manner that enables team members to delineate what is possible and what is not as well as to provide direction in terms of student needs, appropriate support services, and appropriate linkages.

Combining the Theories

Career development theory, social cognitive career theory, and decision-making theory provide both support and rationale for incorporating systematic transition assessment for disabled students transitioning from school to work. Savickas and Lent (1994) state: "The theories of career development need each other in order to comprehensively address the complexities of career development." Additionally, substantial research has supported the premise that combining career development theories through comprehensive evaluation of students enables team members to acquire deeper meaning when they are viewed from the perspective of two or more theories. Ultimately, transdisciplinary transition teams must be aware of and knowledgeable regarding the area of career development theory in order to develop a transition assessment plan and program that is consistent and concretely based on empirically supported theories and information. Primary points to remember for transdisciplinary transition teams include: utilization of multiple theories of transition/vocational development is vital; assessing students is an ongoing, continuous process; and assessing students according to their individual interests, preferences, skills, abilities, and needs increases the probability of successful vocational selections and outcomes.

Transition from School to Work: Informal Assessment Tools

A variety of informal assessment tools should be utilized in the transition assessment of students with disabilities which are not only practical, but provide first-hand knowledge as to the interests, skills, strengths, and needs of the individual student. These assessments include: practical/hands-on assessment, interviews, observations, work samples, and situational assessment.

Practical/Hands-on Assessment

Practical/hands-on assessment is a critical component in terms of assessing students with disabilities in preparation for the work environment. Present levels of functioning are required as part of standard reevaluations, but most often only include present levels of academic functioning. Performance assessment related to the student's skills for employment should also be included. Typically this might include assessment of the student's attendance, writing and reading skills, ability to follow directions, and task analysis which are desired skills possessed by the student's future employers.

Performance Tests

Performance tests are "manipulative tasks that while minimizing the use of language are designed to evaluate a specific ability believed to be related to job performance" (Best Practices in School Psychology III, 1997). One example of a performance task is that of manual dexterity which involves skills that are related to the performance of many trade and technical occupations such as auto mechanics, heating and air conditioning, and construction/manufacturing. Manual dexterity performance tests require the student to work with manipulatives such as nuts, bolts, and drawings. A few examples of commercially developed performance tests available to transdisciplinary transition assessment teams include: "The Crawford Small Parts Dexterity Test, the Minnesota Rate of Manipulation Test, the Pennsylvania Bi-Manual Worksample, and the Purdue Pegboard" (Patton & Blalock, 1996). Additional performance tests that may be used by teams include: "The Bennett Hand Tool Dexterity Test, the Computer Operator Aptitude Battery, the General Clerical Test, the Office Skills Test, the Lincoln-Oseretsky Motor Development Test, and the Personnel Test for Industry-Oral Directions Test" (Berkell, Brown, 1989).

Interviews and Observations

Interviews are most commonly defined as verbal and non-verbal interactions with more than one person working toward a common goal. Interviews with students are one of the most valuable sources of information that cannot typically be obtained through standardized assessments. Although interviews often lack reliability and validity, qualitatively interviews encourage self-assessment and exploration of career opportunities through the transition assessment process. Several types of interview formats may be utilized in the transition assessment process such as standardized interviews, structured interviews, and unstructured interviews. The transdisciplinary transition assessment team should consider incorporating checklists with interviews such as the "Career Education Checklist" (Clark, Patton, Moulton, 2000), the "Self-Determination/Self-Advocacy Checklist" (Clark & Patton, 1998), and the "Skills Checklist for Transition Planning" (Shearn, 1999).

Observations are another useful tool for gathering data in the school to work assessment process. Observations are broadly defined as "the process of gathering information through one's senses" (Levinson, 1993). Best practice for incorporating observation techniques in the transition assessment process involves the use of multiple observers in a variety of practical observational settings. Observations can be utilized to assess a variety of individual student traits as well as specific behaviors such as on-task behavior, spontaneous behavior, ability to follow directions, and ability to work with others, all of which are relevant in school to work assessment. Observation tools that are consistent with Best Practices include: the B.O.S.S. and the Saudargas/Creed Observation Tool.

Work Samples

Work samples are defined as a well-defined work activity involving tasks, materials, and tools which are identical or similar to those in an actual job or cluster of jobs and are used to assess an individual's vocational aptitude, worker characteristics, and overall vocational interest. Work samples are the focal point of a hands-on approach to vocational assessment in transitioning students effectively to the work environment. Three phases are appropriately implemented through work sample assessment: demonstration, training, and assessment. Live audio or video demonstration may occur as well as verbal instruction prior to task completion and subsequent assessment. Through work samples, students can be assessed and provided with feedback in a variety of roles and situations. Therefore, the work sample is not only an assessment tool, but an instructional technique for students preparing for entry into the work environment. A variety of work samples exist as suggested by Levinson (1993) including: cluster trait work samples, indigenous work samples, job samples, simulated work samples, and single-trait work samples. Interested readers are referred to Levinson's description of these various work samples.

Situational Assessment

Situational assessments are designed primarily to assess student's interests, aptitudes, and/or work habits in real or simulated work situations. Observations, interviews, and rating scales are typically used through the course of simulated job stations, production work situations, on-the-job evaluations, job tryouts, and evaluation in a vocational training setting. Transdisciplinary transition assessment team members may find this type of assessment to be time-consuming, but invaluable information is gathered and formulated related to student work habits, strengths, needs, interactional/social skills, response to job demands, and individual dispositions.

Students with disabilities can best be assessed through a situational assessment as there is no truly accurate way to formulate how an individual will respond to certain work environments, work demands, and their identified disability in a given work setting. Simulated job stations and on-the-job evaluations are the best ways to realistically assess students in work-related environments. One disadvantage related to situational assessment techniques is the cost in terms of time and finances in developing this type of assessment. One situational assessment that should be considered by the team is the "Situational Assessment Behavior Checklist" which lists potential employee characteristics in terms of instructional needs, problem-solving, attending to tasks, worker orientation, and interpersonal skills. This situational assessment of employee characteristics can be coupled with the "Situational Assessment Site Description" in identifying potential site demands for the employee in domains such as independent functioning, work habits, interpersonal skills, and organization and planning skills.

Desired Employee Skills and Assessment

Job site analysis is one method through which the transdisciplinary transition assessment team can determine what employers desire most from their employees. McLoughlin, Garner, and Callahan (1987) describe a detailed process for determining desired employee traits and overall job demands of transitioning students. McLoughlin, Garner, and Callahan (1987) suggest several important steps in conducting a job site analysis and developing a task analysis list for transitioning students including: "visiting the job site, observing the job site, participating in standard new employee orientation, meeting with coworkers and supervisors, learning the job from coworkers and supervisors, performing all aspects of the job, developing an analysis of tasks within the work environment, identifying natural cues and consequences, determining additional considerations for training, and developing a written training plan." Listed desired employee traits include characteristics such as stamina, sound judgment, endurance, speed, and experience.

Various checklists are available and can be developed by the transdisciplinary transition assessment team that emphasize evaluation of further desired employee characteristics including, but not limited to: appropriate hygiene and grooming, ability to work with others, effective communication skills, ability to read and interpret information, ability to follow verbal and written instructions, ability to perform manual tasks, ability to problem-solve, ability to make decisions independently, responsiveness to supervision, honesty, dependability, punctuality and good attendance, and responsible use of work property/tools/equipment.

Two assessment tools that are effective in evaluating transitioning students' employability skills in terms of strengths, weaknesses, and areas for further development are the "Employability/Life Skills Assessment" (Weaver, DeLuca, 1987) and "The Environmental Job Assessment Measure: E-JAM" (Waintrup, Kelley, 1999). These assessment tools enable assessment teams to evaluate self-help skills, work habits, task-related skills, work quantity, work quality, relationships with supervisors and peers, work attitudes, general work behaviors, physical demands of the job, working conditions, educational demands, and effectiveness of accommodations and modifications.

Transition from School to Work: Formal Assessment Tools

A variety of useful formal assessment tools are available in assessing students as they prepare for transition from school to work settings. Four assessment tools have been selected for discussion and further consideration in this chapter including: the Self-Directed Search, the

Myers-Briggs Type Indicator, the Strong-Campbell Interest Inventory, and the Employment Readiness Scale. These assessment tools are more formal, standardized assessments as compared to previously discussed data collection tools and assessments such as interviews, observations, work samples, and situational assessments. These formal measures need to be systematically assessed in terms of their strengths, weaknesses, validity, reliability, relevance, usage, administration time, practicality, and cost. A model will be conceptualized for utilizing these tools, in particular, through integration of components of the Myers-Briggs and the Strong-Campbell Interest Inventory. Last, a systematic plan for combining these assessment results in a meaningful fashion for students and families will be highlighted.

Self-Directed Search

John Holland's Self-Directed Search (SDS) will be discussed in terms of its utility and relevance for school to work transition assessment. Briefly, the SDS can be administered to children who are reading at a fourth grade reading level and above. In terms of utility, the SDS can be administered by school psychologists and other transdisciplinary transition assessment team members at the high school level. The SDS is self-administered, interpreted, and scored in approximately 30 minutes and a three-letter summary code is produced identifying students as realistic, investigative, artistic, enterprising, social, and/or conventional which represent Holland's six personality types. The Occupations Finder is then utilized to identify potential job and work opportunities that best match the student's preferences and personality. Good psychometric properties are noted with the exception of lower predictive validity.

Myers-Briggs Type Indicator

The Myers-Briggs Type Indicator, Third Edition (1980), the MBTI, is a tool which was designed to provide insight and understanding into why individuals prefer to engage in certain activities, how they prefer to live life, and how individual differences and preferences are understood. Katherine Briggs, the daughter of Isabel Myers Briggs, developed the MBTI instrument which is a three-part, 126-item assessment that takes approximately 45 minutes to complete. Test-retest reliabilities range from .48 to .87 depending on length of time between retesting. Split-half reliabilities range from .67 to .90 and validity coefficients range from .67 to .79. The work of Jung, Harman, Bloom, Kohlberg, Westcott, and Myers has contributed significantly to the development of the theory driving the MBTI. Carl Jung's theories involving intuition have been most influential, however, in terms of role-taking through perception involving the individual senses. Four dimensions have been developed through this theory that enable identification of eight different preferences or types including: extraversion versus introversion, sensing versus intuition, thinking versus feeling, and judging versus perceiving. The four dimensions work simultaneously to answer four pertinent questions which are relevant to all individuals including students who are preparing for transition into the work setting. These questions reveal individual differences and preferences which have implications for workplace interactions, perceptions of data, developing conclusions based on data, and coping with integration into the world of work. These four questions are: What is the source of stimulation and energy? How do we perceive the world and take in data? How do we reach conclusions on the data? How do we deal with the world around us?

According to Jung's theory of psychological types, all individuals utilize all four functions (sensing, intuition, thinking, and feeling) and all four attitudes are adopted (extraversion, introversion, judging, and perceiving). The types are called preference types because all individuals in each type prefer one of the two perceptive functions (sensing or intuition), and one of the two judgment functions (thinking or feeling). A four letter formula or type is developed and the two middle letters of the type formula are the preferences of the individual. Additionally, types differ in the functions they prefer to use when in the introverted or extraverted attitudes. A total of 16 MBTI types are possible. Further description and explanation of these types can be found in articles by Mary H. McCaulley and Isabel Myers (1985).

In summary of the MBTI, personality preferences, particularly in the areas of extraversion and introversion, can assist in determining jobs that might be most suitable for transition to work students, providing an understanding of leadership styles, and providing valuable insight into how students may respond to particular work situations such as those that may require working in groups, negotiating, problem-solving, using leadership skills, using intuition, being decisive, working alone, and coping with conflict. It is vital to understand that the MBTI is based on strengths of individual personalities and preferences and that the 16 types function on a continuum which is changeable over the course of time. For example, research has indicated that typically as individuals age they move progressively further to the left or right on scales such as extraversion/introversion and judging/perceiving. Last, further description of recommended careers regarding the MBTI results will be discussed later within the context of the development of a systematic plan for integrating the formal assessment results of school to work transition students.

In conclusion, the MBTI is comprehensive in its analysis of individual preferences, dispositions, and strengths. The MBTI is relatively affordable compared to some other assessments, but does require expertise in interpretation and takes additional time to administer and interpret which may be limiting factors in terms of overall utility for the transdisciplinary transition assessment team.

Strong-Campbell Interest Inventory

The Strong-Campbell Interest Inventory, the SCII, may be viewed as an extension of John Holland's theory and the Self-Directed Search. The primary difference is that the SCII is significantly more time-consuming to administer again having limitations in utility for the team. Statistical characteristics of the SCII include: "reliability and validity levels in the .80 range with retest correlations ranging from .91 for three weeks to .81 over three years" (Hansen, 1985). Further statistical research and analysis has demonstrated internal reliabilities ranging from .90 to .95 and a validity coefficient of .76. Statistically, the SCII has remained a popular and well respected career interest inventory over the course of many years.

The SCII contains 325 items which are divided into seven sections that measure respondents' likes, dislikes, and indifference related to varied occupations, school subjects, activities, amusements, types of people, and work characteristics. The interests are correlated with the interests of people in 119 occupations. The SCII provides three types of information including: scores on six General Occupation Themes reflecting Holland's; scores on 23 Basic Interest Scales which specify interests within Holland's arrangement; and scores on the Occupational Scales which indicate degree of similarity between the individual's interests and those of people engaged in a wide variety of occupations.

The basic premise behind utilizing the SCII is two-fold related to assessing school to work transition students. First, the SCII is a valid and reliable measure which examines traits, values, and attitudes in a meaningful manner by determining preferences that enable students to seek an occupation that corresponds to their orientation. Second, through empirical research it has been determined that the SCII is correlated with the MBTI, and hence, further meaningful interpretations can occur through utilization and combination of these instruments.

Research on the part of McCaulley has demonstrated that business professions attract practical and sensing-thinking types as well as realistic and extraversion types when combining the MBTI and the SCII. Additionally, mathematical fields attract intuitive-thinking types, engineering and law reflect thinking-judging types, and intuitive-feeling types are attracted to humanities, arts, counseling, psychology, psychiatry, and journalism. Sensing-feeling types are friendly and sympathetic and are often attracted to careers such as elementary school teaching, nursing, general practice, and patient care.

Additionally, more recent research by Dillon and Weissman (1988) has revealed positive correlations between the MBTI and the SCII related to certain careers. Relationships between the Social Occupational Scales which include helping, guiding, and group-oriented interests and the MBTI scales indicate that both sexes prefer extraversion. Social females prefer intuition and social males prefer feeling. Females prefer perception and extraverted intuitive persons tend to focus their creativity on working with others while extraverted feeling persons tend to concentrate on seeking peaceful resolutions. Enterprising SCII Occupational Scales which include business, sales, and political interests are highly correlated with the MBTI extraversion type for both females and males. The SCII Conventional Occupational Scales involving organized, routine, and clerical interests are associated with the sensing and judging preferences of the MBTI types for both females and males. Lastly, males who score highly in the conventional area are frequently high on the extraversion scale of the MBTI indicating preferences for taking active roles and working with people.

Further research by Apostal and Marks (1990) supplemented the findings in Dillon and Weissman's studies by indicating that "career interests are correlated with two measures of introversion-extraversion on the MBTI." Measures of introversion-extraversion on the Strong-Campbell Interest Inventory and the extraversion-introversion scale of the Myers-Briggs were significant in terms of correlation with the only exception being the realistic type for males on the SCII. Their research involved 219 students including 130 females and 89 males and further supported the premise that there are strong correlations between the General Occupational Themes area of the SCII and the Myers-Briggs types.

Combining the MBTI, SCII, and SDS

Several authors have researched and supported the correlations between the MBTI and the SCII in terms of the selection of careers that are congruent with both Holland's six codes and the MBTI personality/preference types. Both instruments have implications for assessing students with and without disabilities for school to work transition. The MBTI contributes an additional component for disabled students in terms of examining and evaluating preferences related to how individuals will most likely respond to their environment and work setting. The MBTI provides relevant information in terms of how students perceive the world around them. Since it is unrealistic, difficult, and unnatural to change individual personalities and preferences as well as workplace expectations, it is vital that transdisciplinary transition assessment teams accurately identify student preferences and personality to best match them with jobs that are congruent with student attitudes, aptitudes, skills, abilities, preferences, and characteristics of the disability. The implications of the proposed model for transition assessment are that the multitude of aforementioned variables will be accounted for in a systematic fashion. Further research is required related to the proposed model, however. First, additional research should be conducted in assessment of students with disabilities to be certain that the correlations previously mentioned are stable across disabled and non-disabled student populations. Second, further research is required in terms of incorporating the SDS and MBTI in determining their correlations as most research has focused on the SCII which is more time-consuming for students to complete and transdisciplinary transition assessment teams to utilize.

In demonstrating the correlations between the MBTI and the SCII scales, Dillon and Weissman have developed correlation charts for females and males related to the MBTI and SCII types. For example, males demonstrate significant correlation in the career of forester in the SCII realistic type and the MBTI extraversion/introversion type. Females demonstrate significant correlation in the career of banking on the conventional and sensing/intuitive types. In summary, further research needs to be conducted to allow transition team members to replace the SCII with the SDS to produce a more time-effective assessment model for transdisciplinary transition assessments.

Employment Readiness Scale

The Employment Readiness Scale is the last formalized assessment tool that will be considered here. This rating scale should be utilized after potential careers have been identified through the formal assessment process, and it may be used in combination with the informal assessment techniques mentioned earlier in this chapter. The questions on this rating scale assess desired employee traits such as: safety, self-efficacy, dress, response to redirection, respect, responsibility, motivation, timeliness, student feelings about monetary considerations, and goals.

Future Directions in Assessment for Transition from School to Work

Informal and formal assessment tools have been discussed to form a comprehensive model of assessment for transition teams in school to work transition of disabled students. It is assumed that a team should be developed such as a transdisciplinary transition assessment team to assist the student in preparing for the school to work transition. As indicated in research, the earlier transition assessment and plans are developed, the more likely students are to experience success in selecting appropriate vocations and jobs prior to and after graduation. Transition teams are in an excellent position to utilize a number of resources and individuals with expertise in career development and assessment.

Although school psychologists and other trained evaluators are required to administer assessments such as the MBTI, SCII, and SDS, informal assessments, observations, interviews, and rating scales can be completed by any number of individuals on the transition assessment team. Beneficial data will be gathered if responsibilities are divided among team members. Once data is collected in all domains, the transition assessment team should meet again with the student present to discuss assessment results and to develop a transition plan.

This comprehensive method of assessment is consistent with Best Practices in School Psychology III (1997) and Gresham's proposed multitrait/multimethod assessment in which it is understood that not all instruments in assessment are reliable and valid. Therefore, multiple methods of assessing similar traits through use of instruments such as the MBTI, SCII, and/or SDS as well as interviews, observations, and work samples are consistent with the multitrait/multimethod approach. Best Practices clearly states that transition teams need to work cooperatively not only to develop goals for students, but to assist in determining long-term outcomes that are realistic and attainable for students with disabilities. Additional assessment tools and instrumentation exist beyond the tools in the model proposed in this chapter, and transdisciplinary transition assessment teams have the responsibility of determining which tools and assessments are most appropriate and useful in evaluating the students with whom they are working.

Developing Knowledge of Local Employment Options

Acquiring knowledge of the local employment options available for individuals with disabilities is necessary for professionals involved in the transition assessment process. Transition planning options typically include: competitive employment, supported employment, and sheltered employment as determined by individual student needs and skills. Competitive employment typically is comprised of competitive salary community jobs without ongoing support. Supported employment option are those jobs in which individuals typically have "job coaches" who provide support including, but not limited to training, retraining, skill development, monitoring, and problem resolution. Sheltered employment options are those programs in which individuals with disabilities are placed in jobs or businesses operated by human service agencies such as sheltered workshops or work activity centers.

Additional support services are often available in the community and the transition team is responsible for becoming educated about these services, and of the agencies and the roles and functions that they serve. It is recommended that services be accessed from these agencies through formal interagency agreements which will enable representatives of these agencies to attend transition meetings, become aware of students and their needs, and meet needs well before students graduate. Representatives of these agencies often have training and knowledge that will complement the knowledge and training of transition team members. Two examples of agencies that assist students with disabilities in transition from school to work are the Office of Vocational Rehabilitation (OVR) and Career Link.

The Transdisciplinary Transition Team

The transdisciplinary transition team often is directed or chaired by one individual who is identified as the transition coordinator or the transition specialist. Several school districts have now employed transition coordinators on a part-time or full-time basis. This individual should be trained in learning and developmental theories, assessment and interpretation of assessments, and special education laws and procedures. The transdisciplinary transition team members should not only be familiar with the student's strengths and needs, but have a vested interest in assisting students to successfully transition from school to work. Responsibilities of the transition team should be distributed so that all members come to know the student better and can contribute at team meetings in a meaningful fashion. School psychologists are in an excellent position to contribute positively to transition teams because of their training in assessment, learning and behavioral theories, adolescent psychology, developmental psychology, and consultation.

Making the Match

The last step in the transition assessment process after assessment and meetings involving local employment agencies for school to work students is to make the match of individual career interest with the environment and work setting. Supports, accommodations, and instructional needs should be accurately identified and specifically defined as a result of the transition assessment team member reports. If the match is determined to be appropriate, then the student should continue with the job opportunities and subsequent placement with appropriate supports, accommodations, and instruction/skill development needs being implemented in the work environment with the support of the local employment agency and in some cases a "job coach." If the match is not satisfactory or successful, then additional data should be collected on other work opportunities, environments.

SUMMARY

Within this chapter, we have discussed the driving forces and developments that have promoted the establishment of transition assessment and transition programming. Special education and disability laws such as the Carl D. Perkins Vocational Education Act, the Individuals with Disabilities Education Act, the Vocational Rehabilitation Act, the Education of the Handicapped Act, the Vocational Education Amendment Act, and the Career Incentive Act have mandated transition planning and provided federal funding to assist students with disabilities in preparing for work. Additionally, we have discussed some striking statistics that suggest that students with disabilities transitioning from school to work are not having their needs met nor experiencing success to the degree that they could.

In response to the need for improvement in terms of successful transition from school to work, we have presented a variety of informal and formal assessment tools and techniques which can be employed by transdisciplinary transition assessment teams, transition specialists, transition coordinators, and school psychologists. Gathering information through informal and formal assessment, and then matching student interests, strengths, and needs will further improve appropriate and successful career and job selection for students with disabilities.

REFERENCES

Apostal, R., & Marks, C. (1990). Correlations between the Strong-Campbell and Myers-Briggs Scales of introversion-extraversion and career interests. *Psychological Reports, 66,* 811–816.

Berkell, D. E., & Brown, J. M. (1989). *Transition from school to work for persons with disabilities.* White Plains, NY: Longman Inc.

Briggs, K. C., & Myers, I. B. (1977). *Myers-Briggs Type Indicator.* Palo Alto, CA: Consulting Psychologist Press.

Clark, G. M. (1999). Informal assessments for transition planning. *The Career Development Quarterly: The National Career Development Association, 47*(4).

Clark, G. M., & Patton, J. R. (1998). *Transition Planning Inventory.* Austin, TX: Pro-Ed, Inc.

Clark, G. M., Patton, J. R., & Moulton, L. R. (2000). *Informal assessments for transition planning.* Austin, TX: Pro-Ed, Inc.

The condition of education. (1998). Washington, DC: U.S. Department of Education, Office of Educational Research and Improvement, National Center for Educational Statistics.

DeFur, S. H., & Patton, J. R. (Eds.). (1999). *Transition and school-based services: Interdisciplinary perspectives for enhancing the transition process.* Austin, TX: Pro-Ed, Inc.

Digest of educational statistics. (2000). Washington, DC: U.S. Department of Health, Education, and Welfare, Education Division, National Center for Educational Statistics.

Dillon, M., & Weissman, S. (1988). Relationship between personality types on Strong-Campbell and Myers-Briggs instruments. *Measurement and Evaluation in Counseling and Development, 20*(2), 68–79.

Hansen, J. C., & Campbell, D. P. (1985). *Manual for the SBIB-SCII Strong-Campbell Interest Inventory,* 4th ed. Palo Alto, CA: Stanford University Press.

Holland, J. L. (1985). *The Self-Directed Search Professional Manual–1985 edition.* Odessa, FL: Psychological Assessment Resources.

Knight, D., & Rieck, E. (1997). Contracts for careers. *Teaching Exceptional Children, 29*(6), 42–46.

Krumboltz, J. D., & Worthington, R. L. (1999). The school-to-work transition from a learning theory perspective. *Career Development Quarterly, 47,* 312–325.

Learning to work: Making the transition from school to work. (1995). Washington DC: Office of Technology Assessment, Congress of the U.S.

Lent, R. W., Hackett, G., & Brown, S. D. (1996). A social cognitive framework for studying career choice and transition to work. *Journal of Vocational Education Research, 21*(4), 3–31.

Levinson, E. M. (1993). *Transdisciplinary vocational assessment: Issues in school- based programs.* Brandon, VT: Clinical Psychology Publishing Co.

Levinson, E. M. (1998). *Transition: Facilitating the post-school adjustment of students with disabilities.* Boulder, CO: Westview Press.

McLoughlin, C. S., Garner, J. B., & Callahan, M. (1987). *Getting employed, staying employed: Job development and training for persons with severe handicaps.* Baltimore, MD: Paul H. Brookes.

Michaels, C. A. (1994). *Transition strategies for persons with learning disabilities.* San Diego, CA: Singular Publishing Group.

Michaels, C. A. (1998). *Transition to employment.* Austin, TX: Pro-Ed, Inc.

Myers, I. B., & McCaulley, M. H. (1985). *Manual: A guide to the development and the use of the Myers-Briggs Type Indicator.* Palo Alto, CA: Consulting Psychologists Press.
Patton, J. R., & Blalock, G. (1996). *Transition and students with learning disabilities: Facilitating the movement from school to adult life.* Austin, TX: Pro-Ed, Inc.
Power, P. W. (2000). *A guide to vocational assessment.* Austin, TX: Pro-Ed, Inc.
Shearin, A., Roessler, R., & Schriner, K. (1999). Evaluating the transition component in IEP's of secondary students with disabilities. *Rural Special Education Quarterly, 18*(2), 22–35.
Sitlington, P. L., Neubert, D. A., Begun, W., Lombard, R. C., & Leconte, P. J. (1996). *Assess for success: Handbook on transition assessment.* Reston, VA: The Council for Exceptional Children.
Strong, E. K., & Campbell, D. P. (1974). *Strong-Campbell Interest Inventory.* Stanford, CA: Stanford University Press.
Thomas, A., & Grimes, J. (1997). *Best practices in school psychology III.* Washington, D.C.: National Association of School Psychologists.
Waintrup, M., & Kelley, P. (1999). *The Environmental Job Assessment Measure.* Austin, TX: Pro-Ed, Inc.
Weaver, R., & DeLuca, J. R. (1987). *Employability/Life Skills Assessment.* Dayton, OH: Miami Valley Special Education Center and Montgomery County Board of Education.

NAME INDEX

N

O

P

R

S

SUBJECT INDEX